The Montaukett Indians of Eastern Long Island

THE
Iroquois
AND THEIR
NEIGHBORS

Laurence M. Hauptman, Series Editor

JOHN A. STRONG

SYRACUSE UNIVERSITY PRESS

The Montaukett Indians of Eastern Long Island

Copyright © 2001 by Syracuse University Press
Syracuse, New York 13244-5160
All Rights Reserved
First Edition 2001

01 02 03 04 05 06   6 5 4 3 2 1

The paper used in this publication meets the minimum requirements of
American National Standard for Information Sciences—Permanence of
Paper for Printed Library Materials, ANSI Z39.48-1984. ∞™

Library of Congress Cataloging-in-Publication-Data

Strong, John A.
    The Montaukett Indians of eastern Long Island / John A. Strong.— 1st ed.
        p. cm.— (Iroquois and their neighbors)
    Includes bibliographical references.
    ISBN 0-8156-2883-8 (cloth : alk. paper)
        1. Montauk Indians—History. 2. Montauk Indians—Land tenure.
    I. Title. II. Series.

E99.M88 S76 2001
974.7'21004973—dc21

                                                          00-061221

Manufactured in the United States of America

To Olive Pharaoh (1927–1996),
Matriarch of the Montauketts

They take our lands away everyday,
a little and a little

—Delegation of Long Island sachems to Governor Lovelace,
1670, *Department of State Book of Deeds,* 3: 40

JOHN A. STRONG is professor of history at the Southampton College of Long Island University. He received his Ph.D. from Syracuse University. He has written extensively on the Indians of Long Island. His publications include *The Algonquian Peoples of Long Island from Earliest Times to 1700* (1997), and *"We Are Still Here!" The Algonquian Peoples of Long Island Today* (1996). His articles have appeared in *Ethnohistory*, the *Long Island Historical Journal*, the *American Indian Culture and Research Journal*, and *The Encyclopedia of North American Indians*.

CONTENTS

ILLUSTRATIONS

Maps

PREFACE

THE MONTAUKETT Indians are close relatives of the Shinnecocks, Unkechaugs, and Matinecocks on Long Island and
have had long-established relationships with the Pequots,
Niantics, and Narragansetts in southern New England. They survived
the ravages of European diseases in the seventeenth century, two centuries of sporadic attempts to squeeze them off their homeland, a court
ruling in 1910 that declared the tribe no longer existed, historians who
declared they had vanished, and numerous newspaper obituaries
announcing the death of the "last of the Montauketts."

Nineteenth-century Long Island historians, such as Silas Wood
(1826), Benjamin Thompson (1838), Nathaniel Prime (1845),
Gabriel Furman (1874), and Martha Flint (1896), regarded the Indians as colorful background for their celebration of the European settlers' accomplishments. The Indians appear as cardboard images who
emerge briefly and then fade away as the history of the Dutch and
English settlements unfold. These authors dutifully included chapters
on "the Indians of Long Island," and then resumed their focus on the
white communities. Not only were most of these brief references
inadequate, but they also left the reader with the impression that the
Indians all conveniently died by the end of the seventeenth century.
In the twentieth century several lay historians wrote about the Indians of Long Island, but they merely repackaged the material in the
earlier histories, adding very little new information (Schur 1942;
Morice 1949; Bailey 1956, 1982; Coles 1954; Overton 1969). Unfortunately, this material has become entrenched in the elementary- and
secondary-school texts used in most Long Island schools (Sesso and
White 1990; Mannello 1984).

The first historical monograph on the Montauketts by a professional historian was Marian Fisher Ales's master's thesis at New York University (1993, originally 1950). This solidly researched work, titled "A History of the Indians on Montauk, Long Island," reached few readers outside of her own university until Gaynell Stone published it in the 1979 edition of *The History and Archaeology of the Montauk*.

Ales and Stone used the name "Montauk" for both the place and the people. Some of the colonial documents, however, identify the people as "Montauketts." The tribal members today have revived the distinction and refer to themselves as Montauketts. Although Ales's basic research holds up quite well, her approach is now dated, and she ended her account with the loss of the land claims case in 1910. She assumed that Montaukett history was closed at that point. "Thus ended the tribe of Montauk Indians," she wrote (1993, 63).

The Montauk volume marked an important threshold in the study of the Algonquian peoples of Long Island. In 1993 Stone edited a revised and expanded edition of the Montauk book that included my monograph on the process of land alienation culminating in 1910 with the loss of their suit to reclaim the Montauk lands. The new edition brought together an enormous amount of primary and secondary material on the Montauketts. This seven-hundred-page body of documents and essays was a significant part of the database in my research.

Laurence Hauptman, the editor of this series for Syracuse University Press, and several of the Montauketts, including Chief Robert Pharaoh; his mother, Olive; and Robert Cooper, encouraged me to work with the material in Stone's volume and write a more concise history of the Montauketts that would be accessible to a larger audience. The Montauketts were particularly concerned about correcting the impression that they had become extinct. They wanted to remind everyone how they had struggled through very difficult times to survive and how they are now engaged in a campaign to obtain federal recognition.

This book owes debts to many people. The largest, of course, is to the Montauketts themselves: Olive Pharaoh, the Montaukett matriarch; her son, Robert; Robert Cooper; Ralph Bunn; the Reverend Sharon Jackson; John Kenney; Phyllis Brewster-Toone; Jo Ann Leftenant; La Roque Waters Jr.; and Terrie Caldwell, who patiently answered my questions about so many things over the last ten years. Ralph Bunn, in particular, deserves a large measure of credit for his help in documenting the kinship web connecting the Montaukett diaspora on Long Island.

The illustrations give the book an important additional dimension. David Bunn Martine, a member of the Shinnecock Nation and an accomplished artist, contributed some wonderful line drawings that give the reader a visual interpretation of historical Montaukett activities. He researched his subject and took great care to make his drawings as accurate as possible. I am also indebted to my friend and colleague Helen Rountree for her gracious offer to make the maps for the book and for her constructive criticism over the years.

Larry Hauptman's encouragement and constructive analysis as the manuscript went through several drafts played a very important role in this endeavor. James Wherry's critique helped me sharpen my focus and avoid some of the difficulties that often plague scholars who use an interdisciplinary approach to their subject.

I am most grateful to Dorothy King and her assistant, Diana Dayton, at the East Hampton Public Library for their help with my research. They shared with me their knowledge of the historical context of the documents, providing me with many important insights into the relationships between the English settlers in East Hampton and the Montauketts. David Kerkof and Ned Smith at the Suffolk County Historical Society Library, William Asadorian at the Jamaica Queens Library, and David Overton, the Brookhaven town historian, were all very helpful.

By far the largest debt is to my wife, Jane, who not only gave me comfort and support through the whole process of research and writing, but also played a very important role in the editing and reshaping of the final draft.

ABBREVIATIONS

BA   Brotherton Archives, Manuscript and Special Collections, York State Library, Albany, N.Y. (originals at Marian College, Fond du Lac, Wisc.)

BHSL   Brooklyn Historical Society Library, Brooklyn, N.Y.

CP   Cases and Points: The text of *Wyandanch v. Benson* and the appeals were bound by the Daly law firm. One copy is in the East Hampton Public Library, and a second copy is in the Brooklyn Historical Society Library in Brooklyn, N.Y. The case files are also in file no. 3567 in the Suffolk County Law Library, Riverhead, N.Y. The bound volume is not paginated sequentially. In order to avoid confusion, the author prepared a guide that is on file in the Brooklyn and East Hampton Libraries. The citations in the text are coded to this guide.

CPMCP   "Comprehensive Plan for the Preservation and Use of Montauk County Park." Montauk County Park Citizens' Advisory Board, 1995.

CSAIP   Connecticut State Archives, Indian Papers, 1647–1789, Documents 1: 10–23, Connecticut State Library, Hartford, Conn.

DHSNY   *Documentary History of the State of New York.* Edited by Edmund Bailey O'Callaghan. 4 vols. Albany: Weed, Parsons, 1849.

DSBD   Department of State Book of Deeds. Unpublished Documents Office of the Secretary of State, Albany, N.Y. (N.Y. State Archives Series 453, vols. 1–9).

EHPLC   East Hampton Public Library Collections, Long Island Room, East Hampton, N.Y.

FFB-BHSL	Fatting Field Books, 9–27, Indian Documents (ArMs 1974.48), Brooklyn Historical Society Library, Brooklyn, N.Y., 1803–1830.
FFB-EHPL	Fatting Field Books (JG 75), East Hampton Public Library, Long Island Collection, 1843–1879.
JASNY	*Journal of the Assembly of the State of New York.* Albany: John Barber, Printer, 1818, 1822.
JEHT	*Journal of the East Hampton Trustees.* Edited by Harry D. Sleight. 7 vols. East Hampton, N.Y.: Town of East Hampton, 1926–1927.
JSNY	*Journal of the Senate of the State of New York.* Albany: John Barber, Printer, 1808.
LSNY	*Laws of the State of New York.* Seventy-fifth Session of the Legislature. Buffalo: Jewett, Thomas, 1852.
MHSC	Massachusetts Historical Society *Collections.*
MIW	Montauketts in Washington, 1920–1924. Photocopies of twenty-five documents in the National Archives, Washington, D.C., General Service, Montauk Indians (NA-GS Box 30, File no. 7345-21-300). Copies of these documents are on file in the East Hampton Public Library, East Hampton, N.Y. (File no. X-GKG, 38) and in the Suffolk County Historical Society Library, Riverhead, N.Y. (Acct. no. 196.40).
NYCD	*Documents Relative to the Colonial History of the State of New York.* Edited by Edmund Bailey O'Callaghan and Berthold Fernow. 15 vols. Albany: Weed, Parsons, 1856–1887.
NYHS	New York Historical Society. "Proceedings of the General Court of Assizes, 1680–82." In *Collections, 1912.* New York: New York Historical Society, 1912.
NYSDE	Report of the New York State Department of Education, Albany, N.Y., 1872.
PBR	*Portrait and Biographical Record of Suffolk County.* New York: Chapman Publishers, 1896.
QPL	Queens Borough Public Library, Long Island Collection, 89-11, Jamaica, N.Y.
RCC	*The Public Records of the Colony of Connecticut.* Edited by J. Hammond Trumbull. 15 vols. Hartford, Conn.: F. A. Brown, 1850–1890; New York: AMS, 1968.

RCNH	*Records of the Colony and Plantation of New Haven from 1638–1649.* Edited by Charles J. Hoadly. 2 vols. Hartford: Case Tiffany, 1857.
RCNP	*Records of the Colony of New Plymouth.* Edited by David Pulsifer. 10 vols. 1859. Reprint. New York: AMS Press, 1968.
RCRI	*Records of the Colony of Rhode Island and Providence Plantations in New England.* Edited by John R. Bartlett. 10 vols. 1850–1865. Reprint. New York: AMS Press, 1968.
RPCC	Records of the Particular Court of Connecticut, 1639–1663. Connecticut Historical Society *Collections,* vol. 22, 1928.
RTEH	*Records of the Town of East Hampton.* Edited by Joseph Osborne. 5 vols. Sag Harbor, N.Y.: Hunt, 1887.
RTH	*Huntington Town Records.* Edited by Charles R. Street. 3 vols. Huntington, N.Y.: Town of Huntington, 1887–1889.
RTNSH	*Records of the Town of North and South Hempstead.* Edited by Benjamin Hicks. 8 vols. Jamaica, N.Y.: Long Island Farmer Print, 1896–1904.
RTSH	*Records of the Town of Southampton.* Edited by William Pelletreau. 8 vols. Sag Harbor, N.Y.: Hunt, 1874–1877.
RTSM	*Town Records of Smithtown.* Edited by William Pelletreau. 3 vols. Sag Harbor, N.Y.: Hunt, 1898–1931.
SCCCR	Suffolk County Civil Court Records, Riverhead County Center, Riverhead, N.Y.
SCH	Hearings Before a Subcommittee of the Committee on Indian Affairs of the U.S. Senate in Relation to Certain Claims of the Montauk, Shinnecock, Narragansett, and Mohegan Indians, September 22, 1900, New York. Washington, D.C.: U.S. Government Printing Office. Microfilm on file in the State Univ. of New York Library, Stony Brook, N.Y. (SIN, 56C, drawer 14, A32).
SCHDR	Suffolk County Historical Documents Room, Riverhead County Center, Riverhead, N.Y.
SCHSL	Suffolk County Historical Society Library, Riverhead, N.Y.

SHNY	*Second Annual Report of the State Historian of the State of New York*. Albany: Wynkoop Hallenbeck Crawford, 1897.
SIHS	Shelter Island Historical Society, Shelter Island, N.Y.
STA	Southold Town Archives, Southold, N.Y.
USR	*United States Reports*. Vol. 180. New York: Banks Law Publishing, 1901.
VSAB	Van Scoy Account Books, 1829–1838. East Hampton Public Library, Long Island Collection.
WJ	*The Papers of Sir William Johnson*. Edited by James Sullivan. 14 vols. Albany: State Univ. of New York, 1921–1965.
WP	*The Winthrop Papers*. Edited by Allyn B. Forbes. 5 vols. Boston: Massachusetts Historical Society, 1929–1947.

The Montaukett
Indians of Eastern
Long Island

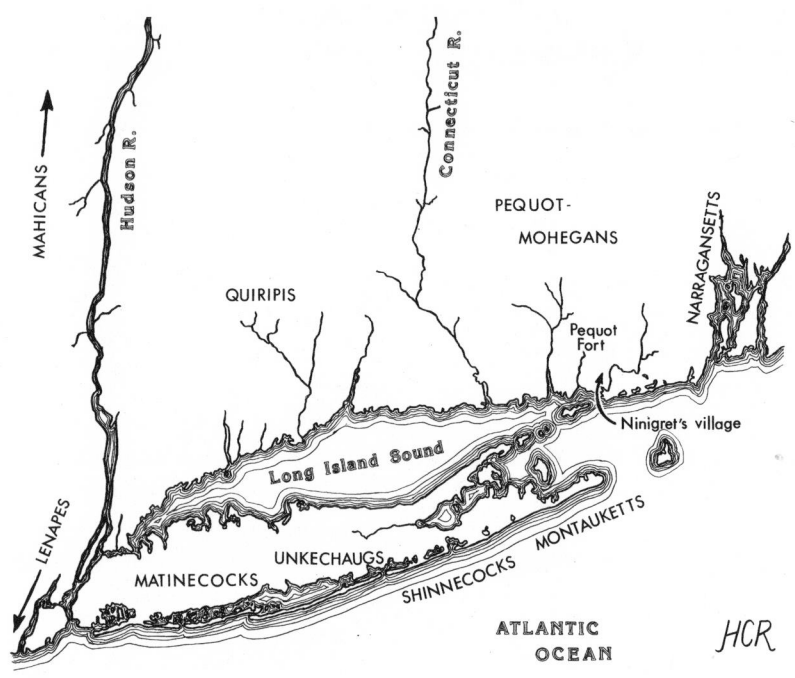

Long Island Before the European Arrival. Map by Helen Rountree.

ONE

A CLASH OF CULTURES

IN ORDER to understand the history of the Montaukett people
we must begin with the land base that provided them with their
livelihood. At the end of the Pleistocene era, the Wisconsin glacier,
a huge wall of ice, ground its way southward and came to rest on
what is today the south shore of Long Island (J. Jennings 1989,
50–53). As the ice gradually melted, it left behind a 120-mile-long
fish-shaped island with tail flukes on the eastern end. These "flukes,"
the northern and southern forks of eastern Long Island, enclose
Peconic Bay. A glacial moraine of low hills, stretching out into the
Atlantic where the Labrador current from the north meets the warm
waters of the Gulf stream, shapes the South Fork. Scattered among
the hills are kettle-hole ponds, broad meadows, and small freshwater streams that flow into tidal wetlands. Nestled in Peconic Bay are
three small islands: Robin's Island, Shelter Island, and Gardiner's
Island.

Near the eastern end of the South Fork, the land narrows to
form a low sandy area called *Napeague,* an Algonquian word meaning "water land."[1] Heavy storms occasionally push water across
Napeague, isolating the remaining land on the eastern end of the South
Fork. This land, consisting of eleven thousand acres, is called *Montauk,* an Algonquian word meaning "place of observation or a forti-
fied place." Eastward from Napeague, the hills rise up to command
the horizon. The Indians called these hills *Nominick,* meaning "land

1. The English translations for Long Island place-names are educated guesses
by William Wallace Tooker, a nineteenth-century amateur ethnographer who devoted
his life to the study of local Indian culture. Although Tooker's word list was dismissed
by Smithsonian scholars, some of his interpretations may be close to the mark. His
Indian Place Names on Long Island, published in 1911 and reprinted in 1962,
remains the basic reference used by the general public.

that can be seen from afar." Just beyond the first rise of hills there is
a body of water in a glacial kettle hole called Fresh Pond, covering
about fifty acres. This area, known as Hither Woods, is a forty-three-
hundred-acre tract of land running east from Napeague to Fort Pond,
a large pond about a mile long by a half-mile wide.

Overlooking the eastern shore of Fort Pond, a high bluff offers
a panoramic view of the South Fork. The Montauketts would later
select this impressive site for a ceremonial center and burial ground.
This two-thousand-acre parcel of land, called "North Neck," sepa-
rates Fort Pond on the west from Lake Montauk, a much larger kettle pond, on the east. A parcel of land south of the two bodies of
water, where the village of Montauk is now located, includes about
one thousand acres of meadowlands and ocean beaches.

To the east of Lake Montauk, an undulating terrain of low
hills, meadows, and two small ponds, covering about forty-two hundred acres, stretches to the end of the island where a high bluff looks
out over the Atlantic. The northeastern section of this area, later
named "Indian Fields," includes twelve hundred acres of land, two
small kettle-hole ponds (Big Reed Pond and Oyster Pond), and some
of the best meadowlands on the South Fork. By the end of the eighteenth century, Indian Fields had become the last refuge of the Montaukett Indians.

As the land slowly took shape, a new ecosystem came to life.
Atlantic barrier beaches protected salt meadows and shallow bays
where waterfowl, seals, and shellfish flourished. Freshwater streams
flowed into the tidal bays, creating an environment rich in plant and
animal resources for the first human inhabitants. Nuts from the oak,
hickory, walnut, and chestnut trees and a variety of edible plants
such as berries, grapes, beach plums, nutritious grasses, and tubers
provided food for human and animal consumption. An abundance
of deer, turkeys, squirrels, and raccoons prospered in the woodlands
and meadows.

This environment soon attracted the first human explorers, the
Paleo-Indian peoples, who began to visit the area about ten thousand
years ago. The first permanent settlers on Long Island established
their villages along the freshwater streams and by the kettle-hole
ponds more than four thousand years ago (Wyatt 1982, 72). These
small communities harvested shellfish, bluefish, flounder, shad, and
striped bass from the tidal bays. The meadows and woodlands provided them with a rich abundance of wild plants and game animals
(Gwynne 1982; Bernstein 1990).

The archaeological data from the Paleo-Indian and Archaic periods (ten thousand to three thousand years ago) on Long Island reveals very few insights into social and political patterns. It is evident, however, that the small hunting and gathering bands did not produce enough surplus to sustain an elite class. Anthropological models of social organization in such small-scale societies suggest that the people shared the food they produced and that their leaders governed by persuasion rather than by force (Brasser 1971; Salwen 1978, 167–68).

A small number of archaeological excavations on eastern Long Island reveal some fascinating insights into the religious beliefs that prevailed during the late Archaic period. Mortuary rituals involving cremations and grave offerings took place on the eastern slopes of high hills overlooking the water (W. Ritchie 1969, 175–78). The site found near Orient Point on the eastern end of the North Fork included a complex of twenty-five small circular pits about five feet deep containing caches of projectile points, gorgets, stone axes, and fragments of steatite vessels.

Nearby was a huge oval-shaped pit about thirty feet long, twenty feet at its widest point, and five feet deep (Latham 1935, 1). Similar pits containing from twenty-eight to forty-one stores of grave goods were found at Jamesport and on Sugar Loaf Hill near the village of Southampton on the South Fork. Large deposits of red ocher, perhaps a symbol of lifeblood, were associated with many of the caches of goods. William Ritchie, the state archaeologist who worked on these sites, said that he sensed "a pervading aura of high religious drama." There is also, he continued, "a good deal of lost symbolism, some of it of a more universal nature, in which high places, the east, the sun, fire, and red ocher figure as elements of a vigorous religious movement" (1969, 178).

The small number of archaeological sites from the Woodland period make it difficult to reconstruct village life. It is possible, however, to document the major changes that mark the close of the Archaic period around three thousand years ago. Evidences of new projectile styles; the development of ceramic pottery technology; the use of tobacco pipes; more permanent, year-round settlements; expanded trade networks; and an increasingly efficient system of exploiting the natural resources are revealed in the archaeological data (J. Strong 1997, 55–77).

The pottery revolution marks a significant technological shift from a reliance on vessels made from gourds, wood, and steatite.

The first vessels had thick walls and very crude decorations. Several of these pots were excavated from sites occupied by the Montauketts' ancestors on Three Mile Harbor near present-day East Hampton (ibid., 55). Later, the Algonquian artisans improved on these early pots by making the walls thinner and decorating them with geometric designs.

Tobacco pipes were undoubtedly used in religious ceremonies during the Woodland period (Ford 1981, 19). A widely held belief among Native American peoples was that the tobacco smoke served as a vehicle carrying prayers to the spirit world (Grim 1987, 127). Pipes were also used for social occasions and to seal agreements. In Algonquian villages, the host usually offered a guest a pipe as a greeting.

During the late Woodland period the eastern Algonquian people began to experiment with domesticated plants such as corn, beans, and squash. The archaeological record, however, indicates that domesticated plants did not play a major role in the diet of the Long Island Algonquians (Ceci 1977, 102–3). The people probably saw no reason to abandon their hunting and gathering practices because the rich variety of wild plants, fish, shellfish, fowl, and game near their villages provided a well-balanced, predictable food supply.

The Long Island communities shared many cultural characteristics with their neighbors all along the northeastern Atlantic coast. These coastal peoples spoke languages with a common Algonquian root, lived in small settlements linked by extended kinship systems, and shared a common belief system. Samson Occom's "Account of the Montauk Indians on Long Island" (1993, 151–53) is one of the few surviving sources of information about the traditional lifeways of the Montauketts available to modern ethnographers. Occom, a Mohegan missionary who lived at Montauk from 1749 to 1760 and married a Montaukett woman, wrote a brief description of what he called the "ancient customs and ways of the Montauk." Occom's account has some significant insights, but it must be read with some caution. Occom wrote more than a century after the Montauketts' first contact with whites. He did not observe many of these practices firsthand, and he himself enthusiastically embraced European culture. Nevertheless, Occom's approach, unlike that of most missionaries, was scholarly and respectful. He did not distort or demean traditional culture, as did some of his fellow missionaries, who wanted to shock their sponsors into sending more funds.

Occom's discussion of the Montaukett gods closely parallels Roger Williams's account of the Narragansetts' religious beliefs in his *Key to the Languages of America* (1973). The Montauketts believed that all nature was alive with spirit forces. They believed, said Occom, that "there were the gods of the four corners of the earth; . . . there was a god over their corn, another over their beans, another over their pumpkins and squashes. There was one god over their wigwams, another of fire, another over the sea, another of the wind, one of the day, and another of the night, and there were four gods over the four parts of the year" (1993, 152). The god Sawwonnuntoh, for example, resided in the west and gave corn, beans, pumpkins, and squash to the Montauketts. One great good god named Cauhluntoowut ruled over all of the other gods, and his rival was an evil god called Mutcheshesunnetooh.

It is quite possible, however, that Occom's own Christian beliefs influenced his interpretation of the two rival gods. Many missionaries looked for parallels with Christianity that might make the process of conversion more palatable to the Indians. Missionaries were very eager, for example, to find the concept of monotheism and some expression of a struggle between the forces of good and evil in the Indians' belief system. As a result, the missionaries often distorted the accounts given by their informants. Occom's description of the rivalry between the good god, Cauhluntoowut, and the evil god, Mutcheshesunnetooh, may be another example of this tendency.

It is more likely that both of these gods were manifestations of Manitou, a powerful spirit force at the center of most Algonquian belief systems (E. Tooker 1979, 16–17). The Lenapes, an Algonqian-speaking people living in present-day New Jersey and western Long Island, told a seventeenth-century Dutch observer that Manitou was "whatever is wonderful and strange that surpasses human understanding" (De Laet 1909, 49–50). Other Indians described Manitou as "a cosmic, mysterious property which is believed to be existing everywhere in nature" (E. Tooker 1979, 13–19; Jones 1905, 190). All of the forms of Manitou had the power to help or harm human beings. There was no concept in the Algonquian religions that paralleled the Christian notion of a duality.

According to Occom, the Montauketts called those people among them who appeared to have sacred powers "powaws." Contemporary anthropologists use the term *shaman* for such people (Laufer 1917). These men and women supervised religious rituals and ceremonies and served as liaisons with the spirit world. The powaws, said Occom, "get their art from dreams." The Montauketts told Occom that spirits visited the powaws in the shapes of animals and spoke to them. Occom did not dispute these accounts of the powaws' powers. He noted that the Christians believed in the power of witchcraft and commented, "I don't see for my part, why it is not as true as the English, or other nations' witchcraft" (1993, 153).

Unfortunately, Occom did not mention anything about the political structure of the Montauketts before the English arrived. Comparative data from other coastal Algonquian communities suggests that the small communities did not produce enough surplus to sustain an elite class or a clearly defined hierarchy of authority. Elders provided counsel to the community and gave legitimacy to village leaders who held very limited authority. These leaders, who could be either male (sachems) or female (sunksquaws), governed by persuasion rather than by force (Salwen 1978, 164–70).

Little permanent political structure existed beyond the village level. On occasion, several villages might form a temporary alliance to accomplish a limited goal, such as a military campaign or a hunting expedition. Once the goal was reached or hopelessly frustrated, the groups went off again on their own (Grumet 1979, 23–28; Bragdon 1996, 40–49; Sturtevant 1983, 13; Campisi 1982, 181; Fried 1975; Fried 1976, 154–84). The kinship networks, however, remained intact and served as conduits for trade and communication on a regular basis. In such systems, families generally shared responsibilities for food production, protection, and religious ceremonies. The kinship networks, which trace their ancestry back to a common founder through the father or the mother or both, are called lineages or clans and are usually exogamous.

The patterns of postmarital residence in northeastern Algonquian communities is not well documented, but there appears to have been a great deal of movement from one village to another, suggesting that a couple could choose to live in the village of either spouse (Salwen 1978, 167; Goddard 1978a, 225; Simmons 1978, 193; Brasser 1978, 200). Two brief references to Montaukett postmarital residence indicate an ambilocal pattern. In 1667 two women living at Montauk testified in court that they had been born and raised at Shinnecock (NYCD, 14: 602). They may have moved to Montauk after marrying a Montaukett. The women also testified that the Shinnecock sunksquaw at the time was the sister of the Montaukett sachem (RTSH, 3: 111). In another case, however, the husband of a Montaukett sunksquaw was a Pequot who had come to live in his wife's village (RTSM, 1: 16–17; MHSC, series 4, 7: 484).

The first mention of the Montauketts in the colonial records referred to them as the Indians from Montauk.[2] It was not until 1655 that their sachem was called the "Montaukett sachem" rather than the sachem from Montauk (RCNP, 10: 50–51). In 1687 an English deed made a clear distinction between the place-name "Montauk" and the "tribal" name Montaukett. In this deed the "Meantauket"

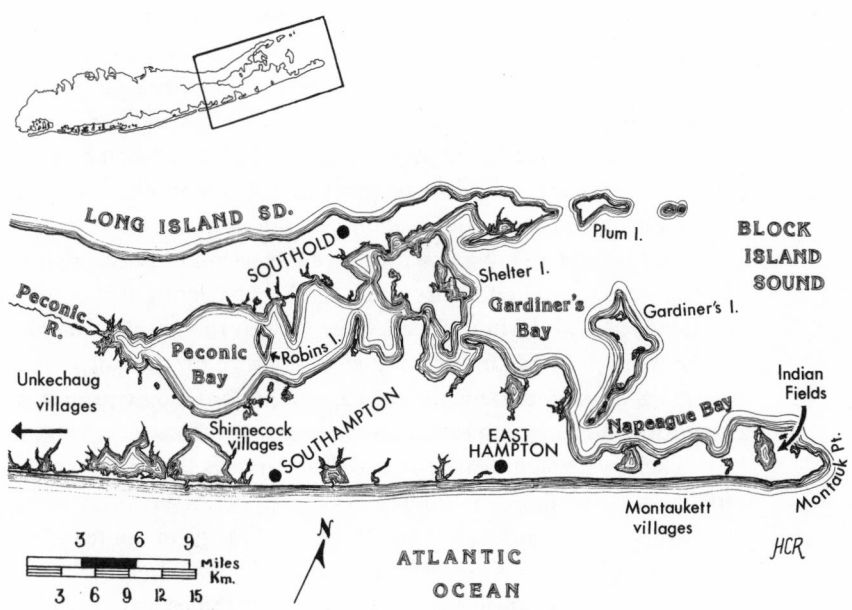

Eastern Long Island in the Seventeenth Century.
Map by Helen Rountree.

2. The first list of names for the "tribes" of Long Island appears in the journal of the Reverend Charles Wooley who served as chaplain to the administration of Governor Andros from 1678 to 1680 (1968, 54). Wooley referred to the Indian communities as "nations which may be more properly called tribes of Indians." He listed seven tribes including the *Mun-tauck* and the *Shin-na-cock* on the east end. Silas Wood, Long Island's pioneer historian, writing in 1826, neatly divided the Indian communities into thirteen tribes based on his reading of the seventeenth-century deeds (J. Strong 1992). Wood's list, with a few minor exceptions, has, unfortunately, become the standard reference for Native Americans on Long Island. The list with Tooker's translations has been repeated by historians, classroom teachers, and the producers of restaurant place mats to the present day.

Indians sold their land at "Meantauk" to the proprietors of East Hampton (R. Smith 1926, 48–49). By the middle of the eighteenth century, however, the modern spelling "Montauk" was used in reference to both the tribe and the land at the eastern tip of Long Island. In the 1990s the community revived the seventeenth-century designation and currently refers to itself as the "Montaukett Nation."

The Montauketts and their neighbors had values and assumptions about such things as governance, gender roles, property, and religion that were in sharp contrast with those beliefs held by the Europeans who began arriving on the Atlantic shores in the sixteenth century. It was the European technological superiority, however, that led the newcomers to conclude that they were destined to take over all of the land. It was just a matter of time. They believed that the land was theirs by natural right because only they could harness the natural resources and make the land productive. European material culture had made it possible for them to get here in the first place and had provided them the weapons of conquest.

The Europeans dismissed Native American culture, with its emphasis on communal values and a spiritual harmony with nature, as backward and dysfunctional. They viewed the native presence, for the most part, as an annoying encumbrance on the Europeans' God-given mission to tame the land and to honor God by producing a bountiful surplus of material goods.

There were significant cultural differences between Indian and European concepts of property and ownership (Grumet 1979, 155–63; Snyderman 1951, 16–29). In the European context land was a commodity that could be bought and sold, often by parties who never set foot on the property in question. Sales were final and absolute. The Indians, by contrast, saw the land as a part of nature that could be used by an entire community. It made no sense to the Indians for land to be divided into privately owned parcels. Could one divide up any part of nature in such a manner? Could one "own" the deer or the water? The Indians did understand the concept of sovereignty over their hunting grounds and would go to war to defend access to them. For the Indians, therefore, the important concern was access and use, not abstract "ownership."

The deeds, therefore, often included clauses allowing the Algonquian villagers to continue living on the land that they had "sold" (Bolton 1975, 7–10). These provisions encouraged the Indians to view these deeds as part of a gift exchange between the two parties. The Indians granted the English the right to use the land and received in exchange some highly valued manufactured goods, such as knives, kettles, coats, and hatchets. The Indian view of such transactions is probably closer to the European concept of a lease rather than a permanent transfer of land.

The Europeans used these misunderstandings to their advantage. They were usually willing to renew the deeds and give the Indians more trade goods whenever they returned to renegotiate or confirm the transaction. This policy suggests that the Europeans saw these payments as a means of buying time until the Indian communities declined in population and gradually disappeared. Most believed that the eventual extinction of the Indians was inevitable. The terrible toll taken by European diseases and the superiority of their armies reinforced their belief that the Indians were a doomed race.

English troops demonstrated their superiority in dramatic fashion during the Pequot War in the spring of 1637. They waged a devastating war against the Pequots and nearly destroyed them. The English attacked a Pequot settlement near present-day Mystic, Connecticut, and massacred nearly seven hundred men, women, and children (Salisbury 1984, 220–25; F. Jennings 1976, 215–27; Cave 1996, 123–67). The Pequots, fighting without firearms, killed only two English soldiers and wounded twenty others. The decisive victory opened up the Connecticut Valley to English settlement.

The English victory also opened up a scramble for control over the Pequots' tributary communities in southern New England and on Long Island. The English, the Dutch, and the Algonquian sachems, such as Ninigret, Miantonomi, and Uncas, now began campaigns of political intrigue to gain influence in the region. The English were particularly anxious to gain a foothold on Long Island before the Dutch expanded their control eastward. The Montauketts and several other Long Island communities who had established tributary relations with the Pequots were now thrust into the center of the scramble.

Shortly after the Pequot massacre, Wyandanch, a young Montaukett sachem, came to Fort Saybrook to negotiate an alliance with Lion Gardiner, the English commander (L. Gardiner 1980, 137–38). They reached an agreement, and Wyandanch joined the English campaign to hunt down the Pequots who were still in arms against the English. One of the reasons that Wyandanch wanted an alliance with the English was because he knew that Ninigret, the Niantic sachem, wanted to bring the former Pequot tributaries on Long Island under his control.

The tangle of conflicting interests became evident in the late spring of 1638 when Ninigret led a war party of eighty men across the sound to convince Wyandanch that he should ally himself with the Niantics, a southern branch of the Narragansetts, instead of Massachusetts Bay or Connecticut (WP, 4: 43–45). Ninigret was attempting to take advantage of what he believed was a power vacuum on Long Island. He hoped to break the newly formed alliance between the Montauketts and the English before it could become firmly established. It was a daring plan that would strengthen his position against his rivals, Uncas and Miantonomi.

The Niantics lived east of the Pawcatuck River between the former lands of the Pequots to the west and Miantonomi's Narragansett territory to the east and north. All three sachems were maneuvering to absorb as many of the remaining Pequot remnants and former tributaries of the defeated tribe as they could (Sainsbury 1971, 115). Ninigret had other problems as well. Both Connecticut and Rhode Island claimed his lands in a border dispute between the two colonies that lasted for several decades.

Shortly after he landed on Long Island, Ninigret sent a delegation to Wyandanch and urged him to abandon the English and accept a tributary status with the Niantics (WP, 4: 43–44). Wyandanch refused and went into hiding to avoid capture, perhaps hoping the English would intervene on his behalf. Ninigret finally did catch the Montaukett sachem and pressed him to reconsider, arguing that Connecticut and Massachusetts Bay would take the Montauketts' wampum, but would not protect them as well as the Niantics could. The Englishmen, said Ninigret, "are liars, they do it but only to get your wampum." The English of Connecticut, he continued, "will speak much but do little" (ibid.).

When Wyandanch refused to abrogate his alliance to the English, Ninigret humiliated him by stripping him in front of his people, seizing thirty fathoms of wampum and other goods, and burning several wigwams (ibid., 44). The Niantics then attacked several neighboring villages, finally convincing some of the Montaukett elders to accept his terms. Ninigret demanded future payments in corn and wampum as terms of the alliance. Although this appears to be a coerced agreement, it is possible that there was some genuine support among the Long Island communities for Ninigret because over the next three decades his agents made several overtures to sachems there.

Ninigret's raid was a strategy Indians commonly used to establish authority over tributaries (Johnson 1996, 40–43). The purpose was not to seize territory or to kill many people. Ninigret wanted to assert his dominance over Wyandanch in a dramatic gesture. Uncas, an ambitious Mohegan sachem who had very little power and influence prior to the Pequot War, employed a similar strategy as well as some cleverly adapted European diplomatic tactics to help him become one of the most powerful sachems in New England. Uncas's raid on the Pequot community at Nameag in 1647 was very similar to Ninigret's actions on Long Island. The intent of the raid was to humiliate the Nameag, who were allies of the English. Uncas stripped the people, burned their wigwams, and stole their goods (ibid., 40–41). The English reprimanded Uncas, but left the Nameag under Mohegan control.

Uncas, Ninigret, and Miantonomi were attempting to establish themselves as the primary intermediaries between the English and the smaller Algonquian communities in each of their areas. They wanted to control the flow of information, trade, and tribute between the English and the smaller bands such as the Nameag and the Montauketts. Each sachem also seized any opportunity to gain control of one of his rivals' tributaries.

Wyandanch went immediately to Roger Ludlow, the deputy governor of Connecticut, and demanded that the English recover his wampum. According to Ludlow, the Montaukett sachem made a compelling argument. How can I pay tribute to the English, asked Wyandanch, if they allow Ninigret to come and steal it from me at will? Ludlow agreed and so did John Mason, the commander of the troops who massacred the Pequots. Mason took an armed guard of eight men to confront Ninigret, telling him that unless he made restitution to Wyandanch the English would send an army against him (WP, 4: 45). The Niantic sachem, whose village was only a few miles from the site of the Pequot massacre, reached a peaceful accommodation with Mason.

Wyandanch must have been pleased with the success of his diplomatic efforts, but he also realized how vulnerable he was to such raids in the future. The following year these fears undoubtedly prompted the eastern Long Island sachems to invite Lion Gardiner to establish the first English presence on Long Island. The sachems decided that they would be safer from attack if an English military man took up residence nearby. The English were very receptive because they wanted to obtain a foothold on Long Island before the Dutch expanded eastward from New Amsterdam.

In May 1639 Gardiner negotiated with a sachem named Yovawam for the first purchase of Indian land on eastern Long Island. Gardiner bought an island called Manchonat, "the place where they all died," located adjacent to the Montaukett lands. The name may refer to an epidemic that possibly wiped out the inhabitants. Yovawam is probably the sachem identified in a later document as "Youghco," from Shelter Island (RCNP, 9: 18). Gardiner promptly renamed Manchonat after himself and moved his family there later that year.

Wyandanch's role in the transaction is not recorded, but he undoubtedly was the one who brought the two parties together. He saw the advantages for trade and military security if the English established a presence near his village. Gardiner and Connecticut governor John Winthrop, Jr., of course, were eager for an alliance that would serve to discourage the Dutch from pressing their claims in this area. These common interests served as the primary basis for Gardiner and Wyandanch to have a close relationship, which later became celebrated in local folklore.

Wyandanch, Youghco (Yovawam), Moughmaitow (the sachem from Corchaug on the North Fork of Long Island), and Weenagamin, who was probably from Shinnecock, came to Hartford in the fall of 1644 for a meeting of the commissioners of the United Colonies, which included New Haven, Plymouth, Massachusetts Bay, and Connecticut. These colonies had formed the union the year before for mutual protection against Indian attacks and to thwart Dutch encroachment on their lands. Roger Williams's Rhode Island, of course, was not invited to join the union. Williams's theology and his Indian policies remained anathema to the Puritans. At the meeting the sachems agreed to become tributaries to the English and granted them exclusive purchase rights to eastern Long Island.

The Hartford Treaty reaffirmed an important principle in English colonial law. The crown and its agencies, the colonial governments, held the exclusive right of purchase. During the early years following the arrival of the English in North America, they applied this principle primarily against Dutch rivals, but they soon expanded it to include private individuals within the settler communities as well. Following the English seizure of New Netherland in 1664, all private entrepreneurs had to obtain permission to enter into negotiations with Indian owners for land sales.

The English required Wyandanch and the four sachems to accept English jurisdiction as a part of their tributary relationship. The sachems promised that any Indians who harmed the English or their goods "upon due notice and proofe they will deliver all such to deserved punishment, or provide due satisfaction for all injuries and offenses donn" (ibid., 19).

In the early spring of 1648, Governors Eaton of New Haven and Hopkins of Connecticut sent Thomas Stanton, a Connecticut merchant, to purchase lands for them on the eastern end of Long Island. The English frequently called upon Stanton to negotiate with the Indians because he was one of the few Englishmen who had mastered any of the native languages spoken in southern New England and on eastern Long Island. The governors were anxious to complete the purchase of these lands because in the fall of 1647 the Dutch had made an attempt to buy land near the English settlement of Southampton, a few miles west of the Montaukett lands (RCNH, 1: 523–24; Ales 1993, 20–21). The English met with Wyandanch; his interpreter, Cockenoe;[3] and three other sachems to negotiate the purchase of a thirty-one-thousand-acre parcel of Montaukett land between the eastern boundary of Southampton and Napeague Bay (map 3).

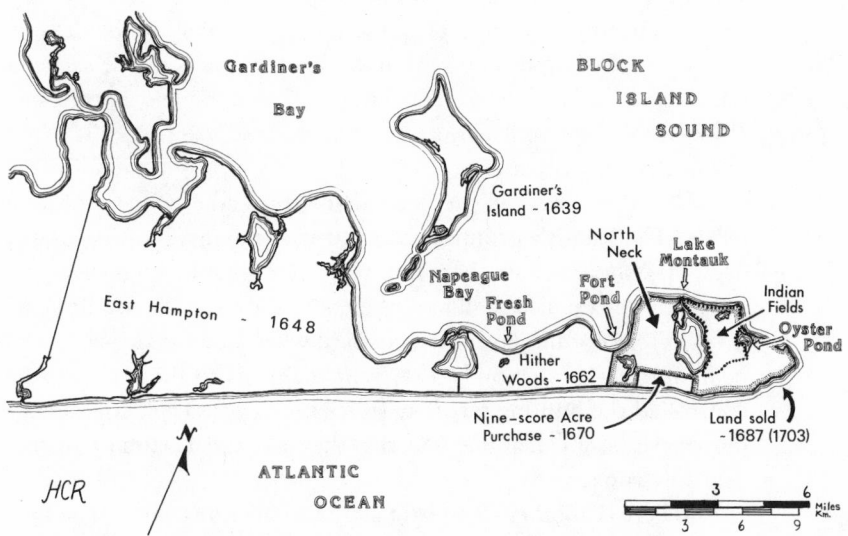

Montaukett Deed Boundaries, 1648–1703. Map by Helen Rountree.

3. This is the first time Cockenoe's name appears in the colonial records. His skill as an interpreter was well known throughout Long Island. He was frequently called in to help negotiate deeds and boundary disputes. In his brief biography of Cockenoe, William Wallace Tooker suggested that he may have learned English while in the service of the missionary John Eliot (1980a, 176–79). Eliot mentioned an Indian youth from Long Island who had quickly mastered English. The young man then helped Eliot in his study of Indian languages. Unfortunately, there is no way to corroborate Tooker's speculation.

Two provisions of the deed reflect patterns found in many of these early transactions. The English gave the sachems twenty coats, twenty-four mirrors, twenty-four hoes, twenty-four hatchets, twenty-four knives, and one hundred small metal drills called "muxes" that were used to make wampum (RTEH, 1: 3). In spite of the clause in the deed stating that the Indians had given up all rights and interest in the parcel, the sachems probably viewed the transaction as a gift exchange in return for the right of the English to use the land. Certainly there was no connection between the value of these goods, which Governor Hopkins had purchased for thirty pounds, four shillings, and eight pence, and the value of the land in the English market.[4]

The second provision in the deed, which allowed for the joint use of the thirty-one-thousand-acre parcel, could also have been interpreted in terms of Native American concepts of land "ownership." The Indians retained the rights to hunt, fish, collect shells for wampum, and take the fins and tails from beached whales. They agreed, in return, not to molest the English or their goods. It is, of course, impossible to know what was in the minds of the sachems who negotiated the agreement, but the arrangement is certainly closer to the Native American concept of land use than it is to the English view of private property.

Another clause in the deed also suggested a concept of joint usage. The English promised that "if the Indians, hunting of any deer, they should chase them into the water, and the English should kill them, the English shall have the body, and the sachems the skin" (ibid., 3). According to Indian custom, when hunters drove deer or bears into rivers or ponds, they sent the skins to the sachem who controlled the hunting territory (RTSH, 1: 157). The Montauketts must have assumed, at the time, that they still had a claim to the parcel (Ales 1993, 21).

There is another significant aspect to the transaction. The English governors who owned the patent purchased the land from the Indians and then later sold it to the local proprietors. This process established a precedent for government involvement in such transactions with Indians. Quarrels both between Indians and the English

4. It is difficult to determine the value of a specific parcel of land in the English market at this time. In 1659 good meadowland in East Hampton cost one pound per acre, and woodland was valued at six shillings per acre (RTEH, 2: 168–70). Later in the seventeenth century land averaged from one to three pounds sterling per acre, unless it was swamp or wetland.

and between rival English purchasers over boundaries and terms in
the deeds frequently forced public officials to intervene. The extent
of public supervision over private purchases of Indian land, however,
remained unresolved until the English established the colony of New
York in 1664.

The New England governors, who had been primarily concerned with the Dutch, did not show any interest in expanding their
own colonies to Long Island at the time. A few families established
homesteads in East Hampton over the next three years, and, finally,
in 1651, they purchased the title from Governor Hopkins, adding
what appears to be an interest payment of eight pounds sterling to
the sum paid by Hopkins for the goods given to the Indian sachems
in 1648 (ibid., 21; RTEH, 1: 4).

This transaction marks a crucial turning point in the history
of the Montauketts. They now had relatively easy access to European
manufactured goods, but there was a price to pay. They would
become increasingly dependent on goods that they could not produce
themselves. The Montauketts were to be drawn gradually into the
web of an economic and political system where they would have less
and less control over their own affairs.

TWO

FROM ACCOMMODATION TO SUBJUGATION 1649–1670

WYANDANCH'S GROWING ties with Lion Gardiner and the East Hampton community increased his status among the sachems on eastern Long Island. The Montaukett sachem, therefore, was careful to fulfill his obligations under the Hartford Treaty of 1644. In 1649 the English put Wyandanch's commitment to a severe test. They asked him to honor a sensitive clause in the treaty that compromised his sovereignty. The clause stipulated that Indians who injured English people or property be turned over to the English courts. When the Southampton settlers accused the Shinnecocks of murdering an Englishwoman, Mandush, the Shinnecock sachem, refused to cooperate with the investigation.

The two communities armed themselves and stood ready for a confrontation (RCNP, 9: 143). The Shinnecocks made a proposal that was in accordance with their custom of providing restitution for the victims and their families rather than punishing the guilty parties. They offered a payment that would be borne by their whole community, but the English rejected this form of restitution.

Lion Gardiner sent Wyandanch to the Shinnecock village and urged him to use his influence to end the impasse. The Montaukett sachem took advantage of the close kinship ties his people had with the Shinnecocks to help him locate and capture the men responsible for the murder. With Mandush's consent, Wyandanch took the accused men to Hartford where they were tried and executed (L. Gardiner 1980, 145). Mandush accepted a tributary status under Wyandanch and granted the Montaukett sachem full control over all of the Shinnecock lands. This diplomacy was a major success for the English policy of indirect rule through local sachems. The English had neutralized a troublesome sachem and strengthened a reliable ally.

The English now held Wyandanch responsible for the actions of the Shinnecocks. The following December when another dispute between the Shinnecocks and the town of Southampton erupted, the English called upon Wyandanch to intervene again in Shinnecock affairs. One of the problems inherent in the "working misunderstanding" about the nature of property had surfaced. Some Indians continued to plant in the meadows near their village on land that had been sold to the English in 1640. The English demanded that the Indians move their planting grounds to accommodate their expanding settlement. Wyandanch negotiated a resolution that required the Indians to remove from the land in question and to build a fence to protect their remaining fields from English livestock (J. Strong 1983, doc. no. 2).

The English repaid Wyandanch's services a few years later. In 1653 when Ninigret, his old nemesis from Rhode Island, raided Wyandanch's village, killing about thirty of his men and seizing his daughter, Quashawam, and fourteen other captives, the Montaukett sachem turned to Gardiner and the English for help. Although the episode is very poorly documented, it appears that Gardiner helped raise money for Quashawam's ransom (DSBD, 2: 119).

The kidnaping of Wyandanch's daughter was later celebrated in local folklore. The story was told and retold, and, of course, embellished over the centuries. In 1840 David Gardiner, one of Lion Gardiner's descendants, wrote the earliest account of the incident. "Tradition has it," said Gardiner, "that the raid took place during the festivities celebrating the wedding of the daughter" (1973, 23). Other accounts further embellished the tragic event, adding that the cruel Niantic warriors had killed her intended husband. Although none of these details are documented, local historians have repeated the story of the wedding feast many times (L. Strong and Karabag 1991, 192).

Ninigret claimed that Wyandanch and the Montauketts were now his tributaries. Wyandanch and his English allies in East Hampton rejected this assertion. The East Hampton proprietors feared that their exclusive right to the future purchase of Montauk would be jeopardized if Ninigret controlled the Montauketts. The Niantic sachem would not be bound by any agreement between East Hampton and the Montauketts. The United Colonies commissioners were concerned about the shift in the fragile balance of power among the Algonquian sachems. Fearing that the growing power of the Niantics might lead to more violence, they rejected Ninigret's assertion that the Montauketts were his tributaries. The New Haven court voted on August 23, 1654, to send twelve pounds of gunpowder and thirty pounds of shot to Wyandanch (RCNH, 1: 117–18).

Wyandanch quickly launched a surprise attack against a party of Niantics who were visiting the Indians on Block Island. The raid was a success, taking the lives of Ninigret's nephew, two Niantic sachems, and sixty of his men (RCNP, 10: 125). The English aid undoubtedly played a significant role in Ninigret's defeat. The military victory also increased Wyandanch's influence with the English and among his own people. This new status, however, was soon to bring the Montaukett sachem serious troubles and new challenges at home.

The relations between Wyandanch and the English reflect one of the patterns that emerged following the defeat of the Pequots. Sachems in New England and Long Island sought alliances with the English, who had displaced the Pequots as the dominant power in the area. The English used this opportunity to gain influence in the internal affairs of the Indian communities by providing military and economic support to selected sachems. The English expected the "alliance" sachems to control their own communities, to keep in close touch with their English allies, to help resolve conflicts between their people and the English, to prevent any of their people from harming English settlers or their property, and to negotiate and enforce the terms of land sales. In return the sachems, who in the past governed primarily by persuasion, were now able to use English support to increase their status and their authority over their communities.[1] The system worked well for both parties, but it was clear from the beginning that the English were the dominant partners in the alliances.

Cockenoe, one of the first Long Island Indians to become fluent in English, very likely played an important role in developing Wyandanch's accommodationist policy with the English. He remained one of Wyandanch's closest advisors until the Montaukett sachem's death in 1659. Cockenoe strengthened his relationship with the Montauketts when he married Wyandanch's sister (RTEH, 1: 261). His familiarity with the English language and customs enabled him to play an important role as a diplomatic liaison between the two

1. Richard White used the term *alliance sachems* to describe the Algonquian leaders who formed alliances with the French in the seventeenth century on the "middle ground" between the two cultures in the Great Lakes area (1991, 36–40). His analytical model works very well for the middle ground on Long Island in the same period.

cultures. He also benefitted materially from his English connections. The colonial documents indicate that Cockenoe was paid for his work as an interpreter and for such services as marking out the boundaries for deeds and tending the grazing lands on Montauk (W. Tooker 1980, 183–84; RTEH, 2: 109–11).

Relations between the Indians and the English generally involved such matters as trade, land sales, labor contracts, conflicts involving livestock, and cultural misunderstandings about the nature of "ownership." The latter two concerns played a major role in Algonquian-English relations during the first few decades after the English established settlements on eastern Long Island. The Indians continued to build their wigwams within the boundaries of the deeds. They saw no reason they should not be able to use any of the unoccupied lands around the English towns. In English law, however, the proprietors who had put up the money to purchase the property owned these "undivided" lands.

The town proprietors in Southampton and East Hampton, for example, allotted to each member of the corporation parcels of land that became their private property. The whole community used the remaining lands for grazing or hunting. Each proprietor held a claim to acreage in the undivided lands. The amount of money contributed to the initial purchase by a proprietor determined the size of a claim. As the communities grew, the proprietors allotted some parcels of the undivided lands to their children and sold others to new arrivals. This process inevitably forced conflicts with the Indians who were living on the undivided lands.

The expansion of these farming communities, of course, caused an increase in the numbers of livestock feeding on the land. The introduction of domestic livestock made a dramatic impact on the ecosystem and was a frequent cause of tensions between the English and the neighboring Algonquian communities (J. Williams 1995, 249–53). The English settlers allowed their hogs to range freely in the woods until harvest time when they brought them in to fatten them for slaughter.[2] Occasionally, when the Indians came upon the hogs, they hunted them like wild game and killed them. Hogs found rooting up shellfish beds were particularly vulnerable. Cattle and

2. As the English settlements grew, the problems caused by free-ranging hogs worsened. Finally, in 1683 the colonial government passed a law requiring people to keep their hogs confined (Kavenagh 1973, 2: 1288–89). Anyone finding a stray hog could kill it. One-third of the meat went to the individual who found the hog, and the rest went to the town.

horses also created problems. The Indians kept their winter food in storage pits near their wigwams. When they moved to another location, they left the pits open. Grazing livestock sometimes fell into the pits and injured themselves. Another problem arose when the animals invaded the unfenced Indian cornfields and destroyed the crops. Fences, of course, were an alien concept to the Indians.

These issues led to tensions about six years after the first settlers arrived in East Hampton. In the spring of 1655 Wyandanch and two of his advisors, Sassakata and Pauquatoun, met with Lion Gardiner, the Reverend Thomas James, John Mulford, and several representatives from East Hampton. The East Hampton people agreed to build and maintain a fence east of the village that would keep their horses out of the Indian planting grounds from early spring until after the fall harvest. The English also agreed that if their horses got through the fence they would pay for the damages. The presence of Indian planting grounds on the eastern portion of the 1648 purchase indicates that the Indians were still living on the land they had sold.

The East Hampton officials, concerned about the possibility that the Dutch or rival English investors might purchase the remainder of the Montaukett lands east of Napeague, pressed Wyandanch and his advisors to give the town exclusive purchase rights. This concession may have been a factor in the English decision to increase their military support to Wyandanch and to bestow upon him a title that greatly overstated his powers at that time. In the text of the 1655 agreement, the English referred to Wyandanch as the "Chief Sachem of Long Island" (Cooper 1993, 174). The term "Grand Sachem" appears frequently in the works of local historians who assume, incorrectly, that it was an indigenous position of authority. It was an empty title, of course, without English support.

When Ninigret again threatened Wyandanch in the fall of 1655, the English moved quickly to protect their loyal ally. The United Colony commissioners ordered John Youngs, an experienced sailor from Southold, to patrol the sound and block any attempt by Ninigret to attack the Montauketts. The commissioners instructed Youngs to take, sink, or destroy Ninigret's canoes (RCNP, 10: 151). The action successfully thwarted any plan the Niantic sachem may have had to retaliate for his defeat on Block Island. He did not initiate any further action against the Montauketts until after Wyandanch's death in 1659. The United Colonies paid Youngs 153 pounds to maintain the blockade for more than a year. In contrast, the colonies paid the missionary John Eliot a yearly salary of only 50 pounds for his "Indian work." Clearly, the English found missionary work far less important than the protection of their alliance sachem. Few Long Island sachems would now openly challenge any leader who could draw on this level of English support.

The importance of a reliable Algonquian ally who had the power to influence the behavior of his fellow sachems became more evident as the scramble for Indian lands continued. English settlers and speculators purchased Long Island real estate from any Algonquian sachem who appeared to have some authority over a given tract of land. These purchases often led to conflicts and court challenges. Some Indians viewed the transactions as leases that could be sold again to another buyer, and others purposely misled English buyers into purchasing land that did not belong to them. Wyandanch proved most adept at resolving these potentially explosive conflicts.

As the East Hampton community grew, the town officials pressed the Montauketts to move from the undivided lands and resettle east of Napeague. They resisted these pressures just as the Shinnecocks had done in 1649. In the fall of 1656, the town asserted its right of ownership by ordering that "noe wigwams shall be set up by any Indians whatsoever within our bounds" (RTEH, 1: 101). This sweeping decree was apparently directed at the dwellings in areas that were desired for new allotments, because a decade later there were many Montauketts still living on the undivided lands near Three Mile Harbor, two miles north of the English village.

In 1657 the Montaukett sachem demonstrated that the role of the alliance chief could be more than that of a passive conduit for English governance. Several Shinnecock men and an African American woman conspired to burn down several buildings in Southampton (RPCC, 22: 175–76; RCNP, 10: 180). The colony of Connecticut levied a fine of seven hundred pounds on the whole Shinnecock community. Wyandanch sent a representative with a written petition to the United Colonies session in Boston the following September and appealed the Connecticut court's fine (RCNP, 10: 180). Wyandanch's decision to go over the head of the Connecticut court and the articulation of his arguments indicate a growing familiarity with English institutions.

When he submitted the petition, Wyandanch also sent seventy-eight fathoms of wampum to the United Colonies' treasurer in New Haven. The wampum was undoubtedly intended to influence the commissioners (RCNP, 10: 194). The sachem began his presentation to the commissioners by reporting that the Shinnecocks had already sustained losses from English horses that destroyed their crops. He then argued that the Connecticut court had not been fully informed about the arson when they imposed the fine. He told the commissioners that the African American woman was primarily to blame for the arson and that the Shinnecock man who was involved was dead. Given these circumstances, argued Wyandanch, the fine was excessive. The United Colonies' commissioners agreed with Wyandanch (RCC, 1: 316–17). When the Connecticut court reconsidered the matter, they reduced the amount to one hundred pounds over a six-year period. Although this was a significant reduction, the amount remained a considerable burden for the Shinnecocks.

Fines of this kind were often used in New England as an effective means of social control. As long as an Algonquian community remained under the shadow of the debt, the English could intervene in their community affairs. The debt was also a strategy used to obtain Indian lands. According to historian Francis Jennings, a favorite strategy of the English was "the imposition of fines for a wide variety of offenses, the Indian's lands becoming forfeit if the fines were not paid by their due date" (1976, 144–45). As we shall see, the English on Long Island were to make equally effective use of this strategy.

In 1656 Wyandanch, along with his advisors—Cockenoe, Sassakataka, and Momoweta (Moughmaitow)—and his young son, Wyancombone, sold Lion Gardiner a large tract of beach land lying west of the Southampton town boundary for an undisclosed sum of money and trade goods (RTSH, 1: 170–71). Gardiner agreed to pay the sachem and his heirs twenty-five shillings a year, each October, forever. The whales that were cast up on the beach, a major source of wealth on the south shore of Long Island, remained Wyandanch's property. The Montauketts took the tails and fins of the whales for their ceremonial feasts and sold the baleen and oil to the English. These commodities could be turned into hard currency on the European market (J. Strong 1990, 17–29). Drift whales were the first cash crop on Long Island. The Indians also retained the right to cut flag grass and bulrushes, which they used to make mats for the wigwams. This transaction with Gardiner was unique in that it guaranteed a continuing return of income rather than a final dispossession. Six months later Gardiner granted the right to use a portion of the tract to a

Southampton man named John Cooper on the condition that he pay Wyandanch the yearly fee (RTSH, 1: 171). There is no indication in the colonial records, however, that Gardiner continued the payments to Wyandanch's heirs after the sachem's death the following year.

The question of drift whales came up again in November 1658 when Wyandanch gave Lion Gardiner and the Reverend Thomas James of East Hampton half of the whales "or other great fish" that drifted onto the beach between Napeague and the far end of Montauk. This was an important grant because it gave the two men an exclusive right to all of the ocean beaches on Montaukett lands. The town of East Hampton owned the whale rights from Napeague west to the Southampton border and held them in common trust. Wyandanch did require a small percentage of their profit, but left it to James and Gardiner to pay "what they shall judge meete and according as they find profit by them" (RTEH, 1: 150).

Wyandanch's generosity to the two influential East Hampton men may have served him well two months later when he brought suit in the town courts against a young townsman named Jeremy Vaile for damages to his large canoe. The vessel, probably one used for trips across the sound, may have been thirty or forty feet long. The suit is significant because it is one of the earliest recorded instances of an Indian plaintiff seeking damages from an Englishman in an English court.

Lion Gardiner testified for Wyandanch against Vaile and charged him with negligence. Vaile and Anthony Waters, another East Hampton man, borrowed the canoe to carry some goods over to Gardiner's Island and ran into some bad weather. They landed the canoe on the island but failed to secure it properly. Gardiner ordered them to return and make sure it was safe, but by the time they got back, the canoe was damaged and full of water. The court ruled for the plaintiff and awarded Wyandanch ten shillings (RTSH, 1: 152).

On July 14, 1659, shortly before his death, Wyandanch signed a most unusual document. It reads almost like a last will and testament. Written in the first person as if dictated by Wyandanch, it acknowledged Lion Gardiner's friendship, counsel, and material aid over a twenty-four-year period. Gardiner, said Wyandanch, "appeared to us not only as a friend but as a father" (RTSM, 1: 3–4). In return for this friendship Wyandanch made him a gift of a large tract of land between Huntington and Setauket that included most of what is now the town of Smithtown in the middle of Long Island. The Nissequogue River, which runs through the center of the tract, was the home of Nasseconset, the Nissequogue sachem. A close examination of the document raises a number of questions about its authenticity. The relationship between Wyandanch and Gardiner was certainly close, but it seems unlikely that Wyandanch, who had previously sold land and whale rights to Gardiner, would now give him a tract of land as big as the one he sold to East Hampton in 1648.

Wyandanch died sometime during the fall of 1659. According to Lion Gardiner, the Montaukett sachem was poisoned, but this allegation is not corroborated in any of the colonial records. It is also possible that he died in the plague, which took the lives of an estimated two-thirds of the Algonquian people on Long Island between 1659 and 1664 (L. Gardiner 1980, 146; J. Strong 1997).

The era of accommodation was coming to a close. There was no longer a need for a "grand sachem." The growth of the English settlements and the declining Indian population shifted the demographics heavily in favor of the whites. The English were now in a position to dominate the Algonquian people. The need for a single Indian leader who could arbitrate disputes and control local sachems, however, was now over. In 1665 Richard Nicolls, the first governor of the newly established colony of New York, officially declared that there was no longer any "grand sachem" of Long Island. "Every sachem," said the governor, "shall keep his particular property over his people as formerly" (DSBD, 2: 127). The English, who had created the position, had now abolished it.

The death of Wyandanch encouraged both the English and the Niantics to take advantage of the Montauketts during the transition to new leadership. Ninigret, whose ambitions for obtaining tributaries on Long Island had never abated, launched several raids on the Montauketts in the spring and summer of 1660. At the same time several East Hampton entrepreneurs attempted to get control over the remaining Montaukett lands. Unfortunately, the colonial records provide only a dim outline of these affairs. The sequence of events is not entirely clear, but it appears that the Montauketts' troubles began when Ninigret's Niantics attacked a group of Montauketts who were on their way across Long Island Sound to visit a village in Rhode Island. The Niantics killed six Montaukett men in an attack that took place on Gull Island, a tiny, barren, uninhabited islet a few miles northeast of Montauk (RCNP, 10: 247–48).

The Montauketts responded by sending a war party to attack

Ninigret's allies, the Manisses, who lived on Block Island. Unfortunately for the Montauketts, the Manisses spotted their canoes and prepared an ambush for the unsuspecting war party. The Manisses sprang the trap after the Montauketts drew their canoes ashore and moved inland. They destroyed the Montaukett canoes, cutting off the possibility of retreat, and proceeded to kill nearly every one of the invaders. The Manisses took one of the Montaukett sachems to Rhode Island where the Niantics executed him (EHPLC, call no. NG 17A–C). The raids by the Niantics and their allies left the Montauketts nearly defenseless by the summer of 1660.

Wyandanch's widow, who, unfortunately, is not named in the colonial records, emerged as sunksquaw of the Montauketts during these troubled times. Female leaders are not unusual in Algonquian communities. Women in "chiefly lineages" often assumed positions of authority over their communities (Grumet 1980, 46–53). Some of the women who became sunksquaws were the wives or widows of sachems, but others were married to men who had no standing.

Wyandanch's widow, however, may have assumed leadership because the Montauketts' enemies had killed so many of their eligible men. Wyandanch's daughter, Quashawam, and his son, Wyancombone, survived him, but the son was too young to assume a leadership role. Although the sunksquaw was a principal party in five major transactions between 1660 and 1663, the English clerks never identified her by name. The same documents, however, always named her son, Wyancombone. This omission is noteworthy because it reflects English attitudes about the status of women and their role in economic transactions. Property and political power in English culture were almost exclusively in the male domain. The English who became involved in negotiations with Algonquian women tended to ignore or understate their roles. The English often identified these women only as the wife, mother, sister, or widow of the man named in the document (J. Strong 1995; J. Strong 1996a).

The Montaukett sunksquaw, her son, and her advisors—Pauquatoun, Cockenoe, Massaquats, Manecopungun (also known as Gentleman), and Powhes—turned to East Hampton for help as Wyandanch had done after Ninigret's raid in 1653. This time, however, the English refused to protect the villages on Montauk from attack. They told the Montauketts that they must leave their homes and take temporary refuge within the bounds of East Hampton. Cockenoe, who had always maintained close personal ties to the English, probably urged the Montauketts to accept the offer.

In February 1662 Gardiner and his colleagues pressed the Montauketts for a gift to show their gratitude for the sanctuary provided by the town. Gardiner asked them to give a small tract of land on the eastern border of the town called Hither (Heather) Woods. The forty-two-hundred-acre tract extends from Napeague eastward to Fort Pond. The sunksquaw and her son were accompanied by nine counselors, including Pauquatoun, Massaquats, and Powhes. Two of her influential advisors, Cockenoe and Manecopungun, however, were not party to the negotiations. It is possible that their absence indicated some dissatisfaction within the Montaukett community over these negotiations. Although Cockenoe generally supported friendly relations with East Hampton, Manecopungun was somewhat ambivalent.

The only source of information about these negotiations comes from a petition written in 1800 by two Montauketts, Benjamin and Stephen Pharaoh (EHPLC, call no. NG 17A–C). Although the account is based on oral tradition rather than written documents, it is one of the few sources that provide insights into the Indians' view of these historic events. According to the Pharaohs' testimony, the East Hampton officials took advantage of the desperate plight of the Montauketts.

The Pharaohs reported that the East Hampton men offered to give the Montauketts powder and shot in exchange for a deed to the southern half of Hither Woods. When the Montauketts took a vote by a raise of hands, the majority were in favor of the exchange. The East Hampton men returned home and drafted a lengthy document, reciting the circumstances of the exchange and, according to the Pharaohs, making significant changes in the terms of the agreement and in the boundary lines as well.

The East Hampton men wrote the deed with a purpose beyond the straightforward description of the transaction itself. It was as much a defense of the deed as it was an account of the terms. They wrote the deed in the first person, as if the document had been dictated by Wyancombone himself. "I Wyancombone, son of [Wyandanch] . . . send greeting [to] . . . my two guardians left by my deceased father viz Mr. Lion Gardiner and Mr. David Gardiner" (R. Smith 1926, 25–29).

The next clause in the deed described the transfer of Hither Woods to East Hampton. The flowery expression of the Montauketts' esteem for the East Hampton inhabitants suggests some embellishment by the English. The Montauketts gave as a gift to the English all of the land from Napeague to Fort Pond "in consideration of the love which we have and do bare unto these our trustie and beloved friends of Easthampton." This statement, of course, is in sharp contrast to the testimony given by the Pharaohs who said that according to Montaukett oral history, only half of the southern half of the tract was involved and that it was sold for powder and shot.

The text went on to describe how the Montauketts had "manifested their consent freelie by a vote not one contradicting ye same," and that Lion Gardiner and his son David, "whom ye deceased father left as overseers and guardians of ye aforesaid Wyancombone sachem," had approved the transaction.

The assertion of guardianship apparently was not deemed sufficient. Shortly after the Montauketts signed the deed, Wyancombone died, probably from smallpox. Either someone challenged the deed or both Gardiner and James feared that such a challenge might successfully be launched, because they shifted grounds a year later and claimed that Wyancombone had been twenty-one at the time he signed the deed. If this were true, according to English law, Wyancombone would not have needed a guardian in the first place. Gardiner and James went to his mother in December 1662 and elicited from her a statement verifying that her son had been twenty-one when he signed the deed (RTEH, 1: 198). The mother's testimony is open to serious question, of course, because there were no written records nor did Indians keep track of time by a European calendar.

In addition to giving Gardiner and James the land, the deed reaffirmed their rights to half of the whales that beached themselves along the shore. The other half, which had been retained by Wyandanch in 1655, was given to the town of East Hampton. This was a significant concession because whale oil brought from one and one-half to two pounds sterling per barrel, and an adult whale produced an average of thirty-six barrels of oil (Edwards and Rattray 1956, 274–75).

The Montauketts also affirmed that East Hampton held an exclusive right of purchase for all of the remaining Montaukett land. "We also stand engaged neither directly nor indirectly to let, give or sell any part of the land without consent of Easthampton." This wording was actually a restatement of a similar clause in the 1655 agreement.

The deed also included an agreement establishing shared land use for Hither Woods and Montauk. The English granted the Montauketts permission to set up their wigwams and gather firewood on the Hither Woods tract, and the Montauketts reaffirmed the English right, set in the 1655 agreement, to graze their livestock east of Fort Pond between the harvest and the spring planting.

The death of Wyandanch and the subsequent "Gift Deed" marked the end of the accommodationist policy. The metaphorical "middle ground" separating the two cultures was nearly gone. The Montauketts and the other Algonquian peoples on Long Island were becoming more dependent on the English for economic survival. The heavy hand of English authority was present in nearly all of the Montauketts' affairs.

The last four decades of the seventeenth century saw a disastrous decline in the Algonquian population on Long Island. The Algonquian peoples suffered military defeats and were decimated by European diseases. As a result, the balance of power shifted to favor the Europeans. The English began to assert their sovereignty over the local Indian communities as the process of dispossession progressed. The imposition of sovereignty, however, involved a continuing struggle, which is still in process today, as evidenced by the continuing conflicts over Indian casinos, child adoption rights, and tax laws.

European diseases, such as smallpox, measles, and several other unidentified viruses, took a frightful toll on Native American lives during the seventeenth century. The psychological impact of the epidemics added to the suffering. The silent killers respected no one. Women, children, the elderly, the weak, and the strong were all struck down in the same relentless manner. The Algonquian shamans were helpless to relieve the fears or the agony of the victims.

The traditional healing rituals and practices actually aided in the rapid spread of the highly infectious diseases. When relatives came to take part in the group healing ceremonies, they crowded around the patient to give support and comfort. The close interaction enabled the virus to infect most of the well-intended visitors and, in a very short time, wipe out the whole village. Samuel Taylor, a Quaker who visited Shelter Island in 1659, about the time that Wyandanch died, recorded an account of such a curing ritual. His guide took him to a wigwam where he witnessed the following ceremony.

[B]y and by came in a great many lusty proper men, Indians all, and sat down; and every one had a short truncheon stick in his hand, pretty thick and about two feet long. So they began to powwow, as they called it; and it was thus; the sick man sitting up as well as he could, and having a dish or calabash of water in his hand, he supped a little of it, sat the dish down and spitted it with his mouth into his hands, and threw it over his naked body . . . and beating himself with his arms and clapping his hands till he was all of such a foam with sweat and did speak something in his own tongue very loud, and as he spoke, they all spoke as with one voice, and knocked on the ground with their truncheons, so that it made the very woods ring and the ground shake. (1980, 285–86)

In 1660, soon after the death of Wyandanch, Lion Gardiner wrote the first direct mention of an epidemic on eastern Long Island. He reported that nearly two-thirds of the Indians on Long Island died in the outbreak (1980, 146). There appears to have been a series of outbreaks over the next four years. Smallpox may have caused Wyancombone's death in 1662. Another outbreak, which also swept through the Montaukett villages, occurred during the winter of 1663–1664. The situation grew so serious that East Hampton passed an ordinance isolating Montauketts from most contact with the English. "It is ordered that no Indian shall come to town . . . upon penalty of paying 5 shillings or be whipped, until they be free of the small poxe" (RTEH, 1: 201). Montauketts who wished to trade with the English had to stop outside the village limits and call to the townspeople to come out to meet them. The devastating loss of population weakened the Algonquian people and undermined their capacity to resist the steadily increasing European intervention into their community affairs.

The English viewed the Montauketts as a troublesome presence on the land, an obstacle to economic growth and development. The only question in the minds of the English was how to get them off the land without getting into legal or political difficulty. Another dimension of the continuing problem was that the English were always putting the proverbial cart before the horse. They purchased the land before the question of Indian residence was resolved. As a result the English were forced into the awkward practice of leasing back portions of the land or acknowledging the Indians' right to dwell and plant on a designated area. These temporary solutions were acceptable to the English because they got the land they wanted at the time without a nasty confrontation. The Montauketts, it was hoped, would eventually "die out" or migrate west. East Hampton rejected the pattern of Native American affairs set in New England, which provided for reservations. Although the reservation system was rooted in the same attitude toward the Indians, it did provide a clearly defined refuge for a time. East Hampton, however, did all they could to prevent the Montauketts from surviving as a separate culture.

The East Hampton settlers no longer gave serious consideration to Montaukett sovereignty. In the fall of 1663, for example, the Montauketts protested against the English practice of mowing hay on the meadowlands at Montauk. The settlers had not considered it necessary to consult with the Montaukett leaders. In an angry response to this practice, the Montauketts threatened to burn the settlers' hay unless they stopped (ibid., 205). Disputes over the use of Montaukett lands became more frequent as the East Hampton population increased.

The following summer the English conquest of New Netherland brought about dramatic changes on eastern Long Island. King Charles established the colony of New York for his brother, James, the duke of York. The king severed the political ties between Connecticut and the English towns on eastern Long Island and placed them under the jurisdiction of New York. The duke authorized Nicolls to draft the laws for the new colony himself without consulting local representatives of the settlers. Nicolls proceeded to write a legal code, which he called, appropriately, the Duke's Laws.

The Duke's Laws, arranged in alphabetical categories, included nine ordinances listed under the heading "Indians" (Lincoln 1894, 1: 40–42). Eight of these laws regulated relations between Indians and Christians, and the last prohibited Indians from holding powwows or other religious celebrations. These laws reflected the new governor's concerns about the potential for conflicts to erupt into violence over land transactions, damage to crops and livestock, and the sale of alcohol. The scramble for Indian land by individual entrepreneurs, such as Lion Gardiner, frequently led the Indians to complain that the English were cheating them. These conflicts often involved rival English purchasers, who often cheated each other as well as the Indians. In an attempt to bring some order to the process, the Duke's Laws stipulated that the governor supervise all land transactions. The governor would now interview both the sachems involved and the English purchaser. In an ordinance foreshadowing the Indian Non-intercourse Act of 1790, the governor's office was required to approve and record all purchases.

Nicolls was also concerned about constant complaints from Algonquian villagers that they could not get proper redress for crop damage by the settlers' domestic livestock and for other injuries to persons and property. Rather than trusting the local colonial courts for redress, the Indians frequently killed and ate the livestock that damaged their fields. Four of the ordinances addressed the issue of damages to a delicately balanced ecosystem that provided the Algonquian peoples of Long Island with a stable food base. Foraging hogs, cattle, goats, sheep, and horses threatened the Indians' hunting grounds and planting fields (J. Williams 1995, 245–64). In 1642 Miantonomi, the Narragansett sachem, warned the Montauketts that "We shall all be gone shortly, for you know our fathers had plenty of deer and skins, our plains were full of deer, as also our woods, of turkies, and our coves of fish and fowl. But these English, having gotten our land, they with scythes cut down the grass and with axes fell the trees; their cows and horses eat the grass, and their hogs spoil our clam banks, and we shall be starved" (L. Gardiner 1980, 142). Miantonomi's speech clearly defined the way economic and ecological imperialisms reinforced each other (Cronon 1983, 162–63).

The Duke's Laws required the English to compensate the Indians for any damages to their crops and to help the Indians build fences where necessary. The governor believed that if he could convince the Indians that the courts would treat them fairly, they would be less inclined to take actions that often led to violence. The second ordinance stipulated that whenever Christians harmed Indians, the injuries were to be redressed "as if the case had been betwixt Christian and Christian" (Lincoln 1894, 40).

Nicolls soon discovered that it was very difficult to enforce the spirit of these ordinances on a settler population with strong prejudices against Indians. The Algonquian people continued to deal with the problem of invading English livestock in their own way. In 1680, for example, the Shinnecocks shot several of the English farmers' horses and buried them (NYCD, 14: 756).

In the fall of 1665, after the harvest, Governor Nicolls called the first meeting of his court. He invited several of the Long Island sachems to confer with him about their concerns. He undoubtedly wanted them to know that his authority superseded that of the local town officials and that they could appeal to him for a redress of their grievances. On the following day he met with Quashawam, the Montaukett sunksquaw, and the East Hampton officials to discuss some of their disagreements.

The first order of business was to set forth the boundaries between the Montaukett lands and East Hampton. It was agreed that East Hampton extended to Fort Pond and that "All the rest to the east end of the island shall belong to ye sunksquaw, daughter of the Montaukett sachem" (Cooper 1993, 166). This important clause acknowledged Montaukett ownership of the land east of Napeague Bay (see map 3), but a subsequent paragraph repeated the agreement made by Wyandanch in 1644 and again in 1655 that gave East Hampton exclusive purchase rights to the remaining Montaukett lands. This time, however, the East Hampton proprietors accepted the new governor's jurisdiction over their land transactions with the Montauketts. Colonial authority over Indian land sales was to become a crucial issue for the Montauketts.

The next concern was the conflict over the use of Montaukett lands by East Hampton. Both parties agreed that English livestock could graze at Montauk from late fall after the harvest was in until early spring when the planting began. The last clause in the agreement called for East Hampton to pay the Montauketts a yearly fee of forty shillings for the grazing rights.

The agreement was a temporary victory for Quashawam and the Montauketts. They had managed to reaffirm title to the land at Montauk and have it endorsed by the governor of the colony. Governor Nicolls had also accomplished his goal by establishing colonial control over the process of dispossession. He continued his active role in Indian affairs the following summer when he warned the towns of East Hampton and Southampton to honor their agreements with the Indians. At the same time he made a concession to the town governments by establishing the Commission of Indian Affairs for Long Island and appointing many of the local men who had been involved in the major purchases of Indian land. Nicolls appointed John Mulford and Thomas Baker from East Hampton and Thomas Topping, John Ogden, and John Howell from Southampton. The governor empowered the commission to summon testimony, authorize the use of military force if necessary, and set up procedures that they believed would improve Indian relations (DSBD, 2: 49–50).

Quashawam disappears from the colonial records soon after her settlement with the governor. She probably died sometime in 1666. The only reference to her death comes from Ninigret, the Niantic sachem, who told the Rhode Island court in 1669 that Wyandanch's daughter was dead (L. Strong and Karabag 1991, 201).

Unfortunately, little is known about the Montaukett leadership during the next four years. The 1664 agreement that endorsed Quashawam's leadership also set forth a line of succession calling for her uncle's son Awansamawge to take her place, but there is no mention of him in any of the surviving colonial documents. Apparently a group of elders, which included Pauquatoun, Sassakataka, and Manecopungun, governed the Montauketts during this period. In 1667, for example, when the town officials met with the Montauketts to determine a boundary location, they spoke with Pauquatoun, who has been identified in various documents as a counselor to both Wyandanch's widow and her daughter, Quashawam (RTEH, 1: 260–61).

Although there are no references to the Montaukett leadership, the records do indicate changes in other aspects of their lifeways. Quashawam's agreement to allow the English grazing rights at Montauk brought the two communities into more and more direct contact. The English needed to have someone at Montauk to tend their livestock and keep up their fences. The result, of course, was that many Montauketts became increasingly involved in the English economic system.

By 1665 relations between the settlers and the Montauketts had gone through many changes. Not only were the Montauketts engaged with the English in tending the cattle near their villages on Montauk, but many had also moved from their homes to live in or near the village of East Hampton where they worked in English households as domestics, unskilled day laborers, or indentured servants.

Many Indians now stayed near the English villages, hoping to get odd jobs wherever they could. One such day laborer, a Montaukett man named Nangenutch and renamed "Will" by the English, had lived as a servant in the house of Richard Shaw, an East Hampton settler. Shaw twice accused Nangenutch of theft, and the second time he turned the young Montaukett over to the town magistrates for a public whipping (Christoph 1980, 71). During the colonial period, masters often gave their servants or slaves over to the public officials for such punishment. Generally, the town officials did not question the word of the master (Kawashima 1986, 215).

A short time later Nangenutch faced more serious charges. In 1669 Mary Miller, an East Hampton housewife, accused him of rape. Nangenutch was tried before the Court of Assizes in New York and found guilty of a lesser charge of attempted rape. The court sentenced him to be whipped and sold into slavery in the West Indies to pay the court costs. With the help of some of his friends, Nangenutch broke out of jail before the sale could take place and fled to Montauk. When the Montauketts refused to turn him over to the colonial authorities, the East Hampton officials placed a fine of four hundred bushels of corn on the tribe (J. Strong 1994b, 576).

The fine on the Montauketts amounted to about ten times the sheriff's expenses. The total debt now imposed on them was forty pounds, about the equivalent of four hundred bushels of Indian corn. Nicolls returned to England in May, leaving his successor, Francis Lovelace, to deal with the problem. Both William Wells, the high sheriff for East Riding (present-day Suffolk County), which included East Hampton, and John Mulford pressed Governor Lovelace to resolve the issue.

The imposition of the fine caused a split in the Montaukett community between the accommodationists and those Indians who were hostile to the English in East Hampton. Pauquatoun remained loyal to Wyandanch's policy of friendly accommodation with the East Hampton community, but other Montauketts, including Manecopungun, Akomias, Massaquats, Papasequin, Nompum, and Nauneyauwant, were apparently angered at the fine. They resolved to pay "no more of the money for ye Indian who ran away" (CSAIP, 1: 19). Some of the Montauketts agreed with them, and in the early summer of 1669 they decided to take a very dramatic course of action.

Manecopungun, an influential elder who had advised Wyandanch's widow when she negotiated the 1660 deed, had apparently become increasingly alienated from the English in East Hampton. He had not participated in the negotiations for the "Gift Deed" that turned over Hither Woods to the English, and now he was to take a much more radical action against East Hampton. He and Akomias headed a delegation to Rhode Island where they negotiated an alliance with the old Montaukett nemesis, Ninigret, accepting a tributary status under the Niantic sachem (RCRI, 2: 270–71; Thomas James to Southold Town, June 29, 1669, CSAIP, 1: 18). The delegation sent wampum to Ninigret and presented him with a gun that had belonged to Wyandanch, perhaps to signify that the Niantic sachem now held authority over the Montauketts. The meeting with Ninigret took place at a great powwow, which included guests from many of the southern New England Indian communities. Manecopungun's motives in this affair are not known. He took a considerable risk in turning to the Niantic sachem who had attacked their villages on several occasions

over the previous three decades. Perhaps he sought to use the threat
of an alliance with Ninigret to gain an advantage in the Montauketts'
negotiations with the New York authorities.

Manecopungun apparently had second thoughts about his
overture to Ninigret because he came back to East Hampton and
reported everything to the Reverend Thomas James and John Mulford. They were quick to turn the affair to their own advantage by
raising an alarm and charging that the Niantic powwow had been
organized by Ninigret to plan a conspiracy to destroy the English
settlements in New England and on Long Island (RCC, 2: 548–51).

The Reverend Thomas James embellished Manecopungun's
account with the allegation that three common targets of English fear
and contempt were involved. In a letter to John Mason, James
reported that French and Mohawk troops, armed by the Quakers,
would aid the Indian warriors.[3] With the help of these allies, wrote
Thomas James, the Montauketts hoped to "have their land again from
the English and be as in former times before the English came."
Shortly after he sent his letter to Southold, James joined Mulford and
Thomas Baker in another letter to John Mason in Connecticut. They
told Mason about the plot and asked him to investigate the matter
(CSAIP, 1: 18, 11).

The East Hampton men then turned immediately to confront
the "Ninigret" faction at Montauk. The actions taken by the town
clearly suggest that they never believed the Montauketts were much
of a military threat. It seems likely that the East Hampton officials
were primarily concerned with restoring their control over the Montaukett community. They sent a delegation consisting of the constable and two other men to tell the Montauketts that because they had
participated in a plot to "wholly destroy the English," they must all
turn over their guns to the English. When some of the Montauketts
"resolutely refused to deliver them," there was an impasse for some
time. Finally they agreed to surrender the weapons as proof that they
were not involved in a conspiracy to kill the English (RCRI, 2: 285).

3. The threat of an Indian uprising was alarming enough, but the suggestion
that the French, who were regarded by the English Protestants as agents of the pope,
were behind it was certain to frighten the English settlers. New York and New England officials frequently voiced concerns about a French and Indian alliance. The
French had sent troops from Canada to the English north of Albany twice during
the winter of 1665–1666, and the Treaty of Breda in 1667 gave France Nova Sco-
tia, raising English fears about the threat of further expansion (Ritchie 1977, 76).
The Quakers, of course, were a favorite target of the English Puritans throughout
New England and in some Long Island communities.

Governor Lovelace now renewed his pressure on the Montauketts to pay the fine. On November 19, 1699, he turned the matter over to the Commission of Indian Affairs, which included John Mulford, and ordered them to immediately arrest the four Montauketts who helped Nangenutch escape. Lovelace told the commissioners to "threaten them severely" and punish them for not paying the fine. The governor told Mulford that he left the "prudent management" of the affair to him and the members of the commission. They were authorized to "find some expedient [means] how to secure at least so much as the late governor [Nicolls] proposed to give which you know was forty pounds" (Christoph and Christoph 1982, 191–92).

The expedient means that they found was to transfer the fine levied on the men responsible for the jailbreak to the whole Montaukett community. To pay the fine, which was the equivalent of four hundred bushels of corn, would take more than the yearly produce of ten Montaukett homesteads (ibid., 200). Although the amount of corn produced by the Montauketts each year is not known, it is likely that their patterns of maize horticulture were similar to other small-scale coastal Algonquian villagers. Most Native American cornfields in this area were on small family plots, usually less than one acre in size, and produced less than forty bushels per year (Thomas 1976, 12–13).

The Montauketts were undoubtedly still recovering from a devastating epidemic, which had reduced their population significantly. If they turned over four hundred bushels of corn, enough to feed about fifty people for a year, they would have difficulty surviving the winter. Mulford and his fellow commissioners must have been well aware of the hardship the fine would inflict on the Montauketts. They proposed that the Montauketts turn over a tract of land as payment for the fine. Sheriff William Wells pressed the Montauketts to accept an offer from three East Hampton men—John Mulford, Jeremiah Conkling, and the Reverend Thomas James—to pay their fine in return for some land (R. Smith 1926, 32–34). Mulford's participation in this arrangement appears to have been a clear conflict of interest, but no objection was raised at the time.

Later that fall the Montauketts regrouped under the leadership of Wyandanch's grandson, Poniute, and a sunksquaw named Askickotantup. On November 3, 1669, Poniute, who was now identified as the sachem, Askickotantup, Pauquatoun, and Akomias signed a pledge of loyalty to Governor Lovelace (NYCD, 14: 627). The Montaukett leaders rejected any connection with Ninigret, stating that they "doe utterly disclayme any such vassalage as Ninigret did declare to the governor of Rhode Island," and promised not to send the Niantic sachem anymore wampum or other gifts. Not surprisingly, John Mulford, Jeremiah Conkling, and the Reverend Thomas James witnessed the pledge.

Now that the Montauketts were firmly under East Hampton's control, it was difficult for them to resist other demands. Fifteen days after the Montauketts signed the pledge of loyalty, James and Conkling asked them to confirm an agreement on the rights to beached whales that Wyandanch had made with James and Lion Gardiner in 1658. The agreement had given Gardiner and James the rights to all of the whales that washed ashore from Napeague to the eastern end of Montauk (RTEH, 1: 150). Conkling now wanted to take over Gardiner's share of the whales. Pauquatoun, Cockenoe, and two other Montauketts, Wassouman and Aukeanit, quickly granted this request (ibid., 2: 321).

The colonial authorities also demanded that the Montauketts and all other Indians on the eastern end of Long Island sell all of their horses back to the original English owners. The sale of horses to Indians, said the order from the Governor's Council, "in time may prove very dangerous and prejudicial to his majesties subjects in those parts" (SHNY, 166). There is no indication, however, that any of the Indians on Long Island ever used horses for military purposes.

Mulford, James, and Conkling now moved to complete their agreement with the Montauketts to take a tract of land on Montauk in exchange for paying off the four-hundred-bushel fine. On December 10, 1670, the Montauketts transferred three thousand acres of beach and meadows south of Fort Pond and Lake Montauk (see map 3), approximately where the village of Montauk is located today, to Mulford, Conkling, and James (Cooper 1993, 166–69). The sachem Poniute, who had taken the name "Mousup," signed along with the sunksquaw Wuchikitaubit, Pauquatoun, Cockenoe, Obediah, and four other elders. Wuchikitaubit may have been a new name taken by Askickotantup, who had signed the pledge of loyalty to the governor the previous year. The deed confirms Poniute's "alias," but does not mention a similar connection between Askickotantup and Wuchikitaubit.

Mulford had taken full advantage of his position as justice of the peace and member of the Indian commission, but the town officials challenged the transaction for a very different reason. Thomas Baker complained to Governor Lovelace that the patent granted the proprietors, as a corporate body, the right to purchase land at Montauk. The three individuals could not, therefore, purchase the land for their own private use. Baker and the other proprietors feared that they might be restricted from using the grazing land in the tract. They turned to the governor because, under the Duke's Laws, he had to approve all transactions involving Indian lands. The existence of three forms of property rights within English law and custom—private, corporate, and public—further complicated relations between the Indians and the English. The issue raised by Baker concerned a conflict between corporate and private property rights. The third form, public property, was virtually nonexistent at this time because the corporation of proprietors who had contributed to the purchase of the deed from Governors Eaton and Hopkins included most of the inhabitants. There was, therefore, no distinction between the corporation and the public until two decades later when the town's population grew to include a significant number of voting freemen who were not proprietors.

Governor Lovelace wrote to Mulford and informed him of the proprietors' opposition to the purchase and withheld his approval. Lovelace's action forced Mulford and his associates to come to terms with their fellow proprietors. The agreement reached called for the proprietors to take over the tract of land at Montauk in exchange for 180 acres of land within the bounds of East Hampton, where the village of Amagansett is located today. The governor then issued his confirmation of the purchase. The Reverend Thomas James did not take the forced compromise very gracefully. He later excommunicated Baker from the Church and told Governor Andros, who replaced Lovelace in 1674, that Baker was unfit for public office (NYCD, 14: 712–13).

The episode had cost the Montauketts about one-third of their remaining land and an opportunity to assert their independence from East Hampton, but it also reaffirmed an important precedent. East Hampton's independence was now limited in matters involving Indian land. The Montauketts were to make use of this small window of opportunity with varying degrees of success over the next three centuries.

THREE

LAND AND LABOR
1670–1740

D URING THE last three decades of the seventeenth century, the Montauketts experienced many changes in their life-ways. Increasing numbers of them became directly involved in the English economy as indentured servants, cattle keepers, whalers, and laborers. A growing dependence on European manu-factured goods and a taste for such commodities as sugar, pork, beef, and alcohol forced the Montauketts to sell their labor for the money to purchase the desired items.

The most common path of entry into the English economy was through the indenture system. The specific terms of the indentures varied widely. One of the earliest records of these labor contracts describes the sale of a six-year-old Indian boy named Hopewell. In 1665 John Kirkland, an East Hampton inhabitant, sold Hopewell to the Reverend Thomas James for fifteen pounds sterling. Hopewell, an orphan whose parents may have perished in one of the smallpox outbreaks, was one year old when Kirkland purchased him from his guardians (RTEH, 1: 229). The child was to serve a twenty-five-year indenture, and, in exchange, his owner would provide him with room and board and a sum of ten pounds at the end of his term.

Adults could also sell themselves into indenture. In 1673, for example, a Montaukett named Isaac hired himself out to William Edwards of East Hampton. Isaac agreed "to live as a servant and do him . . . faithful service during the space of half a year," in exchange for four pounds sterling. Five years later another Montaukett, Tom T. Indian, signed with the Reverend Thomas James for a much longer period. Tom apprenticed himself to James for a term of three years "to do him true and faithful service and to be obedient to all his lawful commands by day or night." In return James provided room and board and one new coat each year and promised to give Tom two more coats at the end of his term (ibid., 362, 411).

John Indian, a Montaukett, bound himself out to Richard Stretton of East Hampton for a two-year term in 1683. John was to serve Stretton faithfully and to be on call at all times day or night. For this service Stretton agreed to pay him twelve pounds at the end of the term. John Mahue, also a Montaukett, indentured himself to Philip Leake of East Hampton for only three months. Leake paid him three pounds, six shillings, about twice the monthly rate paid to John Indian. Another Montaukett, Jeffrey, bound himself out to Richard Shaw for a term of seven years for a payment of twenty pounds, less than three pounds a year, and room and board (ibid., 2: 132–33, 212).

Parents or guardians often negotiated terms of indenture for their children. Many young Montauketts became attached to English households in this manner. In some instances parents who negotiated these indentures received a few shillings when the contract was signed. Papasequin negotiated two such contracts for his children.

Montaukett fence builders. Drawing by David Bunn Martine.

In 1685 Papasequin and his wife bound out their seven-year-old son, Quausuch, to Jacob Schellinger for a ten-year term, beginning in 1688 (ibid., 173). Schellinger paid Papasequin twenty shillings when the child was delivered to him in 1688 and promised to pay ten pounds to Quausuch at the end of his term.

Six years later Papasequin and his wife bound out their daughter, Marget, to Daniel Osborn for a seven-year term (EHPLC, call no. 10 WB, 126). Osborn paid the parents three pounds and gave their daughter room and board and three pounds when she finished her term. Both children probably experienced a rather dramatic immersion in English culture and values, but there was no provision for teaching them to read and write English or preparing them for a trade. The indentures for European children, however, commonly included such benefits. Renock Garrison, a white settler from East Hampton, negotiated a labor agreement that is typical of the English indentures. Garrison bound out his son, Samuel, to Isaack Mills, a carpenter, who promised to teach the youth to read and write and help him master the art of carpentry (RTEH, 2: 133–34). Only in rare instances did the indentures for Indians include such provisions.

Not all Indians entered the English economic system as slaves or indentured servants. English farmers, merchants, and artisans often hired laborers for the day or for a specific job, and paid them upon completion of the task in money or in goods. Some of these jobs, such as fence watching, tending livestock, rescuing livestock from wetland swamps, carrying flour from the mill to the homes, and doing chores around the farm, did not require much skill, but a few tasks, such as the construction of rail fences, guiding hunters and fishermen, and whaling, were skilled crafts.

Fences, of course, play a vital role in any agricultural system. There were serious legal consequences for any farmer who did not keep his fences in good repair. If his livestock got out because his fences were allowed to fall into disrepair, he would be liable for any damage the animals caused. Fence construction, therefore, was a highly valued skill. Settlers often recruited Indians and trained them in the use of iron woodworking tools.

Fences needed constant watching. The weather and the continual probing of the livestock weakened even those fences built "pig tight, horse high, and bull strong" (Hawke 1988, 34). The town of East Hampton hired Montauketts to monitor the fences, day and night, from April to October. The Indians often set up their wigwams near the fences and lived there for the season.

Although the data on wages is sparse, apparently the English generally paid Indians less than English laborers. In the spring of 1698, for example, the town of East Hampton paid two Montaukett Indians, Ben and Pharaoh, seven shillings, six pence for repairing and maintaining the fence around the grazing fields at Montauk for the summer (RTEH, 2: 392). The average daily pay for unskilled English labor in East Hampton during this time was about three shillings (ibid., 220; RTSH, 5: 5). Even if we assume that Ben and Pharaoh were not on duty every day all summer, the pay is well below the daily rate for an English worker.

The English paid the Montauketts in cash, in goods and services, or in some combination of the three. The trustees, for example, hired Ben Indian for three pounds of sugar, two shillings, and a knife (RTEH, 2: 143). Other Montauketts preferred to take coats or duffel cloth. Some, who were beginning to adopt English agricultural techniques, asked the English to plow their planting fields for them instead of taking cash or goods (ibid., 110, 111, 125, 145, 165).

In April 1683 when the trustees hired Quagohi (alias Harry) to watch the fence at Montauk, they gave him ten bushels of corn and arranged to have an acre of land plowed near his wigwam. The following year the trustees hired a Montaukett named Jeffrey and his wife under a similar arrangement, except that the couple were to receive a coat in addition to the plowing and the corn (ibid., 125–26, 145–46).

Cattle tending sometimes involved the difficult task of freeing livestock from swamps and tidal wetlands. In such cases the Indians negotiated for higher pay. When William Sylvester, for example, hired Hannibal Indian to round up the cattle on his Shelter Island estate, the agreement called for Hannibal to search the woods for cattle that had been foraging unattended during the winter. He was to go out "morning and evening, for the space of six weeks," and search the woods, swamps, and wetlands. He was to rescue the cattle that had become mired in the swamps and in mudflats near the tide line. Hannibal received ten pounds "current money" for the six weeks of labor (Rabito-Wyppensenwah 1993d, 355).

Some of the Indian women tended cornfields for English farmers. "Squaws in those days," wrote John Lyon Gardiner in his *Journal and Farm Book*, "were supposed to be the best hands for raising maize" (1798, 142). The employment of women in the cornfields is striking because the English considered such field work to be in the male domain.[1] Unfortunately, we do not have much information about this practice on Long Island. Although some farmers preferred Indian women for field work, many employed Indian men. The East Hampton trustees, for example, hired Cockenoe to grow corn at Montauk for them. He prepared the land in the traditional manner by burning off the planting ground.

Many Indians were attracted to the English towns where they could find odd jobs. The English had hired Nangenutch, the young Montaukett accused of rape in 1667, to carry sacks of flour from the mill to the kitchens where the alleged molestation occurred. Another source of income for the Montauketts was the production of goods such as baskets; scrub brushes; meat from game animals, fish, and shellfish; tanned hides; and feathers. By the beginning of the eighteenth century, many Montauketts were raising livestock of their own. They recorded the earmarks of their cattle, swine, and horses in the town records along with the English farmers' marks (RTEH, 3: 134, 170, 186–87, 271, 317, 423, 24: 9, 124). The owners consumed most of the food from these animals, however, rather than selling it for a profit.

One significant aspect of the Montaukett involvement in the English economic system was the gradual adaptation of the English language and English names. This change, of course, reflects the power relationship that was taking shape between the two cultures. Few of the English were willing to learn the Montaukett language because they regarded it as part of an inferior culture that would soon die out. The Montauketts, however, had to learn English if they wished to find employment or establish any economic ties with the East Hampton community. When the Montauketts came to work in the English homesteads and live in servants' quarters, the employers often renamed them or "anglicized" their Indian names. Jonaquam, for example, became

1. John Lyon Gardiner, the seventh lord of the manor on Gardiner's Island, recorded in his farm ledger that his grandfather John Gardiner III employed Montaukett women in his fields on Gardiner's Island. His journal, however, suggests that the third lord of the manor may have had more personal interests in some of the Montaukett women. He may have been the father of a Montaukett woman named Betty Fowler. George Pharaoh, an elderly Montaukett, told John Lyon Gardiner that his grandfather, "Old Mr. John," spoke Algonquian and "came to their wigwams to eat fresh fish and he liked the young squaws of the old sachem [Wyandanch] breed" (1798, 157–58). Gardiner also reported that the Montauketts had been promised, perhaps by "Old Mr. John," that they could have improvement rights to land on Gardiner's Island. The Montauketts asked Gardiner why they did not have that right anymore. He did not record his answer.

John Aquam. The employer would ignore their Indian names and simply impose names on them as they did with their African slaves and their horses. They were distinguished from the Africans by adding "Indian" to the "first" name. Documents from this period, for example, list such names as "Ben Indian" and "John Negro."

The Montauketts, however, did not abandon their Indian names. In their villages they continued to use their Algonquian names. The English recognized this practice by writing both names on the labor contracts and deeds. A whaling contract, for example, listed a Montaukett man as "Quauquehide alias Harry" (ibid., 1: 408). Not until the nineteenth century did Algonquian names gradually disappear from the records. It is interesting to note that since the 1960s, as part of a Pan-Indian cultural movement, many of the Indians in the East have revived ancient naming rituals and now give their children Algonquian names.

Although the Montauketts were generally forced to find employment in the lowest paying jobs, they enjoyed, for a brief time, an advantage in one area of the labor market. Many of the Montauketts were experienced fishermen who were accustomed to going out past the surf in their dugouts to spear large fish. These fishermen also knew the habits of the whales that frequently became trapped in tidal bays or beached themselves along the shores of eastern Long Island.

Every October, as the arctic freeze reduces its food supply, the northern right whale (*Eubalena glacialis*) migrates south along the Atlantic coast to spawn in the warmer waters off the Carolina and Georgia shores (Kraus et al. 1986, 139–44). The whales remain in these waters until March when they return north. The right whale got its name from the Basque whalers who hunted off the North Atlantic shores in the fifteenth century. It was the "right" whale to hunt because of its physical characteristics and its feeding habits. The whale feeds on the surface, swims very slowly, migrates close to the shore, makes shallow dives for a maximum of twenty minutes, and floats on the surface after it dies.

James Rosier, who accompanied Capt. George Weymouth on a voyage along the coast of North America in 1605, witnessed Native American hunters killing a whale (1930, 392). He reported that the Indian whalers surrounded the whale in their canoes and attacked it with bows and arrows and bone-tipped harpoons attached to rope lines. The Algonquian peoples on eastern Long Island may have used similar tactics to hunt whales as they migrated between their northern habitat and their southern spawning grounds.

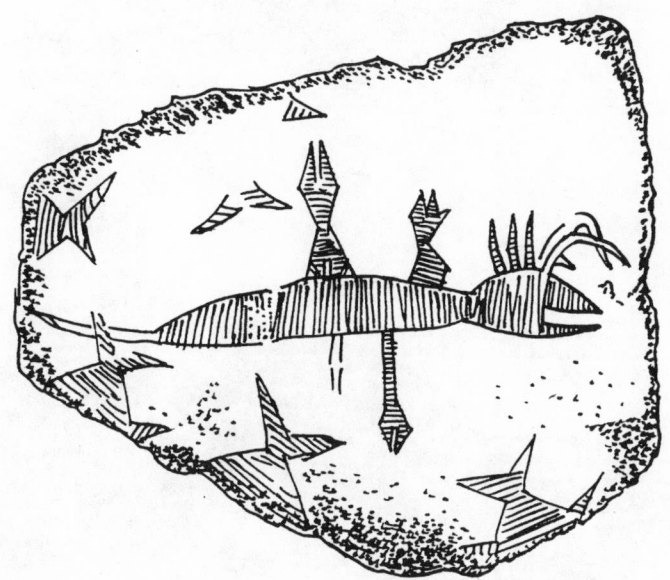

Mica tablet. Drawing by David Bunn Martine.

These whales often accommodated the Indians by beaching themselves along the Long Island shores. The Indians on Nantucket have a myth about a spirit called Moshup who sent these whales to sacrifice themselves on the beaches. Although no Montaukett oral traditions involving whales have survived, they did have a ceremony, mentioned in the previous chapter, to honor the whale spirit.

A curious mica tablet unearthed in the nineteenth century by a farmer plowing his field in the township of Brookhaven, about forty miles west of Montauk, may be related to ceremonies and beliefs involving the whales. The New York State Museum in Albany acquired the tablet sometime later. On one surface of the tablet, which is about seven inches long and tapers from a width of five inches to two inches at its narrow end, there are carvings that appear to symbolize the whale. In the center of the tablet is a whalelike creature with horns. In the margins around the whale figure are finlike images, which probably represent the tail fins of whales.[2]

2. The tablet remains controversial because of its uniqueness. The best guess, according to museum curator Lisa Anderson, is that it was made during the Middle Woodland period, but without knowing the context in which it was found, little more can be said (letter to author, May 23, 1996).

Montaukett whalers. Drawing by David Bunn Martine.

In the 1650s the English in Southampton and East Hampton began to organize companies to hunt the right whales as they migrated along the south shore. These companies combined Indian whaling skills with English technology. East Hampton entrepreneurs recruited Montauketts and supplied them with twenty-eight-foot to thirty-foot cedar-ribbed boats, iron harpoons, and other tools necessary for the enterprise (Edwards and Rattray 1956, 55–63). During the next two decades, the owners paid the Montaukett whalers with such trade goods as coats, duffel cloth, boots, stockings, powder, shot, and alco-

hol. The importance of the whaling industry and the bargaining power
of the Montauketts even forced the English authorities to exempt company owners from the laws designed to prevent Indians from obtaining ammunition and alcohol (NYCD, 14: 608–9).

Most companies sent out two boats, each with a six-man crew
consisting of a harpooner, a steersman, and four oarsmen (Wooley
1968, 38–39). The attack on the whale involved considerable skill
and courage. Boats had to come as close as possible to the whale so
that the harpooner could make a short cast or stab the whale deeply

enough to set the draglines. Once he set the first harpoon, with its razor-sharp point and multiple barbs, he secured the lines to the boat and plunged several narrow, pointed harpoons into the whale. The hunt could be over in an hour or so if the lances hit a vital spot, but it was not unusual for the struggle to take half a day. It was a dangerous undertaking. A man who fell into the freezing waters had little chance for survival unless the other crew members pulled him out immediately.

After the kill the long, exhaustive process of towing the carcass to shore began. A nineteenth-century account of a whale hunt off the shore of East Hampton describes the arduous struggle of a crew bringing in a whale killed about ten miles offshore (Edwards and Rattray 1956, 53–54). It took them about an hour of strenuous rowing to tow the body one mile. After six hours of backbreaking rowing, family and friends came out in small boats with food and water. Another six hours of rowing finally delivered the whale to the beach.

The final stage of the towing had to be coordinated with the tide because the carcass needed to come to rest as far above the low-tide line as possible. The men towed a whale in tail first and anchored it against the pull of the falling tide. Once the carcass was exposed on the tidal flats, the Montaukett crews began the process of butchering. They severed the head with axes and boat spades. The boat spade resembled a shovel with a razor-sharp blade. The workers removed the baleen from the mouth and then turned to the messy business of removing the blubber.

Using the boat spades the men cut the blubber into strips, pulled them off with a hawser and tackle, loaded them into the carts, and carried them to the nearest tryworks. It could take as long as three days to strip the carcass of a large adult whale. At the tryworks the men cut the blubber strips into chunks and boiled or "tryed" them in huge 250-gallon kettles on a stone furnace (ibid., 90–96). As the oil melted out of the blubber, it was skimmed off and poured into cooling vats. The men scooped the scraps of whale flesh out and used them to fuel the fire. When the oil cooled down, they transferred it from the vats to wooden barrels and stored it for shipment to Boston, New York, and London. It was a dirty, smelly business. The odor was so pungent that trying stations were always located some distance from the nearest village or homestead. Boat crews worked in shifts around the clock for as long as a week.

As the number of whaling companies on eastern Long Island grew, the owners found it more difficult to recruit full crews of experienced Indian whalers. The competition for whalers forced up the price of labor. Around 1670 the owners began to offer the crews a half share of the market value of the whale oil. These shares, however, were not paid in cash. Each crew member received a line of credit "laid by" to be used for the purchase of goods or to satisfy old debts. The share or "lay" system was very similar to the sharecropping system in the South during the late nineteenth and early twentieth centuries.

The increased competition for whaling crews encouraged some owners to use alcohol and other bribes to lure away experienced whalers from rival companies. In what appears to have been a response to these tactics, the towns encouraged company owners to draw up written contracts with their crews and record them in the town records. Company owners recorded nineteen such contracts in East Hampton between 1675 and 1684. Sixty-four Montauketts signed on for at least one season during that period.[3] The English abandoned the practice of recording contracts after 1685, perhaps because the owners found another means of controlling the whalers. The lay system drew the Indians into a cycle of debt that forced them to remain with the same employer from season to season.

The whalers signed on for a season and then began to purchase goods on their credit lines. By the time the season began, they might be in debt for more than they would earn that year. The owner entered the value of the goods he gave each whaler in his account book. When the season ended, the owner determined the total value of the whale oil and baleen taken from the whales and set the value of each man's share. Then he deducted the price of the goods taken on credit by each crew member. This system gave the owners complete control over all of the transactions.

The whaling account book of William "Tangier" Smith, whose company operated out of Brookhaven from 1696 until 1721, provides detailed information about the nature of the lay system. None of the thirty-two Algonquian whalers who worked for Smith during those years ever got out of debt. A whaler named Abraham, for example, worked for eleven seasons and ended up ten pounds in debt to Smith. Sacutacca, another whaler, served for ten seasons and ended up owing Smith six pounds, six shillings, and eight pence (J. Strong 1990, 17–28).

3. These contracts are recorded in the town records (RTEH, 1: 373–74, 378–79, 381–83, 407–9, 430–31, 2: 77–79, 86–87, 94–101, 119, 132–33, 152–53, 197).

Many whalers found themselves so deeply in debt that the owners could impose a form of indenture on them for indefinite periods of time. On December 27, 1677, for example, a crew of sixteen Montauketts, led by sachem Mousup, agreed to continue whaling for the owners, John Stretton and Thomas James, "till we have discharged to their satisfaction all former arrears or debts" (RTEH, 1: 408). The debts referred to dated back to a contract signed in 1675.

Papasequin, Weomp, and five others signed a similar contract in April 1679. The men agreed to "bee readie at or before ye fifteenth of November next to goe to sea to kill whales" for Jacob Schellinger of East Hampton, and "to continue in . . . their employment from season to season soe long as wee shall bee indebted unto said owners." Papasequin and Weomp, however, either paid off their debt or ignored the terms of their contract with Schellinger, because they signed with a new owner, John Wheeler, for the following season. The two Montauketts changed to another owner, Benjamin Conkling, for the 1681–1682 season. If Papasequin and Weomp left Schellinger while they were still in debt, they were more fortunate than another Montaukett whaler named Witness, who signed a contract with Wheeler on March 21, 1681. Samuel Mulford, a rival owner, challenged the contract, claiming that Witness was not clear of his debt to him (ibid., 2: 78–79, 86–87, 95–96, 98–100).

Although the system was exploitive, the credit line with the company owners gave the whalers access to such highly valued European goods as guns, powder, shot, cloth, blankets, thread, knives, coats, shoes, and metal tools. The presence of so many more European goods in the Montaukett villages had a significant cultural impact, which is reflected in the seventeenth-century burials. Throughout southern New England, as well as at Montauk, traditional goods intended to serve the deceased in the spirit world were gradually displaced with European goods (Leone and Potter 1988; Sayville 1993, 625–27).

The shore whaling enterprise began to decline by the middle of the eighteenth century. The right-whale population was in decline. Between 1687 and 1707 the number of barrels of whale oil produced on Long Island dropped from more than two thousand to six hundred (Sleight 1931, 7). Although Montaukett crews were still going out in the middle of the eighteenth century, the whaling industry was undergoing some dramatic changes. The near extinction of right whales and the development of advanced technologies prompted the use of larger boats, which went to sea for months at a time and carried their own butchering and trying stations on board. The population of right whales in the North Atlantic has recovered somewhat, but a survey in 1988 estimated that there were only about 350 surviving right whales.

Another source of income for the Montauketts came from the fees or gifts for planting and grazing rights at Montauk. In 1683 the town clerk recorded the payment of a coat to the "Indian sachem" for "grazing at Montauk." Unfortunately, the sachem is not named. The following year the trustees paid two pounds to the "great sachem" and one pound to the "young sachem" (RTEH, 2: 109, 143). Usually they did not record any names, but on a document dated September 30, 1684, they identified the Montaukett sachem as Aquash (Aquaas). It appears that the older sachem, who may have been Mousup, was preparing his son, Aquash, to assume authority over Montaukett affairs. In this agreement the town trustees agreed to pay the Montaukett sachem four pounds per year in perpetuity for grazing rights on Montauk (Cooper 1993, 169–71). The following year the trustees paid Aquash, identified only as "the young sachem," twenty shillings, four pounds of sugar, and a dozen pipes. There was no mention this time of the "great sachem" (RTEH, 2: 159).

In December 1686 Gov. Thomas Dongan issued a new patent to East Hampton that established a town government consisting of twelve elected trustees, two constables, and two assessors. The trustees were responsible for the management of the common lands that had not yet been allotted to individuals, highways, streams, and tidal bays. The patent gave the town exclusive authorization to purchase the remaining Montaukett lands (ibid., 194–203). Only the duly elected trustees, not the proprietors, could negotiate the purchase of the Montauketts' land. Dongan was very clear on this point. "As also I do by these presents give and grant full power, license, and authority unto the trustees of the freeholders and commonality of the said town of East Hampton and their successors, to purchase the said tract of land of the native Indians, commonly called Montauk" (R. Smith 1926, 39; Christoph 1999, 179–84).

The proprietors who put up the money were the owners, but the trustees were to supervise the transactions with the Indians. At first this separation of authority was a mere formality because most of the men elected were themselves proprietors, but as the East Hampton population increased, the proprietors became a diminishing minority, and the common lands came under the control of the larger community of freeholders.

In July 1687 the East Hampton trustees representing the thirty-nine investors met with the Montaukett sachem, who identified himself as Wyandanch. Although there is no confirming document, the sachem was probably the former Aquash, who had now taken the name of his famous ancestor. His counselors, Sassakataka, Obediah, and Cockenoe, accompanied him. Manecopungun and Massaquats may have died because they disappear from the records at this time. The proprietors under the supervision of the trustees purchased the remaining Montaukett lands for one hundred pounds and added a counterbond granting the Montauketts the right in perpetuity to reside at Montauk (RTEH, 2: 213). The counterbond obligated the town trustees to protect the Montaukett residence rights (R. Smith 1926, 48–49).

The Montauketts accepted a payment schedule of two pounds per year in interest rather than the one hundred pounds in full payment for their lands. This arrangement ended the yearly stipend of four pounds for grazing rights set in the 1684 agreement. Although there is no mention of complaints about this loss of income in the town records, by the end of the century the Montauketts had grown quite resentful about their relationship with the town.

In the summer of 1701 the trustees sent a delegation to Montauk to discuss some complaints raised by the Montauketts about the destructive impact of sheep grazing on their lands. The trustees agreed to pay for damages, but the tensions between the two communities continued. Another delegation returned to Montauk in April of the following year. This time the Montauketts complained that they had not been paid their annuity for the preceding year. The trustees apparently disagreed, and there was an impasse. The two parties had still not resolved their differences a month later because the trustees reported that the Montauketts were "obstinate and averse to agreement," and threatened the Montauketts with the use of "the whole power and authority, both offensive and defensive," of the town (RTEH, 3: 7, 29–30, 35–36).

The Montauketts defied the town in spite of these threats. During the fall of 1702 Wyandanch and Sassakataka rejected the 1687 agreement and negotiated the sale of Montauk to two wealthy and influential real estate investors from New York. On October 14, 1702, they sold all of the land east of Fort Pond for a two-hundred-pound bond and a guarantee of permanent residence rights east of Lake Montauk (Ales 1993, 51). This deal was better than the one they had with East Hampton, and they may have also expected that they would have less trouble from a distant landlord.

The East Hampton trustees were alarmed and moved quickly to abort the sale. Forty-seven of the proprietors paid assessments ranging from eleven shillings to three pounds sterling into a common fund to pay the costs of protecting their title to Montauk. John Mulford made three trips to New York where he hired lawyers to work on the case (RTEH, 3: 54–55, 61–62, 65).

The East Hampton trustees called a group of twenty-five Montaukett men together and pressed them to reject the agreement made by Wyandanch and Sassakataka. The Montauketts were vulnerable to such pressure because of the economic ties linking the two communities. The Indians had become dependent on the trade goods that came to them from East Hampton, and many of them had jobs with English employers. The twenty-five men whom the English called together included eight whose names appear on the town records as cattle keepers, whalers, and laborers (QPL Box 325 H, item no. 10; RTEH, 1: 330, 2: 95–96, 98–99, 100, 109–11, 152–53). The English may have employed many more of them at one time or another as cattle keepers. Unfortunately, the references in the town accounts frequently do not give the names of the Montauketts who received wages for such jobs.

The East Hampton officials were not satisfied with the testimonies reaffirming the 1687 deed. They wanted to close off any possibility of another threat to their Montauk title. The following March they opened negotiations with Wyandanch, Sassakataka, and thirty other Montaukett representatives. The two communities concluded four separate documents on March 3, 1703. The first document was an endorsement, once again, of the 1687 purchase (R. Smith 1926, 49–51). The Montauketts acknowledged the deed and stated that any assertion that the transaction was only a "Pretended deed" was false. This language was probably inserted in response to the arguments that were, apparently, raised by Thomas Longworth and Wyandanch the previous fall.

The English designed the second document to make sure that the Montauketts never again challenged East Hampton's title. The trustees forced the Montauketts to accept a bond of two thousand pounds sterling, which they would have to pay if they ever again attempted to negotiate with a third party for the land at Montauk (ibid., 52–53). The English frequently used such tactics to control Indian communities, but this bond was an unusually exorbitant amount.

The third document reflects an important aspect of the trusteeship system imposed by Gov. Thomas Dongan in the East Hampton patent. The trustees guaranteed to the Montauketts that they would supervise the payment of one hundred pounds to make sure that the proprietors met their obligations (ibid., 53–54). The terms for payment set forth in the document gave the Montauketts a choice between taking the full payment of one hundred pounds sterling in one lump sum or receiving an annual payment of the interest that was set at forty shillings. The Montauketts chose the latter. The Dongan patent established the principle that the trustees, as elected officials, were responsible to the whole community. They were supposed to be a disinterested body that would arbitrate conflicting private interests. The trustees' past record, however, was certainly not very reassuring to the Montauketts.

The fourth document was, in many aspects, the most important, because it set forth in specific detail the nature of the Montaukett residence rights at Montauk. The agreement began by acknowledging that there had been "sundry" differences between the two communities (ibid., 54). In order to bring an end to these conflicts, the document set forth a list of resolutions. The first called for the Montauketts to fence in the land that they needed on North Neck (see map 3). All of the land east of Great Pond (Lake Montauk) would be reserved for the English livestock. Second, the arrangement established in 1655 opening up Montaukett planting fields to English cattle from mid-October to April 25 was to be continued with one minor exception. The Montauketts could keep a thirty-acre field enclosed to protect their crop of winter wheat. They were responsible for building and maintaining the necessary fencing at their own expense.

The third resolution stipulated that if the Montauketts decided to move from the lands at North Neck and relocate on Indian Fields east of Lake Montauk they could do so, but they must take all of their possessions with them. They could return to North Neck whenever they wished, but they could not occupy both areas at the same time. Indian Fields includes meadows and rolling hills between Lake Montauk on the west and Oyster Pond on the east. The fields run from present-day Montauk Highway north to Long Island Sound.

Another concern of the English reflected an important change that was taking place among the Montauketts. As their hunting grounds diminished, the Montauketts, as noted above, turned to domestic livestock for subsistence. They began to register their livestock with the town clerk by listing the distinctive earmarks or brands just as the English did. In 1708, for example, Harry Indian "declareth his brand mark to be an 'H,'" Pharaoh Indian declared that the earmark for his swine was "the end of each ear cropped off," Hoppin Indian declared that his earmark for swine was an "L" on the side of the right ear, and Jeffrey's squaw said that her mark for a swine was a hole in the right ear (RTEH, 3: 187).

The English wanted to put a cap on the number of livestock kept by the Montauketts not only to protect their portion of a fixed amount of grazing land but also to make sure that the Montaukett population did not grow. They restricted the Montauketts to 250 swine and a combined total of 50 head of cattle or horses. The Montauketts could not rent or lease grazing or planting rights on their land to anyone but the proprietors. The trustees gave the Montauketts liberty to cut the timber they needed for fencing from Hither Woods west of Fort Pond when they ran out of wood on North Neck.

The restrictive aspects of the agreements and the circumstances surrounding the sale of the land continued to be a source of anger and frustration among the Montauketts. Benjamin and Stephen Pharaoh's petition in 1800 (see chapter 2) denounced the 1703 agreements. They charged that they were still being oppressed by them and that "every line of which is tinged with fraud." They also accused the East Hampton trustees of using alcohol on a systematic basis as a means of manipulating the Montauketts. "The East Hampton people have ever made it one rule when they want to make a bargain with us to attack us on our weak side that is to say they always begin treating of us till they get us pretty well smok'd with white faced rum before they divulge their business" (EHPLC, call no. NG 17 A–C). The Pharaohs also complained that though the English restricted the Montauketts to 50 head of cattle and horses, they set their own limit at 2,000.

The Pharaohs gave their testimony nearly a century after the fact, so it does not carry the weight of an eyewitness account, but it certainly is plausible in the context of Indian-English relations at the time. The Shinnecocks, who negotiated a similar series of agreements in August of the same year, also charged that the English used alcohol to manipulate them. The Southampton town account books recorded among the expenses for the negotiations money for alcohol and several direct payments to individual Shinnecock men, which suggest the possibility of bribery (RTSH, 2: 358–59).

During the first two decades of the eighteenth century, the Montauketts began to grow corn, winter wheat, and livestock. The population base did not decline because the Montauketts took spouses from neighboring tribes on Long Island and in southern New England. Fearing that the Montaukett community would remain stable or perhaps even increase, the East Hampton trustees called for a meeting in the spring of 1719 to discuss a most unusual proposal.

A delegation of fourteen Montauketts met with the trustees, but Wyandanch and Sassataka were not among them. Both had apparently died sometime after 1709 because their names disappear from the colonial records after that. Charles Dayt, John Weomp, John Indian, and Hannibal Indian, whose names appear at the top of the signatures, are not identified as sachems, but they were probably the leaders at the time. Charles Dayt is a new name, but the other three had signed the 1703 agreements, and Hannibal had also signed the 1687 deed. Several of the other men are listed for the first time in the town records. Most notably, this is the first document where the Pharaoh name (spelled "Faro") appears. The family was to play a prominent role in Montaukett affairs up to the present day. Three Pharaoh men took part in the meeting: Faro Indian, Faro P Indian, and George Faro (BHSL, 1974.15, Folder 10).

The trustees wanted the Montauketts to accept a second bond, this time for one hundred pounds sterling, as a guarantee that they would not "let nor take any strange Indians in nor suffer any such to be on Montauk to use or improve any part of said land directly or indirectly by taking of a squaw or squaws" (ibid.). This was a devastating edict for a small, exogamous community that had always depended on marriages with neighboring groups to maintain their population base and reinforce economic, social, and political networks.

The Montauketts apparently had little choice in the matter. There is no record of a protest at the time, but the arrogant attitude of the English was undoubtedly a continuing source of resentment among the Montauketts. A petition carried to Gov. Cadwallader Colden in 1764 expressed a measure of hostility over the pattern of such behavior. Silas Charles, the Montaukett petitioner, stated that the Montauketts had endured "great inconveniences from the contempt shewn to the Indian tribes by their English neighbors at East Hampton" (DHSNY, 3: 236–37).

In spite of the concessions made by the Montauketts, they were not paid the agreed-upon annual stipend for the following five years.

Finally, in 1724 Hannibal and five Montauketts received a payment of ten pounds. Although the receipt does not identify Hannibal as the sachem, his name appears first on the column of signatures. His signature was also at the top on the receipts for 1729 and 1730 (BHSL, 1974, 48). The traditional leadership structure was no longer considered relevant to the English. The trustees could now ignore the Montaukett political system because they did not need to rely on a local leader for support. They were in complete control.

Hannibal apparently left Montauk for several years because his name does not appear on the receipts for 1733 through 1736. He returned in 1737, but his name appears near the bottom of the signature column. There was no Montaukett name that was entered consistently at the top of the receipts during these years. The signatures do indicate, however, that the Pharaoh family was very influential. There is one or more Pharaoh signatures on all of the receipts between 1717 and 1737.

One of the reasons that the trustees were concerned about the Montaukett population became evident in 1741. An entry in the trustees' journal for that year notes that the English were now leasing back land that had been set aside for the Montauketts. The demand for grazing land had grown to a point where the English were now pressing the Montauketts for access to more acreage.

The entry in the 1741 journal and an earlier one in 1737 also reveal that the use of alcohol continued to be part of a strategy to manipulate and control the Montauketts. The trustees listed four shillings, six pence "for drink" as one of the costs of the 1737 meeting. The entry for the 1741 negotiations listed an expenditure for the "customary gallon of rum for bargaining for Indian fields" (JEHT, 1: 85, 94).

By 1740 the English had reduced the Montauketts to a position of tenancy on their ancient homeland. The young Montauketts began to leave the isolated villages on Montauk to find employment in the English towns. Those Indians who remained faced a continuing struggle to protect what was left of their birthright.

FOUR

MISSIONS, MIGRATIONS, AND PROTEST 1740–1800

ALTHOUGH THE Reverend Thomas James once contemplated missionary work among the Montauketts, his worldly concerns with real estate and whale oil profits left him little time or energy for such endeavors. There is no record of any missionary activity on eastern Long Island during the first century after the European arrival. The settlers apparently had little concern about converting the Algonquian people to Christianity.

The first missionary to take an active interest in converting the Montauketts to Christianity was Azariah Horton, a native of Southold, who traced his ancestry back to the original settlers. A missionary organization called the Society in Scotland for the Propagation of Christian Knowledge sponsored Horton's mission to the Long Island Indians. His journals, written during the first four years of his missionary work on Long Island, provide some important insights into the lifeways of the Montauketts (1993, 195–220).

Azariah Horton came to Montauk near the end of the summer of 1741. He met first with a group of twenty Montauketts at Napeague in Hither Woods, which he described in his journal as "a place where the Montauk Indians resort, and sometimes tarry a week or a fortnight together." Horton spent three days in Napeague, preaching in public and conversing with several individuals about the Christian message. On the day he arrived, he wrote, "they treated me kindly, and heard my instructions willingly and seriously." Horton led them in prayer the next day and visited people to discuss the message in his sermon. On the third day he reported that the audience doubled for his second sermon, encouraging him to believe that many of the Montauketts were showing an interest in Christianity (ibid., 196).

Some of the Montaukett women had already had some experience with Christian worship in East Hampton. Horton found that three of these women could sing the popular hymn of the day, "The Blessed Society in Heaven," from memory, having heard it so often in the East Hampton church. It is likely, however, that many of the others may have come out of curiosity, as did many whites who flocked to hear the evangelicals during the Great Awakening. The evangelical ministers could usually be relied upon to stage a great show.

There is also some question about the level of English comprehension among the Montauketts. On several occasions Horton said that he spoke to Indians through an interpreter or struggled to understand their "broken way of talking." Most Montauketts probably knew some English, but the language and delivery of the evangelical minister must have severely taxed his listeners. It seems unlikely that many would have followed the theological arguments Horton presented. Possibly the preacher's enthusiasm and energy stirred more interest than did his message, which was so alien to Algonquian culture and experience. The native shamans also used emotional tones and furious body movements when they conducted religious ceremonies.

Horton moved on to the main Montaukett village, which was probably located at North Neck. He stayed there for the next ten weeks, except for two brief visits to the Shinnecock Reservation. The visit must have been quite an experience for the Montauketts. They had never had this much concentrated and energetic attention from a white man before. Horton carried his message to the Montauketts in public meetings followed by private sessions with individuals who showed an interest in his words (ibid.).

Horton got off to a very successful start at Montauk. He addressed public meetings on six of the first seven days after his arrival. Seventy Montauketts gathered to hear him the first day, and the number grew to eighty on the last day. His pace slowed a bit over the next weeks, but he conducted a total of twenty-two meetings during his visit. He went from wigwam to wigwam, talking with anyone who would listen. The response to his attentions was carefully noted in his journal. He distinguished between levels of consciousness ranging from a "concern" about "the vileness of their hearts" to a full conversion. Several, he said, were "deeply wounded." Some expressed deep concern, and some were "truly awakened," but only eight—six women, a man, and a boy—were "hopefully converted" (ibid.). Unfortunately, Horton seldom mentions the names of the Montauketts he met.

In his third journal he described his return to Montauk in June 1742 to find that the Montauketts were suffering from an epidemic, probably smallpox, which took many lives. Horton displayed great courage in going into the wigwams of the sick and giving them some comfort. One woman, however, was openly hostile to the missionary because she believed that the Christians had once again brought a deadly disease to the Indian people. The woman, said Horton, was "very resolute in her Indian way of living." She warned her people that they should stay away from the Christian meetings, which brought sickness and death (ibid., 209). She may have been correct. If the disease was contagious, it would certainly spread at the public meetings. The woman was not the only one who was resolute in the Indian ways. At Shinnecock a woman kept two wooden gods that her father had worshiped (ibid., 197).

Although many were uninterested and some were openly resistant, there were a few who sought to adapt Christian forms to their traditional ceremonies. Three Montaukett elders approached Horton and asked him to lead them in prayers of thanksgiving for the fall harvest as they had done before the whites arrived. The men told Horton that they used to honor this day with prayers to "their Idol gods, images of wood," but now they would give thanks for the harvest with Christian observances (ibid.).

One consistent pattern revealed in the journals is the disproportionate enthusiasm among the women for the Christian message. Only a small number of men responded with more than polite interest in Horton's mission. The missionary expressed some disappointment in the men's indifference, but he persisted in his task. In September 1742 he again presided over a harvest thanksgiving service. Later in that month he recorded, undoubtedly with considerable satisfaction, that he had even won over the woman who had been so hostile to him.

When Horton returned to Montauk in January 1743, he wrote that he had finally converted a man who had mocked him and his mission earlier. These few successes, however, could not compensate for his frustration with the slow progress of his work. He attributed part of his difficulty to another problem that has universally plagued peoples undergoing the stress of social breakdown and cultural transition. Horton called "the sin of drunkenness" a serious impediment to his civilizing mission, but it should be noted that the civilized Christians from East Hampton were the great "enablers." They made sure that alcohol was always readily available to the Montauketts because it served their interests.

Horton spent the summer of 1743 traveling the length of Long Island, mostly on foot, from Rockaway to Montauk. That fall he preached two thanksgiving services, one at Shinnecock and a second at Montauk. Horton prided himself with having "tamed" the traditional celebration that had customarily involved much singing, dancing, and, to the reverend's dismay, "vain mirth and jollity." Under his influence, he reported, the service was "attended with seriousness and decency" (ibid., 219). Unfortunately, Horton did not document the nature of the celebrations he encouraged the Montauketts to abandon. A record of this transition to a syncretistic religious ritual would be very valuable. In spite of the missionary efforts to suppress all traditional religious expressions, the Algonquian peoples on Long Island did not completely abandon the harvest ceremony. The modern powwows held each fall on the Shinnecock Reservation and in other areas of Long Island keep alive this ancient celebration.

Horton's journal ends on March 8, 1744, but he may have continued to work on Long Island for about six more years. In 1749 he recommended the appointment of Samson Occom as his successor. Horton then abandoned his mission to the Native Americans and took parishes serving the synods of New York and Philadelphia for the rest of his career. Smallpox, the white man's disease to which Horton had unflinchingly exposed himself at Montauk, finally struck him down as he nursed soldiers in the Revolutionary War. Horton's impact on the Montauketts is difficult to evaluate, but his success with several of the women suggests that he did plant the seeds of a new faith among the Montauketts. He baptized nine women and sixteen children, a significant number in such a small population (J. Strong and Torok 1999).

Horton's mission, however, resulted in few changes in the routine of life among the Montauketts. They continued to work as servants and laborers in East Hampton and other Long Island villages. They were also employed as herdsmen on the Montauk grazing fields. In 1744 the East Hampton trustees decided to have a keeper live on Montauk to manage the common lands. They built a small house on the western end of Montauk, south of Fresh Pond, for his living quarters. The man was responsible for keeping the fences in repair, maintaining a detailed record of all the livestock on Montauk, driving the sheep off Montauk each June to be sheared, and herding the calves, beef cattle, and bulls into special enclosures for the inventory.

The keepers hired Montauketts to help with many of these tasks. The proprietors often chose young men from prominent East Hampton families to fill these positions. They gave the keepers a house, grazing rights, firewood, and a garden. Two years later the proprietors built a second house farther east near Fort Pond. The following year they constructed a third house east of Lake Montauk. These houses became known simply as "First House," "Second House," and "Third House." As the numbers of livestock increased and the fields were separated for specialized uses, the management of the Montauk fields became a very complex operation.

The keeper of First House was responsible for preventing the livestock from wandering westward off Montauk. The land between First and Second was primarily sheep pasture. The keeper at Second House had to make sure that the sheep did not stray eastward onto the cattle pastures. The man at Third House had the most important responsibilities. In addition to maintaining the fences and the specialized fields, he supervised the movement of cattle and sheep onto Montauk every May and off again in November. He was also responsible for the "June roundup," when the livestock were all herded in and tallied (Rattray 1985, 5). Inevitably, these developments, which required more administration and control over the land, led to conflicts with the Montauketts.

In 1745 there arose serious questions about the terms in the 1703 agreements. These differences were rooted in the cultural gap separating the two communities. The Montauketts were a nonliterate culture with no written records. None of the men who signed the 1703 documents could read what they signed. They had to rely on the oral explanations from the English, which came while all of the participants were drinking rum. Under these circumstances, it is easy to understand how differences in interpretation could arise.

The Montaukett leaders who emerged after the passing of Wyandanch and Sassakataka were uncertain about the terms of the 1703 agreements, and they wanted the trustees to restate them. They appointed Cyrus Indian and Peter Indian to draft a set of questions for Thomas Chatfield, the spokesperson for the trustees. The Montauketts wanted to know if they could sell their grazing rights to any English purchaser (QPL, Chatfield). Apparently, some individual

Montaukett families wanted to sell their residence rights and leave Montauk.

Chatfield replied that the Montauketts had the right of residence as long as they resided there and that it was a tribal right. In other words, individual Montauketts could leave Montauk, but they could not receive a cash payment because the rights belonged to the tribe as a corporate body. The proprietors held that Montauk belonged to them, and, therefore, no one except them could sell or lease grazing rights. The historical and legal significance of Chatfield's answer is the ruling that the residence rights at Montauk were a tribal right and could not be sold by individual Montauketts.

The other concerns involved the use of lands at North Neck and Indian Fields and the arrangement for opening up the planting grounds between October and April of each year. Cyrus wanted to know if the Montauketts still had equal rights to live at North Neck and at Indian Fields. Apparently, the English were attempting to fence off parts of the areas that the Montauketts believed were reserved to them. Chatfield restated the terms in the 1703 agreement, assuring them that they had rights to both areas and that the agreements about seasonal use of the Montauketts' planting grounds remained intact. Chatfield's answers may have satisfied the Montauketts for a time, but the tensions between the communities continued.

Three years after Cyrus and Peter brought their concerns to the trustees, a new missionary arrived at Montauk, one who would make a very significant mark on Montaukett history. At the age of seventeen Samson Occom (Occum), a Mohegan descended from the sachem Uncas, responded enthusiastically to the preaching of the Great Awakening ministers. His mother enrolled him in Eleazer Wheelock's mission school in Lebanon, Connecticut. Wheelock, who was deeply committed to missionary work, believed that Indian missionaries would be extremely useful in the campaign to convert the Indians on the frontier. He soon became Occom's mentor.

In the summer of 1749 Occom came to Montauk for a visit and returned to spend most of the next decade there as a schoolteacher and minister. The London Society for the Propagation of the Gospel sponsored him, but it paid him at a rate well below the amount granted to white missionaries. Although he deeply resented this discriminatory practice, he continued to work exhaustively at his mission.

Occom served the Montaukett community in the same way ministers functioned in the English towns. He preached sermons, visited

Samson Occom. Drawing by David Bunn Martine.

the sick, and held weddings and funerals. In addition to these duties, however, Occom also served as a teacher; farmed a small plot of land; skillfully crafted furniture, churns, buckets, and other wooden implements; and bound books for the minister in East Hampton.

Occom was a talented and innovative teacher (Love 1899, 42–55). In order to help the children who were struggling with the alphabet, he made a set of wood chips and glued papers marked with the letters of the alphabet to them. Then he played games with the children, mixing up the letters and asking them to arrange them in order (Clark 1993, 239; Blodgett 1935, 44). The children, he said, found this a great pleasure and soon mastered the alphabet.

In 1751 Occom married Mary Fowler, the daughter of James and Betty Fowler. James Fowler may have been a Shinnecock (Ottery 1993, 316). If that claim is true, it indicates that the 1719 prohibition against "strange Indians" was not very strictly enforced. Fowler married Betty Pharaoh, the great-granddaughter of Wyandanch. When Occom married Betty's daughter, Mary, he became another of the exceptions to the 1719 agreement. In Occom's case the support he had for his mission from the Reverend Samuel Buell of East Hampton undoubtedly exempted him from the prohibition against outsiders.

Occom soon found himself embroiled in an issue related to the 1719 agreement. In May 1751 some Montauketts demanded that four Connecticut Indians, Hugh, Nude, James Sachem, and Robin Cineman, be expelled from Montauk. The men were all married to Montaukett women. Their wives protested, and Occom wrote to the East Hampton trustees on their behalf. "I am sick at heart at the noise and contention" (EHPLC, doc. no. RM-63). He said that the Montauketts who demanded their expulsion acted unadvisedly and called for a peaceful solution. Cyrus Charles, he said, "is in the same opinion with me." Unfortunately, there is no other mention of the incident in the surviving records.

Although Occom's role in community affairs is not well documented, he did make a very important contribution to our understanding of Montaukett traditional culture. His observations, based on his interviews with elderly Montauketts, provide modern scholars with an invaluable source of information on precontact Algonquian people (see chapter 1). Occom also kept a diary, which provides rich insights into Montaukett life at the time of his ministry. "I dwelt in a wigwam," he wrote, "framed with small poles and covered with mats made of flags, and I was obliged to move twice a year." He had to be near his planting field in the summer and then move to a place where firewood was readily available for the winter. He had to pay to have his garden plowed and his corn carted to the mill. "I planted my own corn, potatoes, and beans, I used to be out hoeing my corn sometimes before sunrise and after my school is dismissed, and by this means I was able to raise my own pork, for I was allowed to keep five swine" (Blodgett 1935, 47). Occom, an excellent shot, hunted fowl and sold the feathers to the English for their pillows and quilts. He also fished in the tidal bays and freshwater streams. Occom's living quarters and subsistence farming practices were undoubtedly quite similar to those customs of the other family men at Montauk.

Occom's mission was much more successful than Horton's had been, in large part, of course, because the Montauketts probably found it easier to relate to an Indian preacher. The Montaukett community soon began to look to Occom for advice and leadership. His wife's brothers, David and Jacob, responded so enthusiastically to his preaching that they decided to become missionaries. Both of these young men went to study in Eleazer Wheelock's school for Indian missionaries where Occom had studied.

In 1754 the East Hampton trustees again pressed the Montauketts to take measures to prevent the population from increasing through marriage to outsiders. Their concern about the limited resources of wood and grazing land at Montauk was undoubtedly a factor, because on May 28, 1754, the trustees gave notice to the Montauketts that they could no longer cut wood for fencing or for their hearths from the Hither Woods (JEHT, 1: 118). Wood for these purposes was a highly valued commodity for the English as well, and their demands were growing as their population expanded.

The trustees met with a delegation of Montauketts in June and told them that they were trying to eliminate "sundry differences, debates and disputes" between the Montauketts and the proprietors caused by the marriages of "strange or foreign" Indians to Montaukett women. Who else, one wonders, were they going to marry? Apparently, the trustees wanted the Montauketts to marry inside their community of less than two hundred people.

The Montaukett delegation included Cyrus Charles, Hannibal, Long Ned, Scipio, Joseph Pharaoh, Hannibal Sorehand, Little Pharaoh, and Nezer Tom. They signed an agreement, with Occom as a witness, which included a stipulation that forever debarred and excluded from Montauk any Montaukett women who married "a strange Indian" or a man with any African ancestry (R. Smith 1926, 58–61). Their children also lost all rights to live on Montauk. The town also had the authority to prosecute any "mustee, molato, or strangers, or foreign Indians" who came to Montauk and attempted to settle. Some of the Montauketts appear to have internalized the racial prejudices prevalent in the white community. They may also have feared that the appearance of African features among them would give the whites an excuse to deny them their rights to the land.

There is no surviving record of Occom's position on the matter. Although he never mentioned the incident in his diary, he believed that intermarriage with people of African ancestry would make Indian communities even more vulnerable to the whites who wanted their land (Venables 1993, 520). Later, when Occom established the Christian Indian community at Brothertown (Brotherton), he excluded African Americans for this reason. It is quite possible that Occom was the one who urged the Montauketts to adopt the policy against intermarriage with African Americans.

The same year that the Montauketts signed the exclusionary agreement, the French and Indian War began. Several Montauketts enlisted, but there is very little in the colonial documents about their participation. Twenty-five men served with the companies organized in Suffolk County, and several joined companies in Connecticut. Samuel Pharaoh (Pharow) served with Capt. Samuel Handford's company in the Connecticut militia and saw action in the campaign to relieve Fort William Henry in 1757. He was discharged two years later (Rabito-Wyppensenwah 1993g, 433).

During the war David Fowler began his education at Wheelock's Indian mission school in Lebanon, Connecticut (Huden 1946, 153). In 1761, after David had completed two years of study, Wheelock sent him to accompany Samson Occom on a trip to recruit students from the Oneida communities in central New York. This trip proved to be a historic visit, because David established a friendly relationship with one of the Oneida sachems and began to discuss the possibility of moving his people to live among the Oneidas. David related all of the troubles that his people had with the English in East Hampton and with the corrupting influences of white society in general. The sachem listened sympathetically and suggested that the Oneidas might grant the Montauketts a tract of land in their country near the present-day city of Utica, New York. Although historians have usually given credit for founding the community, which later became known as Brothertown, to his more famous brother-in-law, evidently David played a very important role as well (Venables 1993, 515).

The Oneida sachem did not have the authority, on his own, to grant the land to the Montauketts, but he agreed to consult with the other Oneida sachems about the matter. The Iroquois nations often invited other tribes to settle on their land to replace population losses from war and disease. The Iroquois allowed these refugee groups to retain their own customs and their political autonomy in internal affairs. In all matters involving relations with outsiders, however, the Iroquois retained absolute control (Hauptman 1980, 128–39; Venables 1993, 516). Although David returned to Oneida the following year, unsettled conditions on the frontier prevented further negotiations for a land grant to the Montauketts. Pontiac's War (1763–1766) and pressures from English settlers occupied the attention of the Iroquois leaders.

In 1764 the tensions that David Fowler had described to the Oneidas forced the Montauketts to appeal directly to Gov. Cadwallader Colden. Cyrus (Silas) Charles, who may have been the same "Cyrus Indian" who addressed the questions to the trustees in 1745, drafted the petition. The Montauketts chose Charles, one of the signatories on the 1754 agreement, to prepare the petition because of his fluency in English and his status in the community. Unfortunately, little is known about the life of this remarkable man. He served his community as a minister and as a teacher. English visitors referred to him as "Prince" Cyrus, probably because he was a sachem.

Cyrus Charles complained to the governor that the Montauketts were in danger of being "crowded out of all their ancient inheritance, and of being rendered vagabonds upon the face of the earth" (DHSNY, 3: 236). The English, he wrote, kept encroaching on Montaukett lands and denying the people access to wood necessary for fences and for their hearths. Charles may have also had in mind the use of fines to impoverish the Montauketts. In 1756 and again in 1763, for example, the trustees charged the Montauketts for damage allegedly done to English property by hogs (JEHT, 1: 121, 134). The Montauketts paid seven pounds in 1756 and four pounds, six shillings in 1763. These fines were far in excess of the two pounds that the trustees paid to the Montauketts as yearly interest payments under the 1703 agreements. The result was that the Montauketts found themselves in debt to the trustees and even more vulnerable to their manipulation.

The Montaukett dogs were also a source of conflict between the two communities. When some of the Montauketts' dogs killed English sheep, the trustees told the Indians to kill their dogs or the English would do it themselves (ibid., 126). The Montauketts knew that this threat was not idle. In 1727, for example, the trustees sent a man to Montauk for this purpose, and he reported that he killed "all ye Indians great dogs and bitches excepting three." Again in 1742 the trustees sent two men to kill Montaukett dogs (ibid., 46, 95).

Charles also raised an issue that once again underscored the problems inherent in the seventeenth-century deed process. The Montauketts did not believe that the trustees were telling them the truth about the deeds their fathers and grandfathers had signed. Many of the Montauketts remained convinced that the English read selectively from the written documents when they were negotiating the transactions. The documented use of alcohol in all of these proceedings undoubtedly made specific recall of the verbal explanations unreliable.

Charles reminded the governor that the "unlettered state of the American Indians, rendered it impossible for them to keep records, and your petitioners can not ascertain what lands have been [sold] or remain still unsold" (DHSNY, 3: 237). Clearly, the Montauketts did not trust the word of the East Hampton trustees in these matters. Charles wanted the governor to prosecute for trespass any English who resided on any lands between Montauk and Sag Harbor on the western boundary of the town of East Hampton that had not been rightfully purchased, unless they could show some documentation for the property. He requested that all unsold land be granted and confirmed to the Montauketts.

The Montauketts were raising questions about all the deeds beginning with the 1648 sale of the thirty-thousand-acre tract. The East Hampton trustees sent copies of their deeds to the governor in New York. The Governor's Council reviewed the documents and concluded that whatever the Indians may have been told at the time, the language in the deeds was clear enough to the council. The Montauketts, reported the council, had sold all of their land. The council acknowledged the rights of the Montauketts to reside at Montauk, but concluded that both sides may have good reason to be unhappy with the 1703 agreements.

The council called for the governor to recommend "that some new arrangement be entered into between the inhabitants and the said Indians whereby the sole use of the lands to be consigned to the latter, shall be absolutely reserved and timber sufficient for fuel and for fence and for the full enjoyment of fishing and fowling in the most explicit manner secured to them and their posterity" (Gonzales 1993, 70–71). The suggestion here indicates that the council did believe that some of Charles's charges were true and should be remedied. Unfortunately, the governor never pressed the trustees to negotiate a new settlement, leaving the fate of the Montauketts in the hands of East Hampton. The trustees completely ignored the Montauketts' concerns and proceeded to prosecute several Montauketts who were caught taking wood "where they have no right" (JEHT, 1: 134).

When Charles's petition brought no positive results, many Montauketts undoubtedly became more interested in David Fowler's plans for removal to Oneida country. In 1765 Cyrus Charles asked the missionary society to send David back to Montauk because "we are in distress about our children not having a school to go to for we long that our children should be brought up in learning hoping that it may serve to some good purpus" (BA, Charles to Eliphalet Lester, Mar. 4, 1765). Instead, the society sent David to fill a teaching position at a mission school in Mohawk country. David, however, did not have much patience with his students. One of his colleagues on the staff, Joseph Wooley, a Delaware Indian, reported, "Fowler beat his scholars very much, makes their hands swell very much which the Indians don't like very much" (Huden 1946, 153).

David left after a year and returned to Wheelock's school in Lebanon where he married a young Pequot student named Hannah Garrett. David's younger brother, Jacob, also attended the school for a brief time. In 1767 David, Hannah, and their son finally did return to Montauk and take over the school. David wanted to be near his aging parents. He taught in the school for three years, but he often neglected his duties. Perhaps he never did feel comfortable in a classroom situation. When his parents' wigwam burned down in 1770, he turned his attention to family matters and seldom came to the school. The mission society finally decided to replace him. They appointed David Hannibal and paid him an annual salary of twenty pounds.

Jacob Fowler remained at Oneida until 1770 and then moved to Groton, Connecticut, where he served as a schoolmaster in a Pequot community. Both brothers stayed in close contact with Samson Occom, who had become somewhat of a celebrity after his highly successful fund-raising campaign in England in 1766. Wheelock wanted the funds to build another school for the education of Indian teachers and missionaries. Occom expected that his success had earned him a share in planning the new school. He urged Wheelock to place the school on a tract of land near Southold, New York, on the North Fork of eastern Long Island. This land, said Occom, had been offered to the Montauketts sometime in the past in exchange for their lands at Montauk (Richardson 1933, 218–19). This reference is most curious because there is no mention of such an offer in any of the surviving records.

Wheelock ignored Occom's proposal because he wanted to locate the school closer to the Indian frontier in northern New England. In 1769 he proceeded to build a school in Hanover, New Hampshire, and named it Dartmouth in honor of one of his wealthy contributors. Occom never forgave Wheelock and broke off all contact with him. The disappointment probably aroused Occom's enthusiasm for an independent Indian community free from interfering white missionaries.

In 1772 David Fowler wrote to Occom, asking about the progress of negotiations with the Oneidas for a tract of land (Venables

1993, 518). Conditions on the New York frontier, however, still pre-occupied the Iroquois. That same year the Montauketts again appealed to a higher authority for protection from abuses by East Hampton. This time they wrote to Sir William Johnson, the superintendent of Indian affairs for the area that included the colony of New York. They told Johnson that the East Hampton trustees were killing their dogs, fining them excessively for alleged damage caused by their hogs, and prohibiting them from leasing grazing lands to the highest bidder. Johnson responded with an appeal to the East Hampton officials to treat the Montauketts more fairly (JEHT, 2: 7–8). Unfortunately, Johnson had no authority to enforce his recommendations over the English communities. The trustees, therefore, ignored his plea.

The following summer Sir William came to Montauk for a visit and stayed in Occom's old house. In a letter to a friend, he said that he was writing from "an empty Indian house with scarce a table to sit down to" (WJ, 8: 879). He met Cyrus Charles and listened again to the Montauketts' grievances and promised to try to help them as best he could (Ales 1993, 57). This discussion undoubtedly turned to the proposal for resettlement on the Oneida lands as a solution to the problems with the East Hampton trustees. Johnson was in sympathy with David Fowler's plan, and he presented the Montaukett request to the Oneida Council the following fall. The Oneidas agreed to allow the Montauketts and Algonquian refugees from several other tribes to settle on a tract of land ten miles square. The agreement, however, was not unanimous. Several Oneida leaders remained convinced that the land grant was a bad idea and refused to cooperate with the plan. The Oneida Council asked for another meeting with Sir William Johnson before making a final decision.

That same year the Reverend David McClure paid a brief visit to Montauk and preached to the Montaukett converts. He noted that the people at Montauk were still living in wigwams and sleeping on mats made of flag grass. The structures were conical, with a smoke hole in the top. McClure said that he slept comfortably on the mats and enjoyed a fine fresh bass and a tolerable dish of tea for breakfast (Dexter 1899, 139).

McClure estimated that there were about one hundred people living at Montauk, but added that many of the young men were away at sea when he was there (ibid., 137). These men were probably on whaling ships, which often remained at sea for several months at a time. When the whaling enterprise shifted from shore whaling to long voyages on large ships, the companies eagerly recruited Indian whalers, particularly the harpooners (Rabito-Wyppensenwah 1993c, 437).

McClure met Cyrus Charles, whom he described as a teacher and a sensible, sober, religious man, and he stayed the night with James Fowler. Fowler's wigwam, said McClure, was the largest in the community. This home must have been the one James's son, David, had built for him the previous spring.

Curiously, neither McClure nor Johnson mention David Hannibal. He had replaced David Fowler in the Montaukett school and must have been influential in the Montaukett community. In May 1773, Hannibal and Cyrus Charles represented the tribe in their negotiations with the East Hampton trustees. They signed the receipt for the annual payment of forty shillings and for another payment of fourteen pounds for the construction of a field fence (BHSL, 1974.15).

In the summer of 1774 the Oneida Council finally gave full approval for a land grant to the Algonquian refugee community (Hauptman 1980, 128). Samson Occom and David Fowler traveled to Oneida and toured the ten-square-mile land grant in July. That fall Guy Johnson, who had replaced his uncle William as superintendent of Indian affairs for the Northern Department, signed a certificate approving the Oneidas' invitation to the Indians from the Montaukett, Mohegan, Narragansett, Pequot, and Niantic Tribes to settle on Oneida land. The land, however, remained in the Oneidas' possession.

The certificate excluded anyone who was "descended from or have intermixed with Negroes, or Mulattoes" (Venables 1993, 520). Both Occom and David Fowler agreed with this policy, which was consistent with the 1754 agreement between the Montauketts and East Hampton.[1] The British also felt that it was in their best interests to exclude African Americans from joining Indian communities on the frontier (ibid.). The British feared that runaway slaves might seek refuge there and, perhaps, as they did in Brazil and Haiti, use

1. David Fowler and the other Brothertown leaders enforced the racial policy in 1796 when they rejected a petition submitted by Sarah Pendleton for an allotment in Brothertown because she had married a "man of Negro extraction." They stated that it was a long-established custom among them that "if any Indian woman or girl married a Negro man or any who had a mixture of Negro blood, she forfeited all her rights and . . . title to land belonging to the tribe" (BA, doc. SC 11082, 44–45).

the communities as a base from which to launch slave revolts. The fears that Indians and African Americans might join forces against the whites was not new. In 1682 the colonial authorities on Long Island issued a prohibition against large gatherings of Indians and African Americans because "great evils and inconveniences have [been] committed and done by Negroes and Indian slaves" who attended such meetings (NYHS, 37–38). These fears were not unique to the colony of New York. The southeastern colonies also went to great lengths to keep African Americans and Indians apart (Nash 1982, 286–91).

Early in 1776, about five months before the signing of the Declaration of Independence, the Continental Congress issued a memorial requesting information from Jacob Fowler and Joseph Johnson about the movement of the Montauketts to the Oneida country. Unfortunately, there is no record of Fowler's response. The war disrupted all plans for removal. Montaukett complaints about East Hampton continued. In 1778, for example, the Montauketts made their protests known again, this time to Guy Johnson. In addition to the complaints raised previously, the Montauketts charged that the trustees had limited their hunting and fishing rights, making it difficult for them to provide food for their families (JEHT, 1: 20–21). The Montauketts had reason to hope for English support because the year before they had assured Guy Johnson that they stood ready to help the English cause whenever they were called (NYCD, 8: 713). Now that the English troops occupied all of Long Island, the Montauketts expected that their friendly gesture would be rewarded.

Johnson did order the East Hampton trustees to "afford these poor people such liberty and indulgence as they have reasonably required." The trustees, however, ignored the order, and Lord Tryon, the English officer in charge of the troops on eastern Long Island, took no action. That summer the trustees once again fined the Montauketts for damage done by their hogs. This time the trustees fined them eight pounds. The trustees also fined David Hannibal four pounds for fencing off some grassland that was in dispute. The following year the trustees charged the Montauketts eight pounds, ten shillings for more damage from "hog rooting" (JEHT, 2: 97, 100). These mounting debts and the constant harassment convinced many that they should get as far away from East Hampton as possible. They were soon to learn, however, that moving west would bring only a temporary respite from a steadily growing white population hungry for land.

Although many of the Montauketts on Montauk supported the British during the war, Samson Occom and Jacob Fowler advised the Indians to remain in strict neutrality, arguing that this conflict was a white man's war. The Americans held that this policy was in their best interests because it denied the British a military force that they had come to rely upon. The Continental Congress paid Jacob Fowler to travel around Iroquois country and urge the sachems to remain neutral.

After the Revolutionary War ended, the Montaukett removal finally began. The decision to move split the community between the more devout Christians and the traditional Montauketts who did not want to leave their ancestral lands. The prohibition against Indians who had African American ancestry led many local whites to assert that the "pure blooded Indians" all removed to the Oneida country. Photographs of Montauketts in the nineteenth and twentieth centuries, however, indicate that many who remained had classic "Indian" features. The removal split some families apart. Several members of the Fowler and Pharaoh families stayed at Montauk, while others went with Occom. There were some with African American ancestry among those Indians who remained at Montauk, but they often clung more tenaciously to their Indian heritage than did Occom's Christian community. Occom and David Fowler, for example, encouraged their followers to abandon their Indian customs and become more like the English.

Some of the Montauketts resisted Occom's appeal because they did not want to move to a strange place and provide for themselves by farming like the white man. They hesitated to leave a familiar environment, which had always sustained them. Samuel Kirkland, a missionary who worked with the Brothertown community, said that some Montauketts told him that they feared some Indians would not "work like white people. And might . . . suffer and come to poverty if they should move as a body into this part of the world where there were no oysters and clams" (Pilkington 1980, 162; Wonderly 1997, 12).

Hoping for a better future, some Montauketts were willing to take the risk. In the early summer of 1784 about thirty of them went with Occom and his brothers-in-law to the Oneida country where they established a Christian community called "Eeayam Quittoowauconnuck," or Brothertown in English. Occom mentioned that Ephriam Pharaoh, Samuel Scipio, and their families accompanied him to Brothertown, but he did not record the others. Other Montaukett family names, however, such as Peters, Dick, Hannibal, and Charles, frequently appear in the Brothertown records (Ottery 1993, 315–26).

Soon after the war the Montauketts sent another petition to the state authorities. The undated document congratulates the Americans on their newly won independence and recites, once again, East Hampton's abuses. Unfortunately, no Montaukett names appear on the document. The signature simply reads, "the Montauk Indians." The authors reminded the English that their forefathers had come to this country and "soon began to settle and cultivate the land, some they bought for almost nothing, and we suppose they took a great deal without purchase" (Stone 1993a, 505, 512–13).

They followed this general comment on the English occupation and settlement with a specific reference to the 1703 agreement with East Hampton. They raised the same complaint voiced by Cyrus Charles two decades earlier. The English, they said, took advantage of the Montauketts' unfamiliarity with the written language and imposed an inequitable settlement on them. The Montauketts complained about the severe limitations on cattle and hogs, the small amount of land in the reserved areas, and the diminishing supplies of wood for cooking and heating. The petition also raised an issue that Charles had not mentioned: the use of alcohol ("hot water") to manipulate their leaders. The situation worsened with time as the white settlers intruded upon the Montauketts' hunting grounds and harvested enormous amounts of wood. The petition concluded with a request for 150 head of cattle, some sheep, and a few more hogs.

Unfortunately, the document does not indicate whether the authors were from Brothertown or from Montauk. The location of the petition in the Connecticut Historical Society archives with some of Occom's papers and the references to the great spirit who was the "great and good governor of the world" suggest that the authors were members of the Brothertown community. There is no indication, however, that New York took any action on the petition.

The Brothertown community soon came under pressure from aggressive real estate developers. They were harassed by their white neighbors who continually trespassed on Indian land to harvest wood for fuel and for building materials. Between 1831 and 1850 the members moved to Calumet County, Wisconsin, where the federal government set land aside for them. In 1839 the Brothertown (Brotherton) Indians were granted full citizenship but lost their tribal status. Although they lived on individual plots of land, they continued to maintain their Indian identity. In 1990 tribal chairperson June Ezold began the long process of petitioning the federal government for reinstatement of their tribal status as the Brotherton Tribe of Indians (Venables 1993, 529; Cornelius 1993, 565–68).

FIVE

CONTINUITY AND CHANGE
1800–1880

A FTER OCCOM and his followers departed, the life of the community on Montauk continued with relatively few changes. One of the constant themes was the struggle against the erosion of their land base and the endless restrictions imposed on them by the trustees. In 1797 the trustees began to lease grazing rights on the southern half of Indian Fields for an annual fee of twenty-four pounds. Some of this money quickly found its way back to the trustees as the Montauketts paid the numerous fines imposed on them. Later that year, for example, the trustees fined Stephen Pharaoh three shillings for grazing his two horses on North Neck without permission from the trustees (JEHT, 2: 142, 147).

The Montauketts' hogs became an issue again in the late spring of 1797. Apparently, many Montauketts depended on pork as a staple in their diet. Their hogs ranged freely in the meadows and woodlands during most of the year. This time the trustees ordered that all of the hogs had to have rings in their noses, so they could be more easily captured and controlled. Those animals without rings would be rounded up and driven off Montauk to East Hampton to be impounded until the owner came to claim the hog and pay a fine to get it released. Shortly thereafter, before many Montauketts had time to get the rings in place, the threatened pig roundup began. It was done, the Montauketts later testified, in a most cruel manner. "The poor brutes were drove without any respect or mercy, driving off the sows that had young pigs leaving the pigs to starve in the swamp and it is very probable that some of the sows were killed in driving off by their dogs" (EHPLC, call no. NG 17A–C).

In the midst of these acrimonious relations between the two communities, John Lyon Gardiner, the seventh-generation descendant of Lion Gardiner, recorded a brief vocabulary list of the Montaukett language from George Pharaoh, who was sixty-six at the time (1980, 15–16). Gardiner reported that there were only about seven Montauketts left who could speak the ancient language. Pharaoh told Gardiner that the Mohegans in Connecticut spoke the same language. Ives Goddard, a Smithsonian anthropologist who has studied eastern Algonquian languages, also suggested a close connection between Montaukett and Mohegan-Pequot (1978b, 72).

In 1800 the Montauketts asked Benjamin and Stephen Pharaoh to appeal once more for the colonial authorities to intervene and offer them some protection from the East Hampton trustees. The two Montaukett representatives addressed a petition to the New York State Assembly recounting their long history of suffering at the hands of the East Hampton officials (EHPLC, call no. NG 17A–C).

They reminded the assemblymen that Wyandanch had welcomed the first settlers even though some of his people recommended that they be driven away. The petitioners left the clear impression that they thought Wyandanch had made a great mistake, but they realized that it could not be undone. After recounting the charges that the East Hampton trustees obtained the Montauketts' land by deceitful methods, the Pharaohs argued once again that the limits set in 1703 on their grazing rights were arbitrary and unfair. The trustees sent more than two thousand head of cattle to graze at Montauk, while the Montauketts were limited to fifty head for the whole community.[1]

The Pharaohs charged that there was one man among the trustees who was leading a plot to force the Montauketts off the land. He is identified only as the "hard faced old man," who was "determined by his conduct to root us out of existence . . . contriving every plan that he could possibly invent to complete our ruin and he has spared no pains" (ibid.). The man, said the Pharaohs, had talked to all the proprietors and urged them to cut off the Montauketts' supply of wood so that they would not be able to survive the winter.

The Pharaohs also charged that the proprietors had torn down wigwams, and "what is still more serious . . . they have sometimes

1. The average number for the trustees was probably between 1,200 to 1,500 (Rattray 1953, 107), but in some years the number was more than 3,000. The list of names and grazing charges for 1727, for example, indicate that there were 3,424 head of cattle on Montauk that year (Rattray 1985).

burnt them scarcely giving us time to get out of doors" (ibid.). The Montauketts often erected temporary shelters near locations of wild foods, cultivated fields, and hunting and fishing grounds. In the winter they often moved to sheltered areas where there was an abundance of firewood. They continued this practice long after the proprietors set out the boundaries for the reserved areas.

In one such case the Montauketts had set up some wigwams by the cranberry bog at the head of Fort Pond. Each year women and children lived by the bog and gathered cranberries until the season ended. On at least one occasion the proprietors sent a crew of men to pull down the wigwams by the bog. The Pharaohs also mentioned that the men destroyed some wigwams as punishment for gathering firewood in areas set aside for the proprietors.

The Reverend Lyman Beecher, who served as minister in East Hampton from 1799 to 1810, described one abuse that was not mentioned by the Montauketts themselves. He reported that one "grog seller" would go out to Montauk with a barrel of whiskey and "get then all tipsey and bring them in debt" (1993, 289). Then he would take corn from the fall harvest to pay off the whiskey debt. Late in the winter, when their food supplies ran low, the Montauketts who sold him their corn were forced to walk twenty miles to East Hampton to buy back the corn at a very high rate. "Oh it was horrible—horrible!" wrote the reverend in his autobiography. "It burned in my mind, and I swore a deep oath to God that it shouldn't be so" (ibid.). There is no record, however, that the good reverend ever did anything at all to stop such abuses, nor did he provide any aid or counsel to the Montauketts in their struggle with the trustees.

The petitioners did not make a specific request for action by the assembly. The Pharaohs may have embellished their recitation of old grievances somewhat, but the trustees' own records document most of the charges. The trustees, however, believed that they were simply applying the same laws and penalties to the Montauketts that they imposed on their own people. The town officials impounded hogs that ran free in East Hampton and destroyed feral dogs to protect sheep. But the Montauketts were not English, and they were not involved in the decision-making process that produced the laws and regulations.

There is no further mention of the matter in the state records for several years. The trustees continued to enforce the same policies that the Pharaohs complained about. In 1801 the trustees sent two men to "kill all the dogs they could find on the land belonging to the Indians and to drive off of Montauk all strange Indians" (JEHT, 2: 164). They probably killed many dogs, but there is no record of any confrontation with Indians who were not Montauketts.

Apparently, one reaction from East Hampton to the Pharaohs' petition was to raise the issue of miscegenation in a very different context than had been the case in 1754, when they wanted to prevent the growth of the Montaukett community. This time, although the ends were similar, it was apparently being raised to support a claim that the Montauketts were no longer Indians and therefore could no longer claim residence rights at Montauk.

In response to this charge, the Pharaohs presented a census list to the assembly in 1806 with the names of 117 people at Montauk who were identified as "true blooded natives of Montauk not an instance of Negro mixture." They added with a note of irony that there were some Montauketts, however, who had white blood "owing to the honour of our East Hampton neighbors" (Rabito-Wyppensenwah 1993e, 409). The Pharaohs hoped that this list would defuse any attempt to deny them their Indian heritage and, on that basis, to void their residence rights on Montauk. If that point was their concern, they were successful, but only for a time. The question of racial identity became an issue when the Montauketts sued to retain their lands in 1909. The court ruled that the Montauketts had "lost" their Indian identity through intermarriage with African Americans.

Finally, in 1808 the state senate heard the report of a committee that had visited Montauk to investigate the Montaukett complaints. In the summer of 1807 the committee met with a delegation of Montauketts and representatives from the proprietors. The Montauketts told the senators that they did not believe that their forefathers had intended to sell all of their land. The proprietors, however, presented the 1703 documents that clearly stated that, regardless of what the Montauketts' ancestors had understood, they had sold the land.

The senate committee reported that the Montauketts appeared to be satisfied and requested that the land reserved for their residence be clearly marked off "for the separate use of them and their posterity" (JSNY, 21–22). The senate proposal would have established a reservation status for Indian fields where most of the Montauketts were living at the time. The proprietors refused to consider the matter seriously, and the senators, unfortunately, did not press the matter.

The Montauketts repeated most of the charges that had been raised in the earlier petitions, and the proprietors responded to each charge. The East Hampton men killed the dogs, they said, because they were attacking sheep, not as a pretense to harass the Montauketts. The proprietors argued that the wigwams, which were torn down or burned, were placed on the proprietors' property and "at certain seasons of the year were occupied by some Indians and mulattoes, who committed trespass" (ibid.). They acknowledged that some individuals put their livestock on Montaukett reserved lands without paying for them, but denied that these people had the approval of the other proprietors or of the trustees.

The proprietors further claimed that the source of the problems at Montauk was not themselves or their policies at all. It was outside agitators, they claimed, who caused the difficulties by stirring up and confusing the poor Montauketts. "These strangers (not inhabitants of this state) who, for a number of years past, have made a practice of visiting them and have . . . [promised] to assist them in respect to their claims on Montauk" (ibid., 22). These assertions, very similar to those claims voiced by the white South during the civil rights movement, imply not only that the Montauketts' complaints were artificially conjured but also that the Montauketts themselves were incapable of doing the petitioning without outside help.

The senate committee, aside from supporting the Montaukett appeal for the establishment of a permanent area "set off for the separate use and improvement of them and their posterity," concluded that the situation did not warrant state intervention. An entry in the *Senate Journal* for the 1808 session, however, did acknowledge that, according to the attorney general, the Montauketts and other "tribes of Indians within our limits" were to be given state protection "against injuries which, from their particular situation, they may be exposed" (121).

Although the senate committee's response dashed the Montauketts' hopes for immediate aid from the state authorities, the attorney general's statement did provide some hope for the future. However disappointed they may have been at the time, the Montauketts did not give up the struggle. A decade later they again brought their complaints against East Hampton to the attention of the state authorities.

The patterns of accommodation that emerged in the eighteenth century continued as the Montaukett community found itself drawn deeper into the English economic system. The account books for 1829 to 1838, kept by Isaac Van Scoy, the merchant who carried the largest stock of consumer goods in East Hampton, show that the Montauketts were buying the same range of items that the English families were purchasing (VSAB). The Pharaohs, for example, were regularly purchasing such items as cloth, shot, buttons, needles, ax heads, knives, scissors, molasses, tobacco, rum, combs, shoes, and shawls.

In order to pay for these goods, some Montauketts had to leave Montauk to live in the English towns where they could get jobs as laborers and domestics. Indian Fields was isolated. It was about a twenty-mile walk to the village of East Hampton. If a Montaukett wanted to work there, he or she had to live in or very near the village. The Shinnecock and Poospatuck Reservations, in contrast, were located so close to English towns that the Indians could commute daily to work. This factor more than any other enabled these two Algonquian communities to maintain a sufficient population base and a geographic center for their cultural identity.

Many of the Montauketts, however, were forced to relocate throughout Long Island for economic survival. They often bound out their children as indentured servants, and some adults signed themselves into extended contracts as domestics and laborers to pay off their debts (Rabito-Wyppensenwah 1993j, 447–53). Another incentive for moving was to have easier access to the consumer goods they were working to purchase. The closest place with an abundance of goods was Isaac Van Scoy's store at Northwest Harbor near East Hampton.

The families and individuals who migrated out from Montauk formed a diaspora that located in segregated African American communities or moved onto the reservation communities at Shinnecock and Poospatuck. They married into Algonquian and African American family systems. In the process many traditional Montaukett names such as Hannibal, Nimrod, Gunnock, Shine, and Charles, which were listed on the 1741 list prepared by Samson Occom, disappeared. This development did not mean that the Montaukett population was dying out as the reports in the press implied. It simply meant that, in some cases, the male line ran out. When this happened, of course, the new family names became a part of the Montaukett community.

Those Montauketts who married residents on the Shinnecock and Poospatuck Reservations were generally adopted into those communities. Their children became Shinnecock or Poospatuck, enriching and expanding those population bases. There are, therefore, many Shinnecocks and Poospatucks who also have a valid genealogical claim to a Montaukett identity. The Hannibal family, for example, had members in at least three Algonquian communities. The first mention of the family name is on the 1687 Montaukett deed described in chapter four. In 1698 a man identified as Hannibal Indian was living on Shelter Island, where he worked for Nathaniel Sylvester, tending his livestock (1993d, 355). In 1764 Stephen Hannibal was living with his family near Southold on the North Fork of Long Island (STA, Petition of the Southold Indians). Over the next three decades some members of the Hannibal family migrated westward and settled on the Poospatuck Reservation. Charles and Isaac Hannibal were identified on deeds as members of the Poospatuck Reservation.[2]

The Hannibal family migrations were not atypical. Most of the Algonquian families moved frequently in search of unskilled jobs. They often moved to the segregated African American communities where they had a difficult time maintaining their Indian identity. Some moved to Freetown, a settlement of freed African American slaves and Indians on the outskirts of East Hampton; others went to the Eastville section of Sag Harbor, about ten miles west of East Hampton. Members of the Fowler family settled in North Amityville near the center of Long Island. Some went to Southold on the North Fork of eastern Long Island, to Little Neck in Nassau County, and some left Long Island to settle in New Bedford, Massachusetts, and in Providence and Westerly, Rhode Island.

Many of the family members married non-Indians and became active in community affairs. The whites, however, did not distinguish them from African Americans and subjected them to the same residential restrictions and humiliations. The assertion of Indian identity often caused tensions between the Indians and their African American neighbors. As a result of the ridicule from whites and the resentment from African Americans, many Indians refrained from overt public expressions of their Indian identity.

---

2. These men participated in some questionable land deals. Charles Hannibal, the son of Nimrod and Hannah Hannibal, and another family member named Isaac sold their land on the Poospatuck Reservation to William Floyd without consulting the tribe. The transactions, however, were not questioned at the time by the tribe or by the colonial government (Gonzales 1984, 3: 4–5). These purchases foreshadowed events that were to take place at Montauk in 1885.

The Montauketts and other Algonquian families joined in the community affairs where they lived. The most important social institution in many of these communities was the African Methodist Episcopal Church. Richard Allen, an African American minister, founded the AME church in 1787, when the Protestant churches in Philadelphia would not accept nonwhite members. The new church quickly took root in segregated communities throughout the North. Charles Plato and Lewis Cuffee, Montauketts who left Montauk to live in the Eastville section of Sag Harbor, were involved in the founding of St. David's AME Zion Church. Their names are on the plaque commemorating the construction of the church in 1840. George Fowler, another Montaukett, was active in the Bethel AME church in North Amityville, which was founded in 1815. Indians were also involved in the founding of the Lakeville AME Zion church in Nassau County (J. Strong 1996b, 25, 65, 90). James Waters, a member of the Lakeville church, played a leadership role in the later stages of the Montaukett court battle from 1914 to 1924.

For many young Montaukett men, the call of the sea was compelling. Although the reality of a seaman's life in the nineteenth century was far from the romantic picture painted in novels and in the taverns in Sag Harbor where sailors gathered to swap stories, the Montauketts, like many young men, paid little heed. Isaac Cuffee, a young Montaukett, signed on for two whaling voyages in 1818 and 1819 on the ship *Abigail* (Rabito-Wyppensenwah 1993c, 438). Cuffee went out again in 1826 on the *Thames,* a ship owned by two East Hampton men, and returned a year later with 1,450 barrels of whale oil on board. According to Van Scoy's account books for 1832, he outfitted John Hannibal and five or six other men who appear to be Montauketts for a whaling voyage.

It was possible, however, for a small number of Montauketts to earn a living on Montauk. They could herd cattle, tend fences, and sell baskets, fish, and wild game to the English. They also received some income from the trustees and from individual proprietors for grazing rights. The trustees' journals do not provide a clear record of these payments. In 1842, for example, Samuel Pharaoh leased the rights to grazing land to J. Madison Huntting of East Hampton for fifteen dollars (EHPLC, call no. MM 757). This exchange appears to be an individual transaction by Pharaoh, separate from the yearly fees and interest payments the trustees made to the Montaukett community. The Montauketts divided up these funds among the heads of the prominent families in their community.

Many Montauketts were now taking Christian names and getting married in Christian ceremonies (Rabito-Wyppensenwah 1993h, 420). In 1834, for example, Sylvester Pharaoh married Mary Jacobs, and there were twenty-five others entered in either census or church records between 1833 and 1880. There were undoubtedly many more that were never officially documented.

Against the background of these social and economic changes at Montauk were the tensions that continued unabated between the Montauketts and the English communities over the land and its resources. In 1818 the Montauketts again sought help from the state. Gov. Daniel Tompkins sent Isaac Keeler and Richard Hubbell to Montauk to investigate the complaints of the Montauketts that people from East Hampton were trespassing on their reserved lands at Indian Fields. Keeler and Hubbell called the trustees and representatives from the Montauketts together to listen to both sides. Although the Montauketts who were involved were not named in the report, it seems likely that Benjamin and Stephen Pharaoh were among the Montaukett representatives (JASNY, 129–31).

The Montauketts once again charged that their lands had been obtained through fraud, and once again the trustees produced the same documents that had been presented in 1764, 1800, and 1808. And, once again, the state officials concluded that the 1703 documents constituted a valid transfer of land to the trustees. They also agreed that the Montauketts had permanent residence rights at Montauk.

The next concern was the charges of flagrant abuses suffered by the Montauketts. They again accused the trustees of destroying their wigwams. Keeler and Hubbell concluded that the wigwams were on disputed land and that the trustees were justified in their actions. The second issue was the measures taken to control the damage done to the English fields by Montaukett hogs. Keeler and Hubbell agreed that something had to be done, but argued that the impounding of Montaukett livestock was too severe and that there were other means that could have been used to remedy the situation.

Keeler and Hubbell examined the other familiar issues involving the regulations on hunting, fishing, and the gathering of firewood and the slaughter of the Montauketts' dogs. They concluded that though some regulations were necessary, the random killing of their dogs and the restrictions on fishing were unjustified. Two new abuses were added to the charges against the English. The Montauketts complained that the trustees were keeping their cattle on their planting grounds three weeks past the date of April 25, agreed upon in the earlier documents. Consequently, this delay pushed the Montauketts' planting season forward to the middle of May because they could not prepare the land for the crops until after the English removed their livestock.

Keeler and Hubbell confirmed that the abuses described by Beecher were more widely practiced than he imagined. They reported that "sharpers and free-booters" came from East Hampton, bringing the liquor by boat as well as by cart. After the Indians were intoxicated, the "sharpers" took their corn as well as their winter supplies of cranberries, oysters, clams, and fish. The Montauketts, reported Keeler and Hubbell, were left to "stand shivering with wet and cold a spectacle to the world, and those robbers after plundering those poor natives of their living, row off with their boats without remorse" (ibid., 131).

Although they accepted the validity of the 1703 agreements and supported some of the trustees' actions, Keeler and Hubbell were much more sympathetic to the Montauketts' plight than were the officials who responded to the earlier petitions. They included a graphic description of the hardships the elderly Montauketts suffered during the winter months. Addressing the governor, they wrote, "Once more we wish to ask the indulgence of your Excellency, while we state the destitute and almost naked situation of some of their oldest females, several of them eighty years and upwards old, and some of them must freeze to death this winter, unless they have some relief given them in blankets and common clothing, they also suffer from the necessities of life, situated as they are seventeen miles from East Hampton" (ibid.). They reported that several of these elderly Montauketts had perished during the previous two winters.

Keeler and Hubbell recommended that the state appoint an agent to live at Montauk to "teach their children to learn useful improvements and to direct them how to cultivate and improve their lands to better advantage, and to...promote useful industry which would, we believe in a certain degree, restrain and put a check to such impositions being practiced upon them by people who resort to their shores." They also asked the state for some act of benevolence to aid "those poor distressed native Indians of Montauk, who are suffering greatly for many of the conveniences of life" (ibid.). There is no indication in the records that anything was done by the state or by East Hampton to provide the recommended benevolence to the Montauketts.

The trustees, who wanted no interference in their relations with the Montauketts, rejected the recommendation that the Montaukett lands be clearly marked off and that the state appoint an agent to aid the Montauketts and help them protect their interests. Had the governor and legislature responded to Keeler and Hubbell, Montaukett history would have been quite different. The creation of a state agency would have established a de facto reservation at Indian Fields and provided the Montauketts with a protected homeland.

The isolated location of Montauk, however, would remain a serious obstacle to survival. As Keeler and Hubbell suggested, unless the Montauketts had some help in developing some form of industry at Montauk, which could provide a source of income, it would be difficult to stop the population decline as the youth left to find employment elsewhere. Ironically, the forces that brought employment opportunities and the establishment of an English settlement to Montauk were the very forces that finally squeezed the Montauketts off their land.

The East Hampton community was also going through some significant social changes. The proprietors found themselves in the minority as the population of the town expanded to include more and more citizens who owned no shares in the Montauk lands. A majority of residents, many of whom probably had little concern for the interests of the proprietors, elected the trustees. Prior to 1838 all of the money paid to the trustees for grazing, fishing, and hunting rights on Montauk went into a separate account used solely for improvements at Montauk. The money paid the Montauketts for their annual payments —rent for land at Indian Fields and wages for cattle tending and fence construction and repair—came from this account. In 1838, for the first time, the trustees diverted some funds to the town coffers where they used them to pay for improvements to the church parish (JEHT, 4: 10–11). In 1841 fifty dollars was used to pay part of the minister's salary. These actions of the trustees angered many of the proprietors, but they were no longer able to control the local government as they had in the past.

These disagreements between the trustees and the proprietors had no impact on the situation at Montauk. The numbers of Montauketts living there declined to about fifty. Many observers, noting the shrinking population, mistakenly reported that the Montauk Tribe was nearing extinction. This assertion, of course, was not the case at all. The Hannibals and other Montauketts who left Montauk did not cease to exist.

The decline in residents at Montauk left a large portion of land in Indian Fields unused. In 1819 the trustees began to lease individual grazing rights from the Montauketts. The Fatting Field Books kept by the trustees listed proprietors who had leased grazing rights from individual Montauketts (FFB-BHSL, no. 25). The leasing was negotiated on the basis of the 1703 agreement, which allowed the Montaukett community grazing rights for fifty head of cattle or horses. These rights were divided up among the remaining heads of Montaukett households, who then leased them out to individual proprietors. In 1819, for example, Benjamin Hedges leased one cow from David Hannibal, and David Hedges leased one from Stephen Pharaoh (ibid.).

For most of the years between 1820 and 1852, the trustees as a whole leased grazing rights from the Montauketts. The amount changed on occasion, suggesting that some hard bargaining was carried on. From 1826 until 1831, for example, the trustees paid $36.00, and in 1833 it was raised slightly to $36.50, but by 1849 it had increased to $60.00 (JEHT, 5: 61).

The proprietors supported the trustees' arrangement with the Montauketts, but not the use of money from the Montauk account for town expenses unrelated to the Montauk lands. The issue came to a head in 1849 when the trustees took the money George Hubbard paid for a license to hunt fowl on Montauk and put it in the town treasury (ibid., 10). The proprietors brought suit against the trustees, demanding that they withdraw from any further involvement in the management of the Montauk lands. These lands, argued the proprietors, belonged to them, and the trustees were mismanaging them. Not only were the revenues being diverted to the town, charged the proprietors, but the trustees, in their desire to increase the town coffers, had also put too many animals on the grazing lands and sold off far too much of the valuable wood supplies (R. Smith 1926, 176–77).

The East Hampton town trustees responded to the charges, arguing that the proprietors purchased Montauk in 1687 for the whole town, not for themselves as private owners (ibid., 150). The precedent, they said, was set when the first settlers purchased the title from Edward Hopkins in 1651. The town founders never claimed to own East Hampton as tenants in common, nor did Governor Dongan's patent establishing the town of East Hampton recognize such a distinction. There was never any question of individual ownership in any of the subsequent purchases, they argued. The town trustees also reminded the proprietors that they had never paid the Montauketts the full purchase price for Montauk (ibid., 151, 163).

In spite of these arguments, the court ruled against the trustees and ordered them to turn over all of the account books for Montauk to the proprietors. The proprietors now held full title to Montauk in fee simple. The court, however, made no mention of the trustees' obligations to oversee and protect the residence rights granted to the Montauketts in the 1703 bond. The proprietors could not ignore them later, however, when they formed themselves into a corporation called the Trustees of Montauk. The process of incorporation required the approval of the New York state legislature. The act of incorporation, passed in 1852, included a clause stating that "this act shall not affect the Montauk tribe of Indians, nor their right, title or interest in and to said Montauk lands" (LSNY, chap. 139, 175).

The language in the incorporation legislation suggests that the trustees were accountable to the state for any action that involved the residence rights of the Montauketts. The East Hampton trustees' obligations to the Montauketts, set forth in the 1703 agreement, remained intact as well. The court ruled only on the narrow question of ownership in the 1703 deed. The town trustees witnessed and endorsed the proprietors' promise to pay an additional hundred pounds for Montauk.

The shift from town control to the new Trustees of Montauk appears to have made little impact on the Montauketts. When the Civil War started, several Montaukett men enlisted as volunteers. Forty Montauketts from Brothertown also enlisted. They fought in Chancellorsville, Antietam, and Gettysburg. Warren Cuffee and Stephen Pharaoh were among the Montauketts from Montauk who fought with the New York 127th, a white regiment. The army often placed Algonquian volunteers from Long Island with white units (Rabito-Wyppensenwah 1993f, 553–55).

Upon return from the war, the veterans found that little had changed. The Trustees of Montauk continued to keep the Fatting Field Books, which recorded the leasing fees paid to the Montauketts. Now, however, the trustees listed the fees by individual share of the fifty-head allotment set for cattle and horses in 1703. These allocations undoubtedly reflected the individual Montaukett's status in the community. The entries for 1854, for example, listed the division of payments as follows: Sylvester Pharaoh 18, Samuel Pharaoh 12, Elisha Pharaoh 11, William Walter 6 and Charity Talkhouse 3 (FFB-EHPL, 1854). The Montauketts apparently recognized Sylvester Pharaoh as their sachem. The East Hampton records, however, continued to ignore these expressions of Montaukett political structure. Sylvester Pharaoh continued to receive the largest number of shares until his death in 1870. That year his widow received the most shares (ibid., 1870).

Sylvester Pharaoh.
Courtesy of East Hampton Library.

The Fatting Field Book for 1872 marked a transition in Montaukett leadership. The entries indicate that David Pharaoh, who was probably Sylvester's nephew, received sixteen shares, while Jerusha's share was reduced to three. According to a report in the *Sag Harbor Express* for July 14, 1870, following Sylvester Pharaoh's death, "at an assemblage of the whole tribe on the 10th inst., David Pharaoh was elected chief, and George Pharaoh, Elisha Pharaoh and Jeremiah Wright were chosen counselors."

A reporter for the *New York Sunday Sun* described the process for selecting a sachem. "Under the old Indian law," he wrote, "the succession to the throne was supposed, as in Turkey, to go to the oldest living descendant of the old sachem" (quoted in Shepherd 1981, 40). The issue becomes complicated, as it does in all such hierarchies, when there are conflicting lineal descendants who compete for power. The Montaukett elders met in one of the cabins and elected the new sachem, apparently by consensus. The tribal elections, like most elections everywhere, were a time for a great party that lasted long into the night.

Montauketts voted on the candidates by a hand vote and marked the tally on a stick. Those tribal members who lived in the outside communities were eligible to come to Montauk and cast their votes. The two core Montaukett families, the Fowlers and the Pharaohs, were frequently at odds over the choice of a candidate for sachem. David Pharaoh, it was said, won his election by campaigning in Freetown and among the other Montaukett enclaves to the west (ibid., 41). The tension between the two families emerged again during the 1990s when Bob Pharaoh and a Fowler descendant, Robert Cooper, vied for tribal leadership.

Unfortunately, we know relatively little about David Pharaoh, but what we do know is most intriguing. He remained sachem of the Montauketts until his death in 1878, but he also played an important role in the spiritual life of his community. He conducted the June Meeting religious services, which celebrated the change of seasons and the first signs of success of the spring planting.

A newspaper account of a June Meeting in 1871 provides some insights into the nature of the religious syncretism, which had emerged in the middle of the nineteenth century among the Algonquian peoples of eastern Long Island (*New York Standard,* June 6, 1871). The annual meeting drew Algonquian people from all over Long Island to a location in the Shinnecock Hills near the Shinnecock Reservation. David Pharaoh began the service by leading a procession of young men to a platform covered with wildflowers where he took a seat. After he was seated, another procession of men, women, and children filed into the clearing and passed in front of the platform.

Then a white man described in the press as "a 'reduced' white man, who had lived too long with the Indians," gave a long and rambling, sometimes incoherent (to the reporter), prayer. When he finished speaking, the people began chanting and moving around the platform. Then David spoke. He called upon the spirits to prevent the whites from invading his lands at Montauk. When he finished the fires were lit and the people marched around the flames, casting in pieces of evergreen bows as they passed by. David, the reporter said, was "elaborately decorated with colored cloth's and feathers and his face and arms striped with paint" (ibid.).

That same year *Harper's New Monthly Magazine* published an article that mentioned the Montauketts and included a line drawing of David and his wife, Maria, who were described as the "King and Queen of the Montauks" (43: 493). David Pharaoh's influence had apparently spread beyond Montauk to the Shinnecocks and to other

David and Maria Pharaoh, *Harper's New Monthly Magazine,* 1871.
Courtesy of East Hampton Library.

Algonquian peoples on eastern Long Island. This range may have
been due, in part, to the way he effectively integrated his political and
religious messages. Pharaoh had also impressed an American painter
who visited Montauk briefly in 1874. Winslow Homer came to East
Hampton that summer and painted several landscapes. Although,
unfortunately, little is known about the meeting between the two
men, Homer did a line drawing of Pharaoh. The drawing depicts a
man of quiet strength and dignity, looking out pensively at the world
(Hendricks 1979, fig. 169).

In 1870, the year Sylvester died, the Montauketts exacerbated
the ongoing conflict over access to wood for fences and hearths by
closing off the woodland near Indian Fields. They were concerned
about the increasing amount of firewood and timber for buildings
that the whites were taking off Montauk. David and his counselors,
Elisha Pharaoh, George Pharaoh, and Jeremiah Wright, initiated a
historic court case against the Trustees of Montauk. The new generation of Montauketts undoubtedly decided on this course of action
because their predecessors had not been successful when they took

their appeal to the state legislature. The Montauketts sued the Trustees of Montauk on behalf of the Montauketts living at Montauk, charging that the trustees were cutting wood that was vital to the Indians' survival.[3]

David Pharaoh argued that the Montauketts had the right to fence in a general field for their planting ground and to cut the necessary wood for the fence. They also had access to wood for their hearths. The fencing, he said, had to be repaired yearly, and the Montauketts had no other source of wood. The trustees, Pharaoh continued, could easily find enough wood back in East Hampton.

The following fall Downing rendered his decision, which began with a statement recognizing David Pharaoh as "the chief of the Montauk tribe of Indians, occupying the same premises known as Montauk, at the time of discovery and early settlement of that part of America by white people and that said Indians were then entitled to the entire of all said lands, including the premises described in the complaint" (ibid.). Justice Downing recognized the tribe and did not question their right to bring suit in the Supreme Court of New York. He also addressed another significant issue, almost in passing, in his first finding when he declared that Jeremiah Wright was not a member of the tribe. He affirmed that David, Elisha (who had died in 1870), and George Pharaoh were full tribal members. Although he was wrong about Jeremiah Wright, Downing

3. According to the federal census of 1870 there were six family homesteads that included a total of twenty-one people at Montauk. The accuracy of the count is open to question. Jeremiah Parsons, the assistant census marshal, dated his report June 28, 1870. He included the names of Sylvester Pharaoh, Elisha Pharaoh, and Sarah Pharaoh, all of whom died in May of that year. It is quite possible that Parsons did not take his work at Montauk very seriously and may never have actually made the half-day trip to make the count in person. One common criticism of the federal census is that the people responsible for gathering the data in house-to-house visits often avoid neighborhoods where ethnic minorities and poor people live. It is quite possible that he missed some of the Montauketts. David Pharaoh's mother, Amelia, for example, may have been living off Montauk in 1870, but her obituary in 1876 stated that she died in her residence on the Montauk Reservation (*Long Island Democrat,* Aug. 16, 1876, p. 3).

The six families listed were: 1. Sylvester Pharaoh, 65 (deceased May 28, 1870), Jerusha Pharaoh, 40 (Sylvester's widow), and her son by a previous marriage, Ephriam, 24; 2. Stephen Pharaoh, 48, and Samuel Pharaoh, 14; 3. David Pharaoh, 48, his wife, Maria (Fowler), and their children, Wyandank, 7, Maggie, 4, Samuel, 2, and Ebenezer, 5 mos.; 4. Aurelia Pharaoh, 57, and Sarah Pharaoh, 22 (deceased May 10, 1870); 5. William Fowler, 48, his wife, Mary, 49, and their children, John, 25, Hannah, 15, Charles, 11, George, 9, and Herbert, 5; and 6. Elisha Pharaoh, 70 (deceased May 2, 1870) (Rabito-Wyppensenwah 1993e, 409–12).

100

The
Montaukett
Indians of
Eastern
Long Island

set an important precedent with his finding. The Supreme Court of New York had extended its authority into tribal affairs to such a degree that it now determined membership in the tribe.

In his sixth finding Downing affirmed that the Montauketts had not lived on North Neck since early in the eighteenth century and were now settled at a place called Indian Fields. Downing then turned to the primary issue in the suit. He ruled that there was sufficient wood for the Montauketts on Indian Fields and that the trustees were not obligated to give the Montauketts access to any additional woodlands. There is no indication that Downing made any effort to determine how much wood the Montauketts used each year, nor did he make a survey of the available wood supply on Montauk. It seems clear that he simply took the word of the trustees on the matter. The court vacated the injunction and charged the Montauketts for the costs of the trial. The Trustees of Montauk, not satisfied with crushing the hopes of the Montauketts for redress of their grievances, filed a charge of $365.64 for lawyers' fees and damages. Once again the Montauketts found themselves defeated and in debt.

David Pharaoh must have been very disappointed with the outcome. One more avenue to redress grievances against the trustees had proved ineffective. Still he continued to press for the improvement of his people. In 1872, after the state superintendent of the New York public schools visited Montauk, David petitioned the state to establish a school at Montauk for the Montaukett children. The missionary groups that had supported teachers such as Occom, Fowler, and Hannibal lost interest in the school at Montauk after the Christian Montauketts left for Brothertown. Pharaoh realized that an education would help the children become better prepared to make a living. The Trustees of Montauk immediately used their considerable influence to prevent any state involvement with the Montauketts (NYSDE, 25–26). They feared that such attention might erode their control over the tribe. The trustees did not want to allow any improvements that would encourage the Montauketts to remain at Montauk.

David Pharaoh suffered the loss of his father, Samuel, in 1873 and his mother, Amelia, in the summer of 1876. She died, according to the obituary, "upon the floor of her residence on the Montauk reservation" (*Long Island Democrat,* Aug. 16, 1876). David's health also deteriorated after the death of his mother.

In 1878 two proprietors, Robert Grinnell and his wife, sued the other proprietors to force the sale of the Montauk lands. David

Pharaoh, alarmed at the potential threat to the Montaukett entitlement, joined with Stephen Pharaoh and William Fowler to file a complaint to protect their land claims. David, who was suffering from consumption, walked unsteadily into the courtroom to testify (JEHT, 3: 316). Wilmont M. Smith, a young lawyer who had been admitted to the bar the year before, represented the Montauketts. Judge J. O. Dykeman heard the complaint and ruled that the land could be sold at auction, subject to the rights of the Montauketts, which were guaranteed in the 1703 lease. The judge also noted that "a portion of the purchase money of the said lands of Montauk amounting to the sum of 100 pounds sterling, current money of the province of New York, or $250 lawful money of the United States, is still unpaid by the said proprietors and is a lien on the land" (R. Smith 1926, 235). Dykeman reminded all parties that the proprietors had, since 1703, paid only the interest on the purchase price, leaving the principal in trust.

Judge Dykeman's opinion included a "finding of fact," which seemed to be a routine formality when it was announced. His eighteenth and last finding was that "The said tribe consists of David Pharaoh, Stephen Pharaoh and William Fowler and their respective wives and children and of other persons not now residing upon the lands at Montauk. The tribal organization is still maintained and the said tribe now enjoys and is entitled to the privileges set forth in the foregoing paragraph" (ibid., 236). Once again the courts affirmed the existence of the tribe and the legitimacy of its leaders. Judge Dykeman went one important step further than Justice Downing. He affirmed that the Montaukett rights to Montauk belonged to the tribe that included other persons not living at Montauk.

David Pharaoh died of consumption on July 18, 1878, at the age of forty-one.[4] Although he conducted traditional religious ceremonies, such as the June Meeting ritual, he apparently had adopted a belief system that brought together a mixture of Algonquian and Christian beliefs and rituals because the Reverend John D. Stokes, the Presbyterian minister in East Hampton, conducted his funeral. Stokes came out to Oyster Pond to preach the funeral sermon (Shep-

---

4. Consumption was listed as a cause of 36 percent of the Montaukett deaths listed in the East Hampton Presbyterian Church records during the eighteenth and nineteenth centuries. These cases were most likely pulmonary tuberculosis, a common disease among the poor who live in crowded, poorly ventilated dwellings. In a two-year period, from 1877 to 1879, seven Montauketts from eleven months to sixty-three years of age died from "consumption" (Rabito-Wyppensenwah 1993b, 417).

102

*The
Montaukett
Indians of
Eastern
Long Island*

herd 1981, 39). It is likely that the family quietly performed some Algonquian rituals. The Montaukett community he served so well must have deeply mourned David Pharaoh's passing.

Leadership of the tribe now passed to David's close relative, Stephen Talkhouse Pharaoh. Stephen was born in a wigwam at Accabonac, about two miles northeast of East Hampton. Stephen's family was representative of the Montaukett diaspora, who were scattered across eastern Long Island. They often set up their wigwams on land that had been purchased earlier by whites but had never been occupied or developed. The East Hampton people usually allowed the Indians to live in these places because they provided a close, convenient source of cheap, unskilled labor. Stephen's mother, Molly, for example, indentured the young boy to a white neighbor.[5] Stephen joined a whaling crew as a young man and sailed with them to hunt whales in the Pacific. He visited the gold fields of California during the gold rush of 1849, where he was said to have panned for gold. After serving in the Union army, he settled on Indian Fields near Reed Pond.

Stephen was well known throughout Long Island because of his reputation as a great walker. He traveled great distances at a very rapid pace, carrying a pack of hand-carved scrub brushes, which he sold to housewives for their kitchen work. Legend has it that he walked from Brooklyn to Montauk in one day. P. T. Barnum hired Stephen and featured him as the "World's Greatest Walker." In 1976 the town of East Hampton erected a plaque on a small knoll where Molly's wigwam stood to commemorate his birth.

Stephen died in August 1879. His body was found on one of his walking trails near East Hampton (Rattray 1953, 29). His death was attributed to consumption. The *New York Sunday Sun* described his funeral in rich detail (quoted in Shepherd 1981, 38–41). Unfortunately, there is no byline on the *Sun* article, so we do not know who wrote this valuable contribution to Montaukett ethnohistory. The funeral was held in Freetown. Stephen did not convert to Christianity until the last year of his life when he fell sick. The minister hastened to point out that although Stephen had spent most of his life as a non-Christian, he seldom drank, and he lived a peaceful and orderly life.

5. There is a story told by local people in East Hampton that tells more about the plight of the Montauketts than the storytellers realize. They say, with bemusement, that when Stephen was a small child he was indentured out to William D. Parsons for a dollar a pound. He weighed forty pounds, and Parsons paid Stephen's parents forty dollars. Others say Parsons actually paid one hundred dollars.

Stephen Talkhouse Pharaoh. Courtesy of East Hampton Library.

A funeral procession accompanied the body to Indian Fields, where he was laid to rest beside David Pharaoh on the slope of a hill overlooking Lake Montauk. David Pharaoh's widow, Maria, and her five children—Margaret, Wyandank, Samuel Powhatan, Ebenezer Tecumseh, and Sarah Pocahontas—all stood at the graveside. The Montaukett women dressed in bright colors and wore brass earrings. William Fowler also wore brass earrings. The other Montaukett men came in suits.

The reporter for the paper noted that the Montauketts were no longer living in traditional wigwams. William Fowler's house was

104

*The
Montaukett
Indians of
Eastern
Long Island*

a two-story wooden, framed structure. The ground floor was divided into a living room and a washroom. On the wall hung three colored prints: the first depicted a black regiment in the Civil War, charging the Confederate forces; the second showed a naval battle in the War of 1812; and the third, a print, pictured John Brown kissing the child held up to him by a slave mother as he was being led to his execution. The print may have been a copy of Thomas Hovendon's "Execution of John Brown."

William Fowler, who was fifty-six, told the reporter that he had lived through the transition from wigwams to wooden homes at Montauk. He could remember as a child when he could look out over some forty wigwams on Indian Fields (ibid.). He also acknowledged to the reporter that he had a problem with alcohol and opium. He confided that a year earlier he had had thirty or forty hogs, but they had been sold for drugs. He was not destitute, however, because he cultivated a two-acre patch of corn and melons, hunted, fished, and raised fowls to feed himself. There were several guns in the room and a bird dog in the corner chewing a bone. Outside geese, ducks, and turkey gobblers made so much noise that the reporter had difficulty talking with Fowler.

Charles Fowler, William's son, who was about twenty years old in 1879, lived with his wife, Sarah, and their child in a small cabin about twenty-four-feet square. It was sparsely furnished but had a wood floor and a small iron stove (Johannemann 1993, 649–51). Charles worked as a hunting guide for the people who came out to hunt on Montauk for sport. One of his clients was Arthur Benson, who purchased all of Montauk a month after Stephen Pharaoh's death.

Charles's sister, Maria, the widow of David Pharaoh, earned an income doing laundry for East Hampton people in the summer, and in the winter her fifteen-year-old son, Wyandank, earned enough money by shooting game birds to buy pork and cornmeal. Maria had a carpet on the floor of her cabin and a lamp with a porcelain shade on a table in the sitting room. From her house on a small hill she had a spectacular view of Oyster Pond and Peconic Bay.

At that time there were no permanent roads on Montauk, and the cart path to East Hampton was often impassable when the high tides spilled across the narrow beach land at Napeague. Once travelers from East Hampton got across Napeague, they would follow a rough cart path, which went through Hither Woods to the Montauk highlands. Approaches to Montauk by water were equally difficult because no harbor facilities existed. Although a safe and secure anchorage could be found in Fort Pond Bay, there were no deep water harbors.

The small Montaukett settlement on Indian Fields had about thirty acres of land under cultivation on small plots near their cabins. They owned two horses, one of which belonged to David's widow, Maria, but had no other livestock. All of the cattle on Indian Fields belonged to people in East Hampton and neighboring communities. There were only about a dozen Montauketts residing there in 1879, but their relatives throughout Long Island still regarded Indian Fields as their homeland.

Most of the Montauketts living off the reserved land were not able to keep in close touch with the events at Montauk. They were unaware that developers were making plans for the peninsula. The first step in this process came on October 22, 1879, at one P.M., one year after the death of David Pharaoh. The trustees auctioned off all 11,500 acres of Montauk lands to the highest bidder. A flyer announced to the public that 10 percent of the bid must be paid in cash at the auction and that the balance was due on December 1, 1879. The flyer also stated that "the property will be sold subject to the rights and privileges of the Montauk Tribe of Indians" (EHPLC, call no. BG 1-6c). Judge Dykeman's ruling on these rights in the Grinnell case clearly indicated a serious impediment to the sale. Dykeman noted that the trustees had never paid any of the principal on the 1703 purchase, and there is no evidence that the trustees paid the Montauketts between the time of Dykeman's ruling and the auction. One could argue, therefore, that the trustees were selling land they did not own. No one representing the Montauketts, however, came forward with an objection. In fact, there is no record that the Montauketts were involved in any part of the transaction.

By noon on the twenty-second, the town of East Hampton stirred with some excitement as potential buyers made their way to the front of former town supervisor Jehaial Parson's office where a large crowd had gathered. The first bid was $40,000, and then it jumped to $75,000. There followed a series of $1,000 raises until finally Arthur Benson of Brooklyn bid $151,000. The auctioneer tried in vain to get higher bids, but there were no takers. The gavel came down, and Benson became the new owner of Montauk (*New York Times,* Oct. 23, 1879).

By the time he was thirty-seven Arthur Benson had amassed such a fortune in the shipping business that he retired in 1849 to a life of leisure. He came from one of Brooklyn's oldest, wealthiest, and most respected families. Benson, who frequently came to Montauk to hunt and fish, was certainly aware of the potential for development there. He denied that he was interested in development, saying that he only wanted a place for sporting and, perhaps, for a farm for his son Frank. Benson, however, was deeply involved with Austin Corbin and other developers who had extensive plans for eastern Long Island. In 1882 he joined with Corbin to purchase land in Shinnecock Hills for the development of a resort complex (*Seaside Times,* July 27, 1882).

Everett A. Carpenter, an attorney from Sag Harbor, refereed the transaction. He never raised any questions about Dykeman's findings, and he apparently saw no reason to communicate with the Montauketts about the matter. Carpenter noted in his report only that most of the Montauketts were living on a twelve-hundred-acre parcel of land known as Indian Fields. The Montauketts were a small, isolated community. It was easy to ignore them in the midst of one of the largest real estate deals in the town's history.

SIX

THE ENGINE OF PROGRESS
1880–1900

DURING THE last two decades of the nineteenth century, the country witnessed the closing of the western frontier, an increasing enthusiasm for progress and economic development, and a growing belief that the most humane solution to the "Indian problem" was to force the Indians to assimilate into the mainstream of American society. The last major conflict with the Plains Indians occurred in 1890 at Wounded Knee. By this time the railroads, America's first "big business," had linked the country, providing a means to move goods and people quickly over long distances. The Dawes Act, passed in 1887, was designed to end the reservation system and push the Indians into a "civilized" way of life as farmers and tradesmen.

Although the policy won widespread support, some critics warned that the Dawes Act would rob the Indians of their lands (Weeks 1990, 220–21). In spite of these warnings, the process of dividing up many of the western reservations began. The government carved small homesteads out of tribal lands and allocated them to reservation families. In the end, however, white ranchers took over thousands of acres of reservation land, causing the Indians considerable hardship.

On Long Island the forces of progress and the conviction that Indians were better off when they assimilated into the "melting pot" of mainstream America played major roles in the Montaukett dispossession. In 1881 the Long Island Railroad began to push its way eastward toward Montauk under the brilliant and ruthless direction of Austin Corbin Jr., an archetypal business baron of the late nineteenth century.[1] Walt Whitman called railroads the "emblem of

1. Corbin's great wealth, affluent lifestyle, and arrogance were frequently

108

The
Montaukett
Indians of
Eastern
Long Island

motion and power." They were necessary for the kind of economic growth the vast majority of Americans wanted. Eastern Long Island enthusiastically welcomed the eastward extension of the railroad.

The majority of white Americans on Long Island viewed the Montauketts as anachronistic obstacles to the great ideas and forces of the day. Many of the whites also questioned the Montauketts' "Indian identity." Racial prejudice and negative stereotypes led them to assume that miscegenation between Indians and African Americans resulted inevitably in the loss of Indian identity. In contrast, miscegenation between Indians and whites received very little comment at all. The many Iroquois who came from mixed families, for example, seldom had their "Indianness" challenged.

The contemporary press discouraged public sympathy or support for the Montauketts by publishing stories that referred to them in very negative terms. In 1882 an article in the *New York Evening Post,* for example, described the Montauketts as "idle, ignorant, and dissipated, none of them of pure Indian blood. They live from hand to mouth by hunting and fishing and doing odd jobs" (Morice 1949, 126). Similar descriptions appeared in local papers over the next three decades. These reports undoubtedly had considerable influence on the court decisions involving Montaukett land claims.

Arthur Benson began to develop Montauk as a hunting preserve soon after he completed the purchase in 1879. Benson, accustomed to having the best of everything, hired one of America's leading architects, Stanford White, to design summer cottages for his guests. He contracted Frederick Law Olmstead to do the landscaping. His

---

reported in the press. These reports may have influenced Rudyard Kipling to use Corbin as a model in *Captain's Courageous* about a railroad baron who owned "every railroad on Long Island." The similarity was so thinly veiled, said a reporter for the *Brooklyn Daily Eagle,* that "the name [of the character] might just as well have been plain Austin Corbin" (Nov. 8, 1896).

Corbin, who was born in New Hampshire, began his financial career in the Midwest, buying up the lands of homesteaders who could not pay their mortgages. He founded a very successful bank in Iowa and owned a plantation in Arkansas where he used convict labor. Corbin returned east and founded a banking company that soon produced enough profits to enable him to invest in railroads. He built a railroad connecting Manhattan Beach in Brooklyn with New York and then developed two luxury hotel complexes for wealthy patrons. Railroads, in Corbin's view, were to bring wealthy people from their homes to luxurious resorts as comfortably as possible. He admired the English and harbored sharp prejudices against Jews, all nonwhites, and the working class in general (Seyfried 1974, 6: 19–23). He paid low wages and took great satisfaction in crushing unions and replacing their members with newly imported immigrants. One can easily imagine what he thought of the Montauketts.

guests included many of the wealthiest businessmen of the day. Among them were Austin Corbin Jr. and Standard Oil executives Charles Pratt and A. C. Bedford.

Benson entertained his guests in great style. On one occasion he attempted to prohibit all of the East Hampton residents from hunting on Montauk so that he could introduce "English style" fox-hunting (Rattray 1938, 58). Public outrage prevented him from going ahead with the plan. Hunting rights on Montauk continued to be a source of contention between Benson and the townspeople, who were accustomed to taking seasonal hunting trips to Montauk.

Benson's guests, particularly Corbin, saw the potential for a resort area and an international port of entry at Montauk. It would, of course, be very good business for Corbin's railroad. Corbin first visited Montauk in 1881, the same year he formed the Long Island Development Company and the year before he had purchased the Long Island Railroad. If Benson had ever been serious about keeping Montauk as a sportsmen's retreat and a farm for his son, those ideas were abandoned soon after Corbin's visit.

Benson feared that the Montaukett encumbrance on his deed might cause problems for the ambitious development projects that were now being planned. He approached former proprietors and asked them to place all of the Montauk deeds, accounts, and other papers into his custody. They voted to comply with Benson's request and sent fourteen packets of documents to him (EHPLC, file JJ, 49).

In the summer of 1882 Corbin began plans to extend the Long Island Railroad from Bridgehampton to Montauk. He met with Benson and purchased the right-of-way and a small parcel of land on the north end of Fort Pond for a terminal station. Corbin paid Benson one hundred thousand dollars for this package. Benson was getting a very quick return from his Montauk investment (Seyfried 1974, 6: 7).

While all these high-powered machinations were taking place in corporate boardrooms, Wyandank, who was in his nineteenth year, was involved in a prank that got him into trouble with the law. He and Silas Cuffee, who was probably a Montaukett from the Eastville band in Sag Harbor, stole a barrel of whiskey from a white man in East Hampton (SCHDR, file 1402, 1476). The court found them guilty and required them to pay for the whiskey. Cuffee spent some time in jail, but Wyandank, perhaps because of his age, was released (Rabito-Wyppensenwah, letter to author, July 10, 1996). When the judge asked Wyandank what his business was, he answered "most anything, farming, fishing" (SCHDR, file 1476).

110

The
Montaukett
Indians of
Eastern
Long Island

Although the incident itself was not a serious matter, it does raise once again the problem of alcohol abuse in the Montaukett community. The first point to be made is that many Montauketts—including Wyandank; his mother, Maria; Stephen Pharaoh; and others —were not alcoholics. The accounts in the local press, however, tended to reinforce a stereotype of a "dissipated race." Visitors and tourists were often quoted in the press remarking on what they perceived to be evidence of rampant drunkenness. Occasional incidents reported in the newspapers encouraged these perceptions. The *Sag Harbor Corrector,* for example, placed a report on the front page about Jerry Wright, a Montaukett in the Freetown band, who was arrested in East Hampton and fined for "being drunk and disorderly" (Aug. 27, 1892, p. 1). Nevertheless, such incidents did occur, and although exaggerated in the minds of many whites, alcohol abuse did pose a serious problem for the Montaukett community.[2]

In the meantime, plans for Montauk were moving along rapidly. In 1883 Corbin incorporated the rail link between Bridgehampton and Montauk under the name of the Fort Pond Bay Railroad Company. The new company was capitalized at $5 million (Seyfried 1974, 6: 7). Corbin went to England to raise more money to establish an international steamship line between a port in Wales and Montauk. He believed that European goods would enter Montauk and be carried to the New York markets on his railroad. The English investors began plans to build four steamships, which would make weekly trips between Wales and Montauk. The following year Corbin began lobbying in Albany and in the United States Congress for bills to open a seaport and a customs facility at Montauk, register the ships, and establish a permit to carry the U.S. mail to England.

Back on Montauk Arthur Benson began his campaign to remove the Montauketts from Indian Fields. The number living there in 1884 is not easy to document. An article in a local newspaper, the *Patchogue Advance* (May 3, 1884, p. 2), gave a figure of thirteen,

2. In 1895 William Butler was hit by a train as he walked the tracks while intoxicated and was nearly killed (*Sag Harbor Corrector,* Sept. 7, 1895). Ebenezer Pharaoh, Wyandank's younger brother, was involved in several alcohol-related incidents. He was arrested twice for intoxication, and on one of these occasions he was also charged with an assault on his wife, Hattie (ibid., Oct. 27, 1892, p. 3; June 3, 1899, p. 3). Wyandank's other brother, Samuel, was nearly killed once when he passed out on the railroad tracks and was hauled off just in time. In the winter of 1927 he died of exposure after some heavy drinking. His body was found on a knoll near Three Mile Harbor in East Hampton (*Bridgehampton News,* Jan. 7, 1927).

but Maria Pharaoh testified in court thirty years later that there were thirty Montauketts living on Montauk. The number is probably somewhere in between.

Although there were few families on Indian Fields, there were many Montauketts in Freetown, the Eastville section of Sag Harbor; in North Amityville, about eighty miles west of Montauk; and in other communities throughout eastern Long Island. Although little is known about the internal social structures in these enclaves, the Montaukett families in Freetown and Eastville shared food and herbal medicines and visited each other regularly. By the end of the nineteenth century, the Montauketts living in Sag Harbor and East Hampton were identifying themselves as members of the Eastville and Freetown bands. The Montaukett community in North Amityville, however, never adopted a band name. The extended family units, the Devines, the Brewsters, the Steeles, the Fowlers, the Smiths, the Squires, the Greens, the Bunns, and the Hunters, who live there identify themselves as Indians. Their connection to Montaukett ancestors remains a part of their folk tradition (Terrie Caldwell, letter to author, June 28, 1996; Jo-Ann Brewster-Leftenant, letter to author, Dec. 24, 1996).

Although more is known about the Montauketts in these bands, there are occasional references to individual Montauketts in other places on Long Island and in southern Connecticut. The 1860 census for Islip, New York, for example, lists George Pharaoh, who had assisted David Pharaoh in the 1870 court case, and his wife, Hannah. George, a day laborer, was identified as an Indian, but his wife was listed as a mulatto. In 1874 a Montaukett named William Pharaoh was living in Port Jefferson, about seventy miles west of Montauk. William worked as a deckhand on the schooner *Alert*. A newspaper article described William as having "the appearance of a native of the forest, and is very affable, and gentlemanly, and is called a good seaman (*Patchogue Advance*, May 3, 1884). The following year he drowned in Port Jefferson Harbor. The coroner suspected "foul play" but gave no details in the press account (*Sag Harbor Express*, Sept. 12, 1885, p. 2).

Benson was, undoubtedly, well aware of the existence of the Montaukett diaspora and realized that he would have difficulty negotiating with the tribe as a whole. In order to avoid this problem, he sought only the individuals who were currently living on Indian Fields. Benson later argued that those Indians who left Montauk had abandoned their residence rights and did not need to be compensated. He simply ignored Judge Dykeman's ruling in 1878 that the residence rights belonged to all of the Montauketts, including those Indians not living at Montauk, as well as the fact that all of the previous transactions involving these rights clearly indicated that they were given to the Montauketts as a tribe.

Benson hired Nathaniel Dominy VII, an East Hampton man whose family settled there in 1668, to represent him in the negotiations with the Montauketts. Dominy, who was the town assessor at the time, had considerable incentive to help Benson remove the Montauketts from Montauk. He owed Benson a favor for a previous business transaction, and he knew that the right-of-way for Austin Corbin's railroad was going to run through his property (EHPLC, Box BA 4, 1-8).

Dominy had a long association with many of the Montauketts. Over the years some had worked for his family. Benson authorized Dominy to purchase a $150 parcel of land in Freetown, where some Montauketts were already living, and offer plots there to the people still on Montauk for a token fee of $1. This offer was good only if the Montauketts sold their residence rights to Benson. Dominy made the purchase and began negotiations with Maria Pharaoh and her younger brothers, Charles and George Fowler.

Dominy later testified that he assured all of the Montauketts that selling their share in the residence rights at Montauk did not mean that they could never return to Montauk. He told them that this transaction was no different from the purchase of 1662 when they were given the chance to return to Montauk if they wished (CP, 2: 186). This explanation was very confusing to the Montauketts, and it was contrary to the clearly stated language in the deeds they eventually signed.

Dominy went first to Maria, probably because he knew that the other Montauketts held her in high regard. He was also aware that her son Wyandank would soon become chief. Dominy finally reached an agreement with Maria and her brother George on April 21, 1885, in the Dominy home in East Hampton. Benson gave the adults individual cash payments of $100, and Wyandank received $10 (BHSL, 1974.48, no. 28).

In addition to the individual payments, Benson agreed to pay an annual fee of $240. He divided up the payments, just as the grazing fees had been. There is no record about the discussion of this matter among the Montaukett families, but it appears that Maria Pharaoh, George Fowler, and Charles Fowler each received $80 a year. Maria testified during the trial in 1909 that she was still receiving her $80 annuity.

In the agreement signed by the Montauketts, Benson gave them deeds to the plots of land in Freetown and agreed to move their houses from Indian Fields for them. In her autobiography Maria Pharaoh said that Benson also promised to pay for the education of all of her children. She said that he never made good on that promise. She recalled bitterly that Benson "offered me so much money and told such sweet lies" (Rabito-Wyppensenwah 1993i, 366).

The bill of sale identified Maria, George, and Wyandank as "members of the tribe known as the Montaukett Indians." This clause is important because it acknowledges that Benson recognized the Montauketts as a tribe at the time of the purchase. The next clause stated that the "parties of the first part by reason of their belonging to the said tribe of Montaukett Indians have and enjoy certain rights and privileges on the portions of the said Montauk, known as the North Neck and the Indian Field." Maria, George, and Wyandank, therefore, enjoyed these residence rights as members of the tribe, not as individuals.

The Montauketts were faced with the same disadvantage that their ancestors had faced in all of the previous land sales. They could not read the text of the deed. Maria later testified that "the deed was not read over to me. I can't read or write very well. I can write my name" (CP, 2: 177). When Maria composed her brief autobiography years later, she dictated it to her daughter Pocahontas. None of the other Montauketts who sold their homes to the Bensons were able to sign their own names. They signed all of the documents with an X and a legal stamp.

The bill of sale included a clause in direct contradiction to Nathaniel Dominy's verbal assurances to the Montauketts. The clause stated that the Montauketts "do hereby further covenant and agree to remain away permanently from the said Montauk and not to enter upon the same for any purpose whatsoever" (BHSL, 1974.48, no. 28). Maria's charge that Benson's agents took advantage of the Montauketts' inability to read the documents for themselves is the same one raised by Benjamin and Stephen Pharaoh, Cyrus Charles, and the other Montaukett petitioners over the years.

Maria Pharaoh's decision to sign the agreement may have been a factor in Charles Fowler's reluctant acceptance of a similar agreement with Dominy on October 1, 1885. Another factor, undoubtedly, was Benson's offer to give Charles a twenty-seven-acre parcel of land with a house and barn in Freetown. Benson gave the other Montauketts small plots ranging from two to six acres in area. Benson

114

The
Montaukett
Indians of
Eastern
Long Island

also agreed to pay the property taxes, build appropriate fencing, and make repairs on the house. Charles and his wife, Sarah, had rejected all of Dominy's overtures prior to this offer. Charles was loath to give up his rights on Montauk where he often worked as a guide. Dominy continued to press his assurances that they could return to Montauk if they did not like living in East Hampton. Charles and his wife, who were identified in the bill of sale as "belonging to the said tribe of Montaukett Indians," received $100 each and the small farm in East Hampton. The deed took note of the fact that Charles was to receive an $80 share of the annuity payments (CP, 2 plaintiffs exhibit E).

Dominy testified twelve years later before a United States Senate committee hearing on the Montaukett land claims that he objected to doing business the way Benson had asked him to do it with the Montauketts (SCH, 52). Dominy did not elaborate on what procedures he objected to, but Maria Pharaoh recalled in her autobiography that someone broke into her house and stole her husband's papers. Dominy may also have had some second thoughts about Benson's haste in moving the Montauketts off Montauk. Dominy supervised the removal of Maria's house from Montauk to Freetown. Benson ordered that the buildings that could not be moved were to be burned down (EHPLC, call no. DH 22).

In 1890 Arthur Benson died at the age of seventy-seven, and his widow, Jane, and his children, Frank and Mary, took over his estate. That same year Wyandank's mother, Maria, took her third husband, Edward Banks. Her second husband, Theodore Johnson, had died sometime earlier. Little is known about her marriage with Johnson, except that they had a daughter, Edith. Maria and Edward Banks had a son, Junius, who was her tenth child.

In the summer and fall of 1893, the Bensons hired as their new agent Frank Stratton, who was from a local family that settled in East Hampton even before the Dominys. Stratton had lived on Montauk for thirty-four years in one of the houses that the proprietors had built for caretakers. His father had employed Montaukett men to tend livestock, build and mend fences, and do odd jobs. He also hired women to do domestic chores.

Stratton negotiated deeds with Maria's other children, Samuel, Ebenezer, and Margaret Pharaoh, and with Jerusha Pharaoh's son, Ephriam. These deeds were very similar to the earlier ones negotiated by Dominy (SCH, 53–54). The Montauketts received cash payments, $350 to Ebenezer, $100 to Margaret, $200 to Ephriam, and $100 to

Samuel, and plots of land in Freetown. There is no explanation in the deeds for the distribution of the payments, nor is their any record of the interpretation that Stratton gave them about the possibility of their return to Montauk. None of the Montauketts were able to write their own names on the deeds.

Austin Corbin and Charles Pratt revealed their plans when their lobbying efforts, begun nearly a decade earlier, resulted in the introduction of a bill in Congress in 1894 asking for the authority to operate a duty-free port facility at Montauk. There were some serious problems with their plans, however, which were revealed in a report by the Army Corps of Engineers. The report stated that the route for large steamships entering Fort Pond Bay was risky because of sunken rocks and fog conditions. Corbin, however, continued to push the project with his characteristic drive and enthusiasm. While the bill was being considered, he published an attractively illustrated monograph with maps, titled "Quick Transit Between New York and London" (Seyfried 1974, 6: 18). In June 1895 Corbin and Pratt purchased four thousand acres of land in Hither Woods and around Fort Pond. The following month the two developers founded the Montauk Company, a multimillion-dollar corporation, to take the lead in their ambitious plans.

When the word of these transactions spread to the Montaukett people living in New England, Pennsylvania, and Long Island, several of them contacted the Pharaohs and the Fowlers to find out what had happened. Some were very angry with Maria and her family for signing individual deeds. The Pharaohs and the Fowlers, stung by the criticisms, raised questions about some of their critics' claim to Montaukett ancestry.

Although these tensions were never entirely resolved, Wyandank Pharaoh and two Montauketts from the diaspora, the Reverend Eugene Johnson, a Presbyterian minister from Philadelphia, and his brother, Dr. William H. Johnson, a physician from New York City, joined forces to reclaim the Montaukett lands. The Johnson brothers had grown up in Eastville, and Maria, Wyandank's mother, had lived with their family when she was a child. The decision to fight for the land at Montauk had revived a sense of unity among the Montauketts. Ironically, the Montauketts who had left Montauk because of its isolation and the lack of employment opportunities began to consider returning to take advantage of the economic boom envisioned by Austin Corbin.

Wyandank Pharaoh. Courtesy of East Hampton Library.

The Montauketts held a community meeting in September 1895 and established a committee to seek and hire a lawyer to open a suit against the Benson estate. Reverend Johnson served as secretary, but, unfortunately, no minutes of the proceedings have survived. Two decisions, however, must have been made at the meeting. The people confirmed Wyandank Pharaoh as the chief of the Montauketts and mapped out a strategy for a court challenge that involved a token reoccupation of Montauk by the Montauketts. The plan was to have several Montauketts arrested for trespass and then to appeal the arrest (*Sag Harbor Corrector,* Oct. 12, 1895, p. 3).

Wyandank was the obvious choice for chief. The young Montaukett, who had been named after his famous ancestor, was described by a reporter as being "noticeable by his dignified bearing, erect carriage, copper colored skin, high forehead, prominent cheekbones and straight, raven black hair" (*Brooklyn Daily Eagle,* Oct. 20, 1895).

Although he never had much of a formal education and could expect only meager financial support, he set forth to challenge the combined strength of several large corporations.

Corbin, hearing of the Montauketts' decision to challenge the Benson purchases, took measures to prevent anyone from trespassing on Montauk. The *Sag Harbor Corrector* (Sept. 14, 1895, p. 3) reported that Corbin had hired guards to patrol the area. After issuing an edict prohibiting all hunting, fishing, and pasturage on Montauk, he rounded up all of the remaining livestock and returned them to their owners. An era had ended. Montauk was now closed to the citizens of East Hampton, who had been accustomed to having access to the land for two and a half centuries (Seyfried 1974, 6: 11).

On Saturday, October 5, 1895, Wyandank's brother Ebenezer, Charles Fowler, and Ephriam Pharaoh went to Montauk to test Dominy's promise that they could return to Montauk whenever they wanted. They said that they were there to pick wild grapes and cranberries as their ancestors had done (*Brooklyn Daily Eagle,* Oct. 8, 1895). East Hampton constable James Grimshaw confronted the Montauketts and asked them to leave. Charles Fowler told the constable that he had the right to come there any time he wanted and that he would continue to do so. After this exchange Fowler and the others complied with the constable's orders but promised to return.

About a week later Wyandank went to New York to find a lawyer to take their case. The Montauketts had very little money for his expenses, so he found lodging with a friend who served as a coachman for a wealthy family. Wyandank was quoted in the *Brooklyn Daily Eagle* as commenting that he enjoyed being with his friend tending the horses more than he did dealing with white men because you could always trust the horses. He went on to tell the reporter that he was not "the last of the Montauketts. . . . There are from one hundred to one hundred and fifty of our tribe still left, and although they are scattered all over the country from Montauk to California, they are all interested in this suit" (Oct. 20, 1895).

There is no surviving record of his meetings in New York, but Wyandank apparently found some support and counsel, because, according to a *New York Times* report, he went on to Washington and returned to Montauk at the end of October. Wyandank told the reporter for the *Times* that he had found evidence that justified the Montauketts' challenge to Benson. He said that he was going to take a hunting trip to Montauk, and if it was interfered with, "legal proceedings" would follow (Oct. 31, 1895). He held no fault with Corbin and Pratt, he said. Benson was the real culprit because he took the land by deceit.

The attempt to get the case in court on appeal from a trespass charge was abandoned by the Montauketts, who moved instead to bring their own charge of trespass against the Long Island Railroad. When the word of the Montauketts' intentions reached the public in East Hampton, many whites openly ridiculed them. A letter from one of these people, printed in a Brooklyn paper, referred to the Montauketts as "darkies" who were claiming to be Indian to get more money from Benson (W. Tooker 1993, 287).

William Wallace Tooker, a prominent citizen in Sag Harbor and one of New York's pioneer ethnologists, answered the letter. Although the linguists at the Smithsonian criticized Tooker's translations of Algonquian place-names on Long Island, his ethnographic monographs have stood the test of time (Grumet 1991). Tooker said that he was surprised to read that a person who had lived all his life in East Hampton could possibly make such uninformed statements about the Montauketts.

Tooker emphasized three major points in his letter: First, Native American features were still prominent in many Montauketts. Second, Judge Dykeman had confirmed Montaukett tribal status in the Grinnell case. And third, the sale of land by individual tribal members had no standing in law (1993, 287–88). Tooker's third point was the most important because it spoke to a well-established legal precedent, which could not be ignored. Federal and state law required that all sales of Indian lands be negotiated with representatives endorsed by the whole tribe.

The Montauketts began to gather evidence for their case. The Reverend Eugene Johnson wrote to Nathaniel Dominy on February 7, 1896, asking him to come to Washington with him and testify about his role in negotiating the individual deeds. Johnson instructed Dominy to send his reply to "the Montauk Nation," in care of Eugene Johnson at his brother's New York address.

Johnson said that the Montauketts would pay for Dominy's expenses if he would come with all of his papers (EHPLC, Box BA 4, 1-8). Dominy had broken his ties with Benson and had apparently indicated that he was now willing to help the Montaukett cause. Johnson later testified that Dominy and Nathan Cuffee went to Washington with him to speak with the senators who were involved with the bill to establish a duty-free port at Montauk. At the meeting one of the senators told them that Austin Corbin was one of his friends and that he would be talking with Corbin the following week about the Montaukett claim (SCH, 85). Johnson provided no further details of the lobbying effort, but it appears that it was not very successful.

On June 4, 1896, a dramatic event doomed Corbin's ambitious plans. On a trip to his family home in New Hampshire, Corbin suffered a fatal accident. The horses pulling his carriage bolted and ran away, causing the carriage to overturn and throw Corbin against a stone wall. In spite of the problems raised by some critics, the Fort Pond Bay project probably would have been approved by Congress if Corbin had lived. Without his personal prestige and energy behind it, however, the other investors soon abandoned the plan for a port facility (Seyfried 1974, 6: 13, 23). Only the railroad's development plans for a tourist recreation area remained intact as work continued on the docks.

After their return from Washington, Wyandank Pharaoh and Eugene Johnson sought the advice of Francis Morrison, a lawyer from Worcester, Massachusetts, who was experienced in Native American law. Morrison in 1879 had successfully argued for the rights of Indians in Massachusetts to be enfranchised and to be eligible for some monetary compensation from the state (*Sag Harbor Corrector*, Dec. 16, 1899). Since that time he had been involved in cases for many other Native American groups, including the Mohegans, who were close relatives of the Montauketts. Morrison advised Wyandank and Johnson to get permission for the Montauketts to sue in the New York Supreme Court.

Morrison expected that the lawyers for the Long Island Railroad would challenge the Montauketts' right to sue in the state courts. He knew that the New York courts severely restricted the right of a tribe to bring suit. In 1841 the state legislature had passed a law that enabled the leaders of a tribe to sue trespassers on their lands and have them ejected. Four years later, however, the state appellate court ruled, in the case of *Strong v. Waterman*, that a special act of the state legislature was required to bring a suit of ejectment against non-Indians in possession of Indian lands. The United States Supreme Court gave Indian tribes the status of wards or "dependent states," and as such, said the New York Appellate Court, they had no standing in the legal system by right. The tribes, therefore, could not enter the courts without a special invitation from the legislature. Apparently, the East Hampton trustees had not raised this point in

120

*The
Montaukett
Indians of
Eastern
Long Island*

the 1871 case involving access to firewood on Montauk because the Montauketts' right to sue was never questioned by the court.

The tribe held their annual meeting in Sag Harbor in August 1896. More than two hundred Montauketts attended to hear the report of the Committee on Tribal Rights, headed by Nathan J. Cuffee. The committee included Chief Wyandank, the Reverend Eugene Johnson, Aaron Cuffee, Dr. William H. Johnson, Maurice Mitchell, and John Lewis. Aaron Cuffee, the captain of a steamship, and Nathan J. Cuffee, coauthor of *Lords of the Soil,* a novel about Indian life on eastern Long Island, were both from the Eastville band of Montauketts.[3] Mitchell lived in Hartford, and Lewis came from New York City, but little else is known about them. The committee took Morrison's advice and recommended that the tribe sue to reclaim Hither Woods, North Neck, and Indian Fields rather than to limit the case to their residence rights on Indian Fields. The Montauketts voted to approve this strategy and reelected the committee to serve for another year (*Brooklyn Daily Eagle,* Aug. 20, 1896).

The Montauketts filed their suit against the Long Island Railroad on February 5, 1897, charging the company with unlawful possession of all the land from Napeague Beach to Montauk Point. In his response to the suit, William Kelly, the attorney for the railroad, set the strategy that would become the cornerstone of their defense against the Montauketts' claims. Kelly filed a demurrer, objecting to the plaintiff's case on the grounds that a Native American tribe had no standing before the New York Supreme Court and could not, therefore, bring suit. He further charged that there was not sufficient evidence that the Montauketts were a tribal community. Kelly argued that the small group of individuals who brought suit were not members of an existing tribe of Indians (SCH, 125). He stated in his concluding points that the tribe of Montauketts was not a party to the

3. *The Lords of the Soil* is a romantic blend of folklore, myth, and history written by Nathan Cuffee and Lydia Jocelyn, the daughter of a missionary. The plot involves Lion Gardiner and Wyandanch from the end of the Pequot War until Wyandanch's death. In the book Gardiner is a villain who intrigues to obtain Montaukett land by devious means. This theme may come from Montaukett folk history. The accusation of devious plots to get Montaukett land is reminiscent of the eighteenth- and nineteenth-century petitions drawn up by Montaukett leaders.

The authors were an unusual pair, drawn together by an interest in the historical relationship between the Indians and the first English settlers. Jocelyn, nearly seventy years old when they began the project, had lived for many years on a Sioux reservation and was an experienced author. Although the nature of the collaboration is not known, Nathan probably served as the source for the historical setting and descriptions of native customs.

suit because "the names of the members of said tribe being unknown to this defendant." Kelly believed that the Montauketts could not produce such a list with addresses that could be corroborated.

Morrison objected to Kelly's request, arguing that the Montauketts were a tribe of Indians with a long history of relations with the colony and state of New York. If the state legislature recognizes a tribe through its official interaction with them, said Morrison, "the courts must follow the political department" (SCHDR, file 2171). It was not necessary, therefore, to present a list of the names and addresses of all the tribal members.

Judge Samuel T. Maddox listened to both sides, but he sustained the demurrer. He agreed with the defendant that the tribe lacked the standing to bring suit in the New York courts. Maddox ruled that the plaintiff, the Montauk Tribe of Indians, was "not a natural person, nor a corporation, nor an incorporated association permitted by law to maintain an action in the name of any of its officers" (SCH, 125).

At every turn, it seemed, the efforts of the Montauketts to get their day in court were blocked. In spite of these frustrations the small community, with its meager resources, refused to concede defeat. They remained convinced that once they got into court their case would be strong enough to finally win back their land.

These years had been very difficult for the Montauketts. One of the few positive events was Wyandank Pharaoh's marriage to Florence Van Houton, the daughter of jazz musician James Van Houton. The couple established their home in Freetown in 1898, where they lived for several years. Wyandank continued to work as a carpenter and a mason. Although he was reputed to have been an excellent craftsman, his earnings were undoubtedly meager. In spite of the difficulties he faced, Wyandank resolved, with the help and enthusiastic support of his new bride, to carry on the struggle.

SEVEN

THE TRIAL
1900–1910

I N T H E fall of 1901 more than one hundred Indians from the
Montaukett, Shinnecock, and Narragansett Tribes attended a
meeting held in Sag Harbor to discuss their situation. Their
lawyer, Francis Morrison, and tribal committee member Aaron Cuffee had both passed away the previous summer. The Montauketts
decided to hire a new lawyer and to continue lobbying for state permission to bring suit in court (*East Hampton Star*, Sept. 6, 1901).
The following February the Reverend Eugene Johnson wrote an
open letter to all members of the committee, informing them that he
had taken three trips to Albany and had been in Washington twice
lobbying for the Montaukett cause. He reminded his readers that
many of them had not paid their dues and called on them to pay
$1.50 for six months' dues. Those members who did not pay, he
said, would be removed from the list.

The lobbying activities in Washington and Albany drew the
attention of the *Brooklyn Daily Eagle*. On February 16, 1902, the
newspaper published a lead article on the Montauketts, Shinnecocks,
and Poospatucks in a special section with photographs of the three
chiefs, several members of the three communities, and some buildings
on the reservations. With some minor exceptions, the captions under
the photographs expressed the tone of the article. The captions identified photos of the simple wooden buildings with insulting titles
such as "Palace of the Queen Dowager" (Maria Pharaoh-Banks) and
"Palace of Late King of the Poospatucks." One person in a photo is
identified only as "A Pure Type of Shinnecock."

The article reported that W. J. McGee, from the Bureau of American Ethnography, was going to visit the Poospatuck, Shinnecock, and
Montaukett communities to determine whether they were "authentic

124

The
Montaukett
Indians of
Eastern
Long Island

Indians."[1] McGee did visit New York to work with Franz Boas at the American Museum of Natural History in 1902, but there is no record of any such ethnographic research ever being done on eastern Long Island. The *Eagle* sent a correspondent out to interview the chiefs of the three tribes and "to obtain information concerning their tribal customs, organization, future and aspirations." The reporter noted that many of the whites who lived next to the Shinnecocks, Montauketts, and Poospatucks knew very little about them, yet were convinced that they were "lazy, shiftless, drunken and generally useless" and were "Negroes," not "real Indians."

In fairness to the reporter, it should be noted that he did say that "careful investigation failed to bear out the justice of many criticisms." He described the Freetown band of Montauketts, for example, "as decent, intelligent people, willing to work hard when they get a chance, but making a living under decided disadvantages." He added that Maria Pharaoh-Banks was a woman of sobriety and intelligence, who was well spoken of in the East Hampton community. The reporter drew an interesting portrait of Wyandank for his readers:

> He has a long narrow head, with a high, fairly prominent and rounded forehead. The nose is long and straight, with nothing of the African about it; the nostrils are thick, but sensitive. The ears are small, well shaped and set close to the head. He wears a thin, tweedy mustache. . . . His hair is the straight, wiry, coarse, black hair of the Indian or Malay. He wears it trimmed in the American fashion. The eyes are large, brown, and thoughtful, with a tinge of melancholy that saves the face from being ordinary. (Ibid.)

The remainder of the article, however, is quite negative. The reporter asked Wyandank to tell him what traditional Indian customs

---

1. The reporter did not do justice to William John McGee (1853–1912) in this brief reference. McGee was John Wesley Powell's assistant at the Bureau of Ethnography and later became president of the American Anthropological Association. He was a very influential scholar at the turn of the century. Had he come to eastern Long Island, however, he would not have helped the Montaukett cause. McGee was a social evolutionist who firmly believed that the "lower" or more primitive societies represented earlier stages of human development. He was also convinced that the inferior races were developing at a much slower rate and needed help from the more advanced European races (Hoxie 1984, 120–21). McGee most certainly would have applauded Benson's actions for forcing the Montauketts off the reservation and into "civilized" life in East Hampton. Benson was doing exactly what the Dawes Act was designed to do to the Plains Indians.

the Montauketts still followed. Wyandank was not very helpful, perhaps because he had never really thought much about the matter. His answers to questions about marriage, birth, and funeral ceremonies were vague and noncommittal. There is no way to know if Benson's lawyers read this article, but their line of questioning at the trial was very similar to the one the *Eagle* reporter took.

A modern anthropologist would have drawn Wyandank into a discussion about the annual June Meetings, such as the one his father supervised in 1871 (see chapter 5), Stephen Pharaoh's funeral procession to the Montauk burial ground, extended family systems, or the herbal remedies used by his mother (Stone 1993b). Unfortunately, the press, rather than the professional scholars, described and defined the Montauketts for the public.

Wyandank's mother, Maria, who objected to any cooperation with the press, forcefully interrupted his interview. She was justifiably concerned about the negative tone of many articles about the Montauketts. Unfortunately, Maria was not experienced enough to realize that a refusal to cooperate can never correct negative press coverage. The reporter ended his article with a condescending description of the Montaukett tribal meetinghouse in East Hampton as a "crude shack that is hardly good enough for a mule stable," around which were scattered empty whiskey bottles and liquor flasks. He finally concluded that the only aspects of "true Indian culture" that survived among the Montauketts were laziness and alcoholism. These remarks certainly left the reader with a very negative feeling toward the Montauketts. Few of these readers would note the contradiction between the reporter's positive comments about the Montauketts at the beginning of his article and his closing comments.

In spite of the negative images of the Montauketts projected in the press, they continued to lobby for permission to sue. They managed to get another bill introduced in Albany in February 1903. As soon as it was announced, an editorial appeared in the *Brooklyn Daily Eagle* and was reprinted in the *East Norwich Enterprise* (Mar. 21, 1903, p. 5) urging that the bill be defeated. "We sorrow for the sufferings of the Montauk Indians, yet we advise the legislature to examine carefully all measures designed for their relief." The editorial went on to assert that "there aren't any Montauk Indians." The racial strain, continued the editorial, "no longer runs pure. It is blended with that of Negroes and white folks. . . . [T]he reservation of a few house lots for savages in our settled and peaceful land is a farce. . . . [W]e do not believe in supporting a band of pauperized

Negroes on a reservation, and calling them Indians. Throw the reservation open to settlement." The editorial writer's attack on the Montauketts' cultural identity served to justify the dispossession of the Montauketts. The tone and content of the editorial indicate the difficult nature of the challenge faced by the Montauketts.

The editorial expressed the feelings of a majority of whites at the time. Both liberal reformers and conservatives shared these stereotyped attitudes, which were based on flawed perceptions of race and social change (J. Strong 1992). The idealized "true Indian" dressed in buckskin and feathers, and rode on horseback or stood in the woods staring stoically at the horizon. The general public questioned the "Indianness" of Native Americans dressed in contemporary clothes and working as laborers or domestics in a white community. This view, frozen in time, assumes that social change and cultural adaptation discredit "authentic Indianness." The more significant assumption here is that the dominant white group has the right to certify the cultural identity of all nonwhite groups.

The "disappearance" of the Indian "race" is a recurring theme in local history books. Daniel Denton, the son of a minister in Hempstead, Long Island, wrote in 1670 that the Indian population had been "decreast by the hand of God" (1968, 7). A divine hand, wrote Denton, removed the Indians to make way for the whites to settle and prosper. It was the Europeans, however, who introduced the epidemics of smallpox, cholera, and measles, not the divine hand. In spite of these plagues, the Algonquians of Long Island did not dwindle and die out as Denton and others suggested. Other writers, including the author of the *Brooklyn Daily Eagle* editorial, asserted that the Indians disappeared as a result of intermarriage with African Americans. They blended culture and "blood" into one concept in spite of the fact that blood has nothing to do with either physical appearance or culture.

The disappointments and ridicule in the press took their toll on Wyandank's younger sister, Pocahontas Pharaoh. On December 16, 1903, she sold her rights on Montauk to the Benson family for one hundred dollars (CP, 2: 395). This must have infuriated the other Montauketts who were struggling so desperately to regain their rights, but there is no record of any public statement about her action.

The other Montauketts, however, had not lost sight of their cause. The following fall a group of Montauketts, including Wyandank's younger brothers, Ebenezer and Samuel, and their cousins

John J. Butler and his brother George, again tested their right to reside at Montauk. The men built a wigwam and stayed there for a few days, hunting, fishing, and, according to the charges brought against them, "committing various other forms of trespass and roundly cursing out the arresting officer" (*Brooklyn Daily Eagle,* Nov. 18, 1904).

The town entered a charge of malicious trespass against the men, but they refused to answer the charge, remaining silent throughout the proceedings. The judge believed that Ebenezer, the only one of the group who had been involved in the previous "sit-in" nine years before, was the leader and sentenced him to pay a fine of five dollars or spend five days in jail. He gave the others suspended sentences. Ebenezer continued his refusal to cooperate and spent the five days in jail. Wyandank testified later that he had also tested the residence issue in 1906 when he stayed on Montauk long enough to plow a garden and plant a crop. The town, however, never arrested him or ordered him to leave (CP, 2: 188–99).

In March 1906 the lobbying efforts finally came to fruition. The legislature passed an enabling act, but Benson's lobbyists managed to add an amendment that stipulated that "the question as to the existence of the Montauk Tribe of Indians shall be a question of law and fact to be determined by the court" (J. Strong 1993, 141). The clause put a weapon in the hands of the Bensons, which they used to their great advantage.

The *Brooklyn Daily Eagle,* true to form, ran a story announcing the legislative action with a subheadline stating that "A Full Blooded Montauk May Not Exist Today" (Apr. 1, 1906). The paper did acknowledge that the people living in Freetown were at least part Indian, but it played on stereotyped images of the Indians in a strained attempt at humor. "The Indians," it said, were again going to make "heap much trouble for the palefaces."

The Montauketts' new lawyer, Charles O. Maas, an attorney from New York City, had been primarily responsible for getting the enabling bill through. Maas promptly left for Washington where he applied for federal permission to bring suit. The Office of Indian Affairs of the Department of the Interior granted its consent on July 7, 1906 (CP, 2: 362). Later that month Wyandank Pharaoh, as chief and head of the Montauk Tribe of Indians, plaintiff, notified the defendants, who this time included the Benson family, the Montauk Company, the Montauk Dock and Improvement Company, Alfred

Hoyt, the Montauk Extension Company, and the Long Island Railroad Company.

In the notice the Montauketts restated the terms of the 1703 agreement and asked that the Benson deeds be set aside and declared void. They also asked for an accounting of the profits that the defendants had made from the property. The Montauketts wanted Indian Fields, North Neck, and part of Hither Woods returned to them (ibid., 358–62). The notice was met with one more frustrating delay. The defendants asked that the proceedings be postponed for four months because Frank Sherman Benson had died in February, and they claimed that they needed time to get his papers in order.

The New York Supreme Court finally scheduled the case for October 12, 1909, at one P.M. in the Riverhead County Center. The defendants hired the law firm of Daly, Hays, and Mason. The firm appointed George Carpenter and Joseph Belford to argue the case in court. Carpenter, who had served as court referee for the sale of Montauk to Benson, was very familiar with all of the relevant documents. He also knew all of the local people who might be able to help as witnesses or consultants. Belford, a retired judge who had served as chairman of the Republican Party committee for several years, was a fluent and convincing orator (PBR, 588–89). His important position in the dominant political party of the region, his long experience in the courtroom, and his oratorical skills combined to make Belford a most daunting adversary.

The case was tried before Judge Abel Blackmar, without a jury. Blackmar, a political liberal from a distinguished family, graduated from Hamilton College, as had his father and grandfather, and then went on to Columbia Law School. He was an independent-minded jurist who would not be intimidated by the money and power wielded by the defendants in this case. In a case involving the constitutional right of the state of New York to impose limitations on the working hours of women in factories, the mill owners argued that such state intervention violated the sanctity of private property rights. Blackmar responded that the state's obligation to the women carried greater constitutional weight than the property rights of the mill owners. He ruled that the state could intervene on behalf of the women to protect them from exploitation by factory owners (Snyder 1979, 57). Ironically, his belief in the ideals of the reform liberalism of his time proved disastrous to the Montaukett cause.

Charles Maas opened with two primary points. First, he argued that the tribal status of the Montaukett Indians was well established.

Wyandank Pharaoh was their chief, and their legal existence had been affirmed in the findings stated by Judge Dykeman in the case of *Grinnell v. Baker.* Curiously, Maas did not cite the 1871 trespass case where Wyandank's father brought suit in the state court against the East Hampton trustees, charging them with trespass.

Maas's second point focused on the validity of the Benson deeds. They were invalid, he said, for three reasons. First, Benson obtained them under fraudulent circumstances. He led the Montauketts to believe that they would be able to return to Montauk whenever they wished. He encouraged them to view the sale of the rights as no different from the leases of pasturage traditionally sold to whites on a yearly basis (CP, 2: 100–101).

The second reason was that the 1777 state constitution required state approval for all transactions involving Indian land. The state legislature reaffirmed this principle in subsequent actions. John Jay, one of the authors of the *Federalist Papers,* had written the law to protect Indians from "frauds too often practiced towards the said Indians in contracts for their lands" (Lincoln 1906, 4: 153). This provision was a continuation of Gov. Richard Nicolls's policy established in the Duke's Laws. James Kent, the eminent New York jurist, affirmed the role of the state authorities in the protection of Indian property rights a generation after the state constitution was ratified. "The protection of the property of the feeble and dependent remnants . . . within our limits," wrote Kent, "is . . . a fundamental article of government" (ibid., 167).

The third defect in the deeds was that they were negotiated with individuals rather than with the tribe as a whole. This action also violated New York state law and a considerable body of legal precedent that could also be traced back to the colonial period. Maas then narrowed the focus of the suit to the land at Indian Fields, conceding that the Montauketts did not have a strong claim for the land at North Neck and in Hither Woods.

The defense lawyers opened their case with an argument that had been abandoned by the English colonial courts two and a half centuries earlier. They asserted that the Montauketts had lost their claim to all their land when John Cabot landed in Newfoundland in 1497 and proclaimed that all of North America now belonged to England. One wonders whether this was a serious contention or simply a gesture to belittle the Montauketts' case (CP, 2: 104).

Their next point, however, was very serious and became the crucial focus of the final decision. Carpenter and Belford denied that

130

*The
Montaukett
Indians of
Eastern
Long Island*

the Montauketts were a tribe of Indians with legal standing before the New York courts. The plaintiffs, argued the defense, were a diffuse social community of thoroughly assimilated individuals who were seeking a lucrative monetary settlement from the Long Island Railroad Company and the Benson estate (ibid., 105).

The claim to tribal status was open to challenge, and the burden of proof was on the plaintiffs, argued Carpenter and Belford, because Judge Dykeman's ruling in the Grinnell case was not sufficient proof of tribal status. The Montauketts' existence as a tribe was never challenged because they were not primary parties in *Grinnell v. Baker.* The fact that Dykeman acknowledged Chief David Pharaoh's claim to be the leader of a tribe of Indians known as Montauketts did not amount to an official recognition of the tribe that would be binding on the court of New York state, said Carpenter. Nor did the enabling act acknowledge tribal status, pointed out Carpenter, citing the disclaimer in the law that left that issue open (ibid.).

The defense now introduced their own criteria for tribal status that went well beyond the criteria for determining tribal existence established by the United States Supreme Court. In the case of *United States v. Montoya,* the court defined a tribe as "a body of Indians of the same or similar race, united in a community under one leadership or government, and inhabiting a particular though sometimes ill-defined territory" (USR, 261–62). Carpenter and Belford presented a list of characteristics that they asked the judge to apply. In order to be recognized as a tribe, the Montauketts must be in conformity with statutes or a treaty, be governed by a leader whose orders must be obeyed, be able to make war and peace on their own, punish crime, administer civil justice among themselves, be recognized as a tribe by any public agency in the past thirty years, have a continuous history of regularly scheduled meetings for tribal business, and consist of members who have turned their backs on civilized society (CP, 1: 43–44). Such criteria, if universally imposed, would probably deny tribal status to most tribes in North America and Canada.

The Montauketts, continued the defense, had disintegrated and ceased to exist as a corporate entity long before the trial began. The remnants had adopted civilized habits, assumed U.S. citizenship, intermarried with "alien races," and owned property as individuals in fee simple. Mixture with "inferior races" diluted their "Indian blood." Although Blackmar rejected this criteria and paid strict attention to the Montoya ruling, the defense had introduced the emotional race issue, and it dominated most of the trial proceedings.

Even though racial homogeneity had not been a factor in the Montoya case, Belford and Carpenter cleverly played on prevailing racial and class prejudices. The surviving Montauketts were poor and uneducated, and a few had married African Americans. The defense knew that the Montauketts would be easy targets on the witness stands. Throughout the trial references were made to the physiognomies of the Montauketts.

The defense next addressed Maas's assertion that the law required Benson to seek approval from the state of New York for his purchase of Montauk. They referred to the Dongan patent in 1686, which had established the East Hampton trusteeship system and approved the purchase of the rest of the Montauketts' lands. This patent, argued the defense, was similar to a colonial charter granted to Dartmouth College in New Hampshire. In his historic Supreme Court decision, John Marshall ruled that the new state government could not alter the charter. There was no need, therefore, to obtain approval from the state of New York, because Governor Dongan's permission to the proprietors in East Hampton had been passed along to Benson when he purchased Montauk from the proprietors.

There is considerable irony in citing the Dartmouth case against the Montauketts. It was as if the ghost of old Eleazar Wheelock had returned to play one more trick on the Montauketts. He had rejected Samson Occom's plans for a college near Montauk, and now a case involving the charter of that college was being wielded against the Montauketts.

The Dartmouth College case, countered Maas, involved a contract between a government body and a private corporation. John Marshall wanted to guarantee that state governments could not arbitrarily alter private business contracts. Maas pointed out that the Dongan patent was an agreement between a municipality and the colony of New York. There was no private party involved. The East Hampton trustees, not the proprietors, were authorized to purchase Montauk. States have an undisputed right to overrule municipal ordinances and do so regularly. The Dongan patent, therefore, did not absolve the defendants from obeying the state requirement to obtain its permission prior to the purchase of Indian land. In fact, the patent, by its very definition, established the legal precedent of public control over all such purchases. No one could dispute the fact that the

132

The
Montaukett
Indians of
Eastern
Long Island

state of New York assumed all of the sovereign power previously held by the crown.

In answering Maas's last charge that Benson had no right to negotiate individual contracts with tribal members, the defense presented a most novel argument. They contended that "the agreements of 1703 and 1754 did not confer any tribal rights but merely personal privileges granted to individual Indians who should be born on Montauk of Indian blood, to be enjoyed by them as long as they reside on Montauk and no longer" (ibid., 58). Benson, according to this interpretation, had legitimately purchased the land title from individual Montauketts. There was no need to negotiate with the community as a whole. Maas had little difficulty countering this argument. The 1703 deed and lease made clear reference to the Montaukett people "led by a sachem." There is absolutely no precedent in law and no basis in the anthropological record for the defendants' interpretation of these documents. One of the cultural values that has remained unchanged in spite of centuries of assimilation is the Native American concept of collective landownership.

The two sides closed their opening arguments, and the plaintiffs called their witnesses to the stand. Their first witness was Benjamin Barnes, a seventy-year-old white man from one of the oldest families in East Hampton. Barnes had served as an East Hampton trustee for twelve years and had lived for a time on Montauk near Indian Fields. Maas asked him to testify because he was well acquainted with many of the Montauketts, and he could testify about the existence of tribal organization and speak to the issue of race raised by the defense.

Barnes told the court that Sylvester Pharaoh had clearly distinct Indian features and that he was called "king" by the Montauketts. In his capacity as the leader of the Montauketts, Sylvester, according to Barnes, distributed shares of the annual revenues that the tribe received for leasing their land. This action by the Montaukett chief supported Maas's argument that the Montauketts met the Montoya criteria for tribal existence because they were "united in a community under one leadership."

At that point the judge adjourned the trial until 9 A.M. the next day. When the trial resumed on October 13, Belford cross-examined Barnes. He produced the trustees' journals, which listed specific amounts to be given to each Montaukett. Belford then asked Barnes to reconsider his testimony that the Montaukett chief took the money and distributed it. Barnes admitted that he had never seen the chief hand the money to tribal members, but he understood that the chief distributed the money in this fashion. Belford attacked this statement as inadmissible hearsay evidence.

Belford then turned to the question of racial identity. He asked Barnes if Wyandank's maternal grandfather, William Fowler, was an Indian. Barnes said that he was not sure but that everybody at Montauk recognized him as an Indian. Belford asked that the last comment be struck out, and Judge Blackmar then asked Barnes if Fowler was an Indian by blood. Barnes said no. Belford asked Barnes if Fowler had kinky hair and had more of a "mulatto color." Barnes said yes. Maas vigorously objected to this line of questioning, but he was overruled.

The next witness for the plaintiffs was Ephriam Pharaoh. He was asked to testify about the succession of leadership after Sylvester died. Ephriam said that they met at Elisha Pharaoh's house and elected David Pharaoh to replace the deceased chief. There was an election because Sylvester had no children of his own. He was not present, however, when Wyandank took his father's place as chief.

Maas asked Ephriam about the existence of a tribal community. Ephriam said that they did not meet regularly as a group to discuss tribal affairs, but they all visited each other back and forth weekly. When Belford cross-examined him he asked the same questions about Indian culture that the reporter had asked Wyandank in 1902 and got the answer he anticipated. Ephriam said that he knew of no traditional ceremonies associated with marriage, birth, or death. Ephriam, however, had given a good account of leadership succession among the Montauketts.

Maas called Charles Fowler next. He testified that he witnessed the succession of leadership after the deaths of Sylvester Pharaoh and David Pharaoh. Maas then asked him about tribal meetings. He said that the tribe had been meeting fairly regularly since 1895 when they began the court case. Belford then asked Charles to name all of the people who attended the 1895 meeting. Charles, of course, said he could not remember them all. Belford followed with a question about the tribal business discussed at the meetings. He wanted to make the point that the meetings could not be considered evidence of being "united in a community" as stipulated in the Montoya decision. Fowler said he could not remember (ibid., 2: 164–71).

Maas now called Maria Pharaoh-Banks, Wyandank's mother. She also confirmed the existence of a system of tribal leadership with an established procedure for succession. She was not able to confirm

134

The
Montaukett
Indians of
Eastern
Long Island

the chief's role in the division of the tribal shares because she never attended any of the negotiating sessions with the East Hampton trustees. Blackmar and Maas asked questions about the nature of tribal leadership, which clearly indicated their misunderstanding about traditional political systems. They asked Maria if the Montaukett chief "bossed people around." The question puzzled her. "I don't know what you mean by bossing. Yes sir he would tell people, give advice, but I don't know what you mean by bossing" (ibid., 172–79). Although neither Maas nor Blackmar appreciated it, Maria had given a textbook example of leadership in small-scale traditional societies where the sachems or chiefs governed by persuasion rather than by force.

Nathaniel Dominy followed Maria Pharaoh-Banks to the stand. He told the court that he had seen the Montaukett chiefs apportion out the shares of the Montauk revenues to the tribal members. The rest of his testimony centered around the deeds he negotiated for Benson. Dominy said that he had been paid one hundred dollars for each deed. Maas then asked him about the accusation that he had misled the Montauketts about the crucial question of their residence rights on Montauk.

Maria Pharaoh testifying in 1909. Drawing by David Bunn Martine.

Mr. Maas. What I want to know is, did you tell her that after she moved away, and was given this deed, that she could come back?

Mr. Dominy. I told her this.

Mr. Maas. Did you tell Wyandank too?

Mr. Dominy. Yes, sir, every one that called themselves an Indian.

Mr. Maas. Who else did you tell it too? Did you tell it to the Fowlers?

Mr. Dominy. I venture to say, without noting or particularizing any particular minute, I told every one of them.

(Ibid., 186).

This sworn testimony should have been the most important bit of evidence entered into the trial. Here was the smoking gun! Yet, Belford never even cross-examined him in an attempt to shake his account. Dominy was the only witness that Belford did not cross-examine.

After a break for lunch, Maas called Wyandank to the stand. Maas did not ask him about his role as a leader, but Belford hammered away at it in his cross-examination. The trial records have two pages of testimony directed by Maas and nine pages of cross-examination by Belford, who continued his strategy to discredit Wyandank's role as a leader of the Montauketts (ibid., 188–99). Belford asked him who obeyed his orders and when he started calling himself "king." He was successful in leaving the judge and, undoubtedly, many white observers in the courtroom with the impression that Wyandank had assumed an invented title for purposes of the court case.

Wyandank's brother Ebenezer was the last witness for the plaintiffs. He told the court that he had always recognized Wyandank as the Montaukett leader and that he had followed his orders when he staged the two protests on Montauk. He also described the Montaukett community relations as an informal social network of families who made frequent visits to each other's homes (ibid., 201–2).

At this point Maas rested his case, and Belford immediately moved for a dismissal on the grounds that the Montaukett tribe had not presented sufficient proof that they existed as a corporate entity. The plaintiffs, he said, were peoples of mixed blood and had no standing in the court. These "alleged" Indians had voluntarily removed themselves from Montauk and had lost all rights by abandonment. The deeds were all valid, continued Belford, without reference to Dominy's

136

The
Montaukett
Indians of
Eastern
Long Island

testimony. Blackmar refused to grant the request for dismissal, but he did, with Maas's assent, remove the Long Island Railroad from the case because Maas had limited his suit to the land at Indian Fields. The railroad lands were all in Hither Woods and on North Neck.

The defense now called its witnesses. The first was Frank Stratton, who had lived on Montauk when his father was supervisor there for the East Hampton trustees. Belford asked him about Maria's father, William. Stratton said Fowler looked like a "mulatto" but had some features of a white man. Blackmar pressed Stratton about Fowler's skin color, the "formation of his face, the character of his hair." Stratton answered that Fowler had straight hair and a dark complexion (ibid., 208–9).

Then Belford opened another line of inquiry, designed to attack the Montauketts' claim to the status of an Indian tribe from a different perspective. "To all intents and purposes don't they live just as white people live in East Hampton seeking employment as other whites and living the same social life as whites live?" Stratton answered, "Yes," and Maas objected (ibid.). Blackmar acknowledged that it was a very general characterization, but that he had a very good idea about how the Montauketts lived.

The next witness was Joseph Osborn, who had served as town clerk for twenty-seven years. Osborn told the court that the Montauketts were no longer Indians. He said that they lived in town and dressed like everyone else. At this point Maas apparently became angry and frustrated with the direction and tone of the testimony. He objected, saying that he never claimed that the Montauketts wore war paint and shouted war hoops, but that did not mean that they were no longer Indians (ibid., 214–20).

The last witness for the defense was John Mulligan, who had served as justice of the peace for about twenty years. He told the court that the Montauketts were just like any other citizens of the working class in East Hampton. He also introduced hearsay testimony that George Fowler and his brother, Charles, had expressed criticism of Wyandank's leadership. Belford hoped to demonstrate that Wyandank lacked the full support of his people and that there was, therefore, no effective leadership among the Montauketts (ibid., 216–19).

The defense now rested its case, and Blackmar retired to his chambers to examine the testimony and the documents provided by both parties. The case remained with the judge for a year. The following summer Nathaniel Dominy passed away. He never lived to hear the decision rendered. Judge Blackmar finally sent word in the fall that he would announce his findings and conclusions of law on October 10, 1910.

Judge Blackmar acknowledged that the Montauketts had owned Montauk prior to 1660, thereby rejecting the assertion made by the defendants that the English owned Long Island by right of discovery (ibid., 49). The judge also agreed with the plaintiffs that the 1687 and 1703 treaties granted land rights to the Montauk Tribe, not to individual Montauketts.

On the question of the Benson deeds, however, he ruled that they were valid transactions. Blackmar agreed with the defense that the Dongan patent extended to Arthur Benson when he purchased Montauk from the proprietors. It was not necessary, he said, for Benson to seek the approval of the state legislature. The proprietors' purchase rights were private property and were, therefore, protected from any interference by governmental bodies that might replace the colonial government (ibid., 66). Here the judge made a radical departure from the existing interpretations of New York state law cited by Maas in his brief.

Blackmar also ignored the historical context in which Governor Dongan formed his policy. The Dongan patent reasserted the intent of the colonial authorities to monitor all purchases of Indian lands. Under this general policy the colonial authorities granted a license to the East Hampton proprietors. Benson, therefore, bought the land from the proprietors, but he could not buy the license to purchase the Montaukett residence rights because that was a colonial action and the state of New York had now replaced the colonial authority. Blackmar's ruling that this was a private property right is rather strained. Blackmar never addressed the differences between his interpretation and those explanations of such eminent jurists as John Jay and James Kent.

Blackmar did not take the question of Dominy's confessed misrepresentations to the Montauketts seriously. In his decision he stated that "each and all of the releases and instruments of conveyance set forth were voluntarily executed and delivered by the said Indian grantors thereof in good faith and for good and valuable considerations and were not obtained by any fraud, undue influence or duress" (ibid., 65). With those words Blackmar simply passed over what certainly looked like the "smoking gun."

When he came to the crucial question of tribal existence, Blackmar rejected the plaintiffs' arguments that Judge Dykeman's findings in the Grinnell case established the legal status of the Montauk

138

The
Montaukett
Indians of
Eastern
Long Island

Tribe. Blackmar agreed with the defendants that the ruling merely accepted Chief David Pharaoh's unchallenged assertion that he was the leader of a tribe of Indians called Montauketts. The 1871 trespass case might have been more difficult for Blackmar to dismiss because the Montauketts were one of the parties in the suit. Blackmar noted that the New York State Enabling Act and the document from the Bureau of Indian Affairs did not certify the existence of the Montauk Tribe as a corporate entity (ibid., 67–68).

The question of tribal status remained open, and the burden of proof, said Blackmar, was on those claiming to be tribal members. Blackmar did not accept the definition put forward by the defense, but he did apply an artificial standard that reflected the prejudices of the day. He ruled that the plaintiffs had "lost" their Native American traits. Many of these changes had taken place, he argued, since 1885 when the first deed was signed. Now, he said, they "had no internal government and they lived a shiftless life of hunting, fishing, and cultivating the ground, often leaving Montauk for long periods and working in some menial capacity for whites" (ibid., 56). The comments tell us much more about Blackmar and the prevailing prejudices of the times than they do about the Montauketts.[2]

Ironically, this very same description often appears in the colonial records in reference to Native American peoples. Whites frequently commented contemptuously about "lazy" Indians who hunted and fished while their wives tilled the crops in the fields. English observers in the seventeenth and eighteenth centuries commented on the "lack of leadership" and the absence of anything similar to their own governmental institutions among the Indians. The judge took these negative

2. The introduction of expert testimony in the trial might not have had a positive impact on the outcome for the Montaukett case. In the case of *Mashpee v. New Seabury Corporation* (1978), several prominent scholars such as William Sturtevant from the Smithsonian; James Axtell, professor of history from the College of William and Mary; and Jack Campisi, associate professor of anthropology from Wellesley were called by the Mashpees' lawyers to testify as expert witnesses. The crucial issue here was the same one that faced the court in the Montaukett case. The developers who occupied the Mashpees' lands contended that the Mashpees, who, like the Montauketts, had intermarried with African Americans, had ceased to exist as an Indian tribe. Another prominent scholar, James Clifford, listened attentively to the witnesses and said that the testimony convinced him that "organized Indian life had been going on in Mashpee for the past 350 years" (J. Strong 1994a, 23). The jury, however, took twenty-one hours to conclude that the developers were right: the Mashpees were no longer a tribe. The trial record makes it clear that the physiognomies of some of the Mashpees and their modern lifestyle made a bigger impression on the judge and jury than did all the testimony about subtle and complex anthropological concepts.

stereotypes from the colonial period as evidence that the Montauketts were no longer Indians. In both instances the stereotypes were part of a rationalization defending the alienation of Indian lands.

Blackmar's finding on the "loss of Indianness" ignored an earlier judicial decision on the question of Indian identity. In the case of *United States v. Rogers* (1846), the court established two criteria for determining Indian identity (Hagan 1992, 279). An Indian had to have some genealogical connection with a recognized group that existed before the arrival of the whites, and second, the group must accept the individual as a member. The court made no mention of cultural attributes that could be evaluated by a judge.

The "leadership" criteria is particularly ironic because the hierarchical model presented by the defense had never existed among the Long Island Indians before the English arrived. The concept of an absolute leader or "grand sachem," first introduced by Lion Gardiner as a mechanism to facilitate the purchase of land, was now turned upside down and used for the same purpose. The court now denied the Montauketts their right to protect their lands because they did not have a chief whose every order must be obeyed.

Blackmar had actually demonstrated that there were still many aspects of the Montaukett culture that had survived generations of assimilation. Some of the changes cited by Blackmar as evidence of tribal disintegration since 1885 had actually taken place during the early eighteenth century. The integration of the Montauketts into the fringes of the English economy as menial laborers, for example, was not a pattern that developed in the late nineteenth century as Blackmar implied. This accommodation to the English economy began soon after the arrival of whites in the New World and remains a common pattern among Native American groups throughout North America today. These cultural adjustments to the economic realities have seldom been used in a court of law as a criteria for determining "Indianness."

Blackmar ruled that there was no Montaukett "tribe" subject to the protection of the laws of the state of New York or the federal government. The tribe, he said, "has disintegrated and been absorbed into the mass of citizens and...at the time of the commencement of this action there was no tribe of Montaukett Indians" (CP, 2: 66). The tribe had been in decline for decades, said Blackmar; all Benson did was to give it a final "death blow."

Ironically, Blackmar's ruling, with its grim ring of finality, is similar to the wording in the 1637 treaty ending the Pequot War

140

The
Montaukett
Indians of
Eastern
Long Island

wherein the British announced, somewhat prematurely, that the Pequot Nation no longer existed. The Montauketts who, under Wyandanch, had taken the path of peaceful accommodation in order to survive as a people now found themselves pronounced extinct. The Pequots survived the English obituary notice and have emerged as a thriving community today with a flourishing reservation economy. The surviving Montaukett remnant groups may also give the lie to their untimely death notice.

EIGHT

APPEAL AND DEFEAT
1910–1936

THE EARLY decades of the twentieth century were difficult ones for all Native Americans. When the annual Lake Mohonk conference met in 1910, there was general agreement that reservation lands in the West should be leased out or sold to white ranchers and homesteaders whenever possible (Hoxie 1984, 174–87). The government divided the Indians into two categories: competent and incompetent. "Competent Indians," deemed ready and capable of leaving the reservations to live in white communities, were encouraged to divest themselves of their traditional culture. "Incompetent" Indians, whom the government judged incapable of integrating into the American mainstream, remained on the reservation. Many whites came to view the reservation Indians as an annoying burden on the taxpaying public (ibid., 177).

The government now opened up reservation lands to mining companies, which received generous leasing terms. Aggressive entrepreneurs viewed the reservations as a source of valuable raw materials rather than as a sanctuary for Indian peoples. The actions of the Bensons and the Long Island Railroad on Montauk were in harmony with the prevailing climate of opinion in the United States.

In spite of the unsympathetic mood of the times, Wyandank and the other Montauketts decided to continue the struggle. They began the next stage of the court battle by obtaining a new lawyer. On January 28, 1911, Allen Caruthers, a New York lawyer, filed an appeal on behalf of the Montauketts (CP, 2: 1–33). The tribe was hard-pressed to obtain the necessary funds to finance the expensive legal process. The appeal procedures required the appellant to pay the court costs of printing all of the records of the original trial that were then submitted to the appeals court and the respondents.

Caruthers sent the papers to the printer, but he was unable to raise the funds to pay the printing costs. The printer refused to release them until he was paid, causing yet another frustrating delay for the Montauketts. Benson's lawyers tried to take advantage of their predicament by asking the judge to dismiss the case on the grounds that the papers had not been presented in a timely fashion (SCCCR, file 3567). In desperation, the Montauketts sent out an appeal for financial support to the Brotherton community in Wisconsin; to the enclaves in Freetown, Eastville, and Little Neck; and to the scattered households in southern New England and on Long Island. Curiously, the list of contributors has few names from the North Amityville area (Miller and Cuffee 1993). The funds arrived just in time to get the records delivered to the appellate court and avoid the dismissal of their case.

The court did not hear the Montaukett appeal until two years later. The long delay must have placed quite a strain on the Montaukett patience and resources. In February 1912 Nathan J. Cuffee, who had been one of the leaders in the court struggle, died of Bright's disease. His brothers, Lewis, Melanchton, and Christopher, and his

Wyandank Pharaoh presiding at a Montaukett meeting.
Drawing by David Bunn Martine.

married sisters, Amelia Halsey and Nellie Brown, survived him. Nathan, whose book *Lords of the Soil* had given him widespread recognition, was a great loss to the Montaukett community.

In the fall of 1914 Wyandank called the Montauketts together in Sag Harbor for their annual meeting. He urged them not to give up hope and to keep up their financial support for the court case by paying their annual dues of three dollars. They had spent nearly seven hundred dollars over the past two years, he reported. He acknowledged that there had been "much to discourage and little to encourage," but reminded them that justice was on their side.

The Montaukett tribal council now included James E. Waters (Wild Pigeon), who claimed Montaukett and Matinecock ancestry, Walter Halsey, Mrs. Melanchton L. Cuffee, Israel Quaw, and Nathan's brother Christopher. Some of the Freetown and Eastville Montauketts viewed Waters, who lived in Little Neck, with some suspicion. He was intelligent, forceful, and experienced in Indian affairs, but he may have been a bit too aggressive for some of the people in the Pharaoh family.[1] They realized, however, that they needed the support and enthusiasm that Waters brought to them.

Although some of the Pharaoh and Fowler people were cool toward Waters, many of the Algonquian families on Long Island knew and respected him. His connections with the scattered households in Suffolk and Nassau Counties were very important because the core Montauketts in Eastville and Freetown had become somewhat isolated over the years. Waters developed a membership roll of 506 contributors to trial costs (ibid.).

Many of the people on the list were from southern New England and the Brotherton community in Wisconsin, but there were more than 170 with Long Island addresses.[2] These residences were widely dispersed from Brooklyn to East Hampton. The list reveals two characteristics of the Montaukett diaspora. They did not live in cohesive, community-based enclaves, and most had family connections

1. Waters traced his lineage back to his grandmother Sylvia Hicks, who was said to be part Montaukett, and to his great-grandmother Jerusha Larkin, who was also said to have been part Montaukett. This genealogy was worked out by the Waters family. A copy was given to the author by James Edward Waters (Wati Wampatoques), the great-grandnephew of James Waters.

2. The list has not been located, but three membership lists based on dues payments have been published (Miller and Cuffee 1993, 489–500). The lists come from the papers of Eugene Cuffee, a Shinnecock Indian. A fourth list from the papers of Karla Miller, an Unkechaug woman from the Poospatuck Reservation, is a tribal roll arranged in alphabetical order. This list includes 505 adults and 176 children.

with two or more of the surviving Algonquian communities on Long Island. Forty-four of the people on the list, for example, lived on the Shinnecock Reservation, and one was from Poospatuck.

Most of the Algonquian families on Long Island are in this kinship network. They have tended to intermarry with each other, as well as with African Americans. Many of the families, therefore, believe that they have a legitimate choice of tribal identities (Ralph Bunn, letter to author, January 1998). This is also true in many Indian communities in the United States. The federal government, for example, has had to rule that an Indian can claim membership in only one tribal community because so many were eligible for government benefits from more than one tribe.

The two-year wait for a decision on their appeal ended in one more frustration for the Montauketts. Appeals Court justice Joseph Burr affirmed Blackmar's decision. The burden, said Burr, was on the Montauketts to prove that there was sufficient tribal structure to satisfy the criteria in the Montoya definition. Burr revealed his own prejudices when he stated that the Montauketts were "impaired by racial miscegenation, with the Negro race," and were not living together as a tribe (CP, 2: 507). Burr's affirmation reflected the same racial bigotry and anthropological inaccuracies that distorted the arguments in the original case.

The Montauketts responded with another appeal in 1915. This time Caruthers attacked the arbitrary and highly subjective denials of Montaukett Indian identity and tribal existence. They were not valid, said Caruthers, because the court had ruled in *Buttz v. Northern Pacific Railroad* (1911) that "neither the lapse of time, allotment of a portion of the tribal lands in severalty, immigration of a majority of the tribe, nor the fact that the habits and customs of the tribe have changed by intercourse with whites will authorize the courts to disregard tribal status" (CP, 3A: 26). Caruthers could have cited two more relevant cases here. In *Tiger v. the Western Investment Company* (1911) and *United States v. Rickert* (1903), the courts held that only Congress can determine when changes in custom are sufficient to invalidate tribal status (Weatherhead 1980, 9). The historical fact, continued Caruthers, is "that the tribe at the present time consists of over 377 beings, 237 adults, 48 minors, all of whom are accounted for and 92 whose place of residence is unknown, this appears in the files in Washington" (CP, 3A: 28). Caruthers's list has been lost, but he probably used Waters's roll and may have included only the names that he believed could be verified. Blackmar, therefore, had overstepped his authority when he declared the Montauketts extinct.

Caruthers again reminded the court that Nathaniel Dominy had testified that he had misled the Montauketts during the negotiation over the deed in 1885. The Benson lawyers dismissed this charge with a patronizing reference to Dominy. He was, they said, a nice "old man of 83 years whose testimony and memory were of questionable reliability" (CP, 3B:55). They knew, of course, that Dominy could not be recalled for further investigation of the matter.

While awaiting the decision the Montauketts continued to meet and discuss tribal business. On August 31, 1916, they held the annual meeting in Sag Harbor. James Waters, who was now identified as chief of the tribal council, was becoming more directly involved in Montaukett affairs. He and Chief Wyandank, however, never established a good personal relationship. The tribal council membership remained the same as it had been in 1914, but it appears that many of the Montauketts were giving their support to Waters. The report of the meeting stated that about one hundred tribal members attended.

The agenda for the 1916 meeting included a brief presentation by Allen Caruthers, who explained the current status of the trial. He stressed the need for keeping extensive written records of all their tribal affairs (Stone 1993a, 469–72). In the evening session Waters appealed to the members to pay their dues as promptly as possible. He also encouraged them to teach their children about the tribal history and customs.

The development of a more formal tribal structure was an important step forward, but the press was still giving them problems. When an article about the Montauketts in the *East Hampton Star* mentioned, in passing, that the Montauketts had lost their land and their status as a tribe many years earlier, Wyandank wrote an angry response telling the public that the case was still in court and reviewing the arguments presented by the lawyers (EHPLC, file JJ275). In 1917 the court, however, denied the Montauketts' appeal without an opinion. Caruthers appealed again, but the long legal battle finally ended when Judge James Van Sicey dismissed that last appeal at a special term of the court in Brooklyn on March 8, 1918. The loss was a severe blow to the small Montaukett community. The long years of struggle had drained their meager finances. Most families were not even able to provide for the elderly when they required professional

146

The
Montaukett
Indians of
Eastern
Long Island

care. Both Ebenezer and Ephriam Pharaoh, for example, died in the county almshouse in Yaphank.

Mary Benson, the last of the Benson family involved in the claims case, died that same year. She left ten thousand dollars to the American Church Institute for Negroes, twenty-five thousand dollars to Sean's Church Institute, two thousand dollars to the Grace Church of Brooklyn Heights, five thousand dollars to the Society for the Prevention of Cruelty to Children, and, along with most of the papers relating to the trial, five thousand dollars to the Brooklyn Historical Society (BHSL, Benson Papers). The Montauketts, denied their inheritance by the Benson family, were ignored.

The Montauketts did not give up. At a tribal meeting in April 1919, they elected James Waters to serve as chief of the Montauketts and gave Wyandank the office of assistant chief. The tribe reelected Israel Quaw, Walter Halsey, Christopher Cuffee, and Mrs. Melanchton L. Cuffee to the Montaukett Council. Wyandank, who apparently lost the support of the council members, protested the election, creating a split in the small group. He wrote a letter to the *Brooklyn Daily Eagle* (June 1, 1919), stating that he knew nothing of the meeting and that he was still the chief of the Montauketts.

Letters of May 15 and 16, 1919, from James Waters to the council indicate that he went on with his plans to give the Montauketts a modern political structure in spite of Wyandank's opposition (EHPLC, file BA-9-3064). "One hundred Montauk have voted for me to be sachem and Dank to be assistant chief," he said, and urged them not to fight among themselves. Waters included a draft of a constitution and asked the group to consider it for adoption at the annual meeting in August. The new government was to be a union of small bands, which would incorporate several scattered Montaukett enclaves primarily on Long Island. The tribe established a membership roll and charged dues of one dollar per year. Much of the new structure simply put into writing practices that had been followed for many years. The executive council under the new constitution, for example, continued to consist of a sachem, an assistant chief, who served as chief of the Tribal Council, and four tribal councilpersons (ibid.).

Waters called a tribal meeting on August 29, 1919, and opened the gathering with an enthusiastic rallying call to rekindle their spirits and not to despair over the defeat in the courts. The ancestors, he said, held ceremonies at this time of the year to thank the great spirit for the coming harvest. He urged his listeners to study their tribal history and customs and to rebuild their unity. He then called for the new constitution to be read and discussed. After a lengthy debate over each clause, the Montauketts adopted the document (Stone 1993a, 473–86).

Waters continued stressing his view that the Montaukett community included more than the small number of people who lived on Montauk in 1885. This emphasis may have been a factor that caused the split with the Pharaohs and the Fowlers, who viewed some of the Montaukett diaspora with suspicion. Articles four and five in the constitution provided for the recognition of the enclaves as bands with leaders appointed by the tribal chief. These leaders were to serve on an advisory board to the tribal council. Waters announced the appointment of leaders for bands in New Bedford, Massachusetts; Providence and Westerly, Rhode Island; Hartford, Connecticut; Brooklyn and New York City; and the Long Island bands in Little Neck, Sag Harbor, East Hampton, the Shinnecock Reservation, and Brothertown, Wisconsin. The Pharaoh and Butler families had no representation among these appointees (ibid., 486).

Waters urged the Montauketts to take their struggle into a new arena. He urged them to take their case to Washington and lobby Congress to redress their grievances. Waters recommended that they get help in Washington from Dr. Charles Eastman, a Sioux Indian who had earned a national reputation as a writer and as a lobbyist for Indian causes. Eastman was also one of the founders of the Society for American Indians.

Wyandank remained alienated from Waters and withdrew from tribal affairs. His failing health was undoubtedly a factor as well. The announcement of the annual meeting in 1920 did not list his name among the tribal officers. The Pharaoh and Fowler families, however, continued their efforts to regain their land. Maria; her two children Samuel and Pocahontas; her brothers, Charles and George; and George's two children, John and Marguerite, went to Washington on their own. Unfortunately, the only surviving record of their trip is a photograph of the delegation and a brief reference in a letter from Wyandank's wife, Florence, to the commissioner of Indian affairs dated April 4, 1921 (MIW, item 8). There is no mention of their visit in the commissioner's files for that period. It is quite possible that they were given a polite audience and then ignored.

In January 1921 Waters and Eastman met with several senators and representatives in Washington and finally convinced New York's

Montaukett delegation to Washington, 1921. Courtesy of Pharaoh family.

Republican senator, James Wadsworth, and New York Congressman Homer Snyder to introduce resolutions calling for the secretary of the interior to provide Congress with a report on the tribal status of the Montauketts and the legitimacy of their land claims (ibid., item 2).

When Waters met with John Reeves, the commissioner of Indian affairs, he gave him a list of tribal officers, which included Wyandank as "assistant chief." Even though Wyandank was no longer directly involved with tribal business, the Pharaoh name still carried weight. The Pharaoh family, however, resented Waters's actions, and the split in the Montaukett community widened. Waters asked the commissioners for a full review of the Montaukett case and presented all of the arguments that their lawyers had prepared during the long legal battle (ibid., items 3, 5).

Wyandank's health continued to deteriorate as he struggled with Bright's disease, the same affliction that had taken the life of Nathan J. Cuffee. On Wednesday, March 9, 1921, Wyandank had visited his sister-in-law and then returned to his house. His wife, Florence, who worked as a live-in domestic in a nearby community, was not at home during the week. When she came back on Saturday, she found her husband had died, alone, sometime between Wednesday and Saturday (*Brooklyn Daily Eagle,* Mar. 14, 1921).

The community mourned his passing, and it may have encouraged the Montauketts to press on with the campaign in Washington. The assistant commissioner of Indian affairs, E. B. Meritt, sent a letter to several Montauketts, asking them to send him tribal papers, records, membership lists, and photographs of leading Montauketts. James Waters and Florence Pharaoh both responded to the request. Florence replied in a handwritten letter, which included some photographs and a list of twenty-five Montauk descendants of families who had lived on Montauk in the late nineteenth century. In her letter of April 4, 1921, Florence Pharaoh attacked Waters as a "bogus Indian," and defended her identity as a Montaukett (MIW, item 8). Wyandank's obituary described her as "a negress from Sag Harbor," and never even mentioned her by name.

Waters was furious when he learned of Florence's comments to the commissioner. He wrote to the commissioner asking for a copy of the letter and asserted that Florence Pharaoh, herself, was not a tribal member and had no business intruding into their affairs (ibid., item 11).

Meritt, who, understandably, did not want to get involved in the dispute between the Montaukett factions, ignored the charges and countercharges. He assigned the investigation to his staff, who reviewed the records of the tribe and the relevant deeds and papers used in the 1909 case. They also studied Blackmar's verdict and the appeals. They did not complete the process until the following April.

Word apparently reached Waters in January that Meritt's office had nearly completed the report. He sent out an urgent appeal for donations to all of the tribal members and urged them to write to Senator Wadsworth and to Representative Snyder asking them to support Senate Resolution 62 and the House Joint Resolution 55 calling for a full review of the forthcoming report on the Montaukett grievances (ibid., items 1, 2).

The Montaukett families who were listed in Florence's letter— the Pharaohs, the Fowlers, and the Butlers—apparently decided to go back to the New York state legislature and ask for some measure of compensation for themselves. Unfortunately, there is no record of their lobbying efforts, but they were successful in getting John J. O'Connor, the state assemblyman from the twelfth congressional district in New York City, to introduce a bill on February 14, 1922, titled "An

150

The
Montaukett
Indians of
Eastern
Long Island

act making an appropriation for the benefit of the members of the Montauk tribe of Indians living at Montauk in 1876, and the heirs of such members" (JASNY 1922, 149th session, 2: 1150). The fact that the bill specifically excluded Waters and all the Montauketts in the diaspora suggests that the Pharaohs, the Fowlers, and the Butlers from Sag Harbor and East Hampton were behind the lobbying effort.

The bill authorized funds for reimbursements and called for a commission of two members of the assembly and one senator to investigate and "to determine members of such tribe who in the year 1878 were legally entitled to the real property known as Indian Field aforesaid and the members of such tribe who are now legally entitled to the same" (ibid., 1151). There was not enough support for the bill, however, and it never reached the floor for a vote.

Back in Washington the commissioner of Indian affairs gave Charles Eastman a preliminary copy of the report they were going to submit to Congress. Relying heavily on the file of the 1909 case, the thirty-nine-page paper included a history and chronology of the deeds and agreements between the Montauketts and East Hampton from 1648 to 1909 (MIW, item 16). The report agreed with every point made by Judge Blackmar and the appellate court judges and endorsed Blackmar's finding that the tribe had become extinct. The report ignored the existence of Montauketts in the neighboring Long Island communities and stated that the eight Montauketts living in Sag Harbor were the only ones left.

The report then went on to defend its conclusion by citing three local historians, Gabriel Furman (1874), Henry Hedges (1897), and Peter Ross (1902). These men all agreed that the tribe had, in Furman's words, been "reduced to a beggarly number of ten or fifteen drunken and degraded beings" (MIW, item 16, 33–34). The interpretations of these and many other local historians, however, were distorted by ignorance about anthropological concepts, racial prejudice, and, in some cases, a desire to preserve a sanitized account of the local "founding fathers" (J. Strong 1992, 63–69). Gabriel Furman, for example, told his readers that miscegenation between Indians and whites created a generation that would gradually "waste away" (1874, 52). Furman apparently believed that the mixing of the two races was similar to the union of a horse and a donkey and would produce an impotent offspring.

The fact that the Commission of Indian Affairs chose to include these quotes indicates the prevailing climate of racist attitudes that permeated all levels of American society in the 1920s. In Suffolk County, Long Island, during this period, the Ku Klux Klan was drawing thousands of people to their outdoor meetings. In 1923 the Klan claimed to have twenty thousand members in Suffolk County (Gombieski 1993, 42–43; SCHSL, KKK Collection). Both racist perceptions and a naïve nostalgic view that the Indians were the "vanishing Americans" worked to influence the whites who were involved with making crucial decisions about the status of the Montauketts during this period. The media as well as the local history books continually reinforced the "vanishing American" theme.[3]

Eastman was furious when he read the commissioner's report. He called for James Waters to come to Washington as soon as possible and bring all the tribal papers relating to tribal membership, organizational structure, and meetings for the commissioner's staff. Waters came with the information, and Eastman wrote immediately to the commissioner asking him to meet with the Montaukett delegation (MIW, item 14). Eastman and Waters wanted to respond to the assertion that the tribe was extinct.

The commissioner agreed to insert this material into the report. Eastman and Waters submitted a list of names and addresses of 649 members, most of whom lived on Long Island and southern New England. Along with the list they gave the commissioner a description of the tribal organization that included the location of Montaukett enclaves and the names of the leaders. They also wanted the commissioner to reconsider Judge Blackmar's finding that the Dongan patent had exempted the Benson purchases from a government review (ibid.).

The commissioner accepted the information and inserted it into the report, but summarily dismissed it without comment. Following the insertion the report simply stated, "At this juncture we again refer to the conclusion of the New York Supreme Court in the case of Pharaoh v. Benson, that there is now no tribe of Montauk Indians"

3. Local newspapers usually announced the death of an elderly Indian with a "boilerplate" caption reading "the last of the full-blooded Indians." Although the wording might change slightly, the message conveyed is always designed to evoke a sense of nostalgia and draw reader interest. Winslow Homer, for example, titled his drawing of David Pharaoh *The Last of the Montauks*. When Mary Walkus died at the age of 100 in 1867, she was solemnly identified as "the last full-blooded squaw and oldest of the Shinnecocks." She was actually a Montaukett who married a Shinnecock and lived on the Shinnecock Reservation (J. Strong 1992, 64; RTSH, 8: 356). When Wickham Cuffee died in 1915 he was anointed as the "last of the Shinnecocks." In 1936, when Mary Rebecca Kellis died at the age of 102, she was heralded as "the last full-blooded Indian living on Long Island." More recently, a fourth-grade text on Long Island history, published in 1991, includes a photograph of Stephen Pharaoh, who is identified as "the last full-blooded Montauk" at the time of his death in 1879 (J. Strong 1992, 64, 65).

152

The
Montaukett
Indians of
Eastern
Long Island

(MIW, item 16, 35–36). The Senate Committee on Indian Affairs accepted the report on April 22, 1922, and introduced Wadsworth's bill in June. The committee, however, showed little interest in pursuing the matter.

At the annual meeting of the Montauketts on August 31, 1922, Waters called for renewed efforts in Washington. As long as the committee took no action on the report, Waters clung to the very slim hope that there might be a favorable outcome. The defeats and long delays, however, cost Waters the support from the tribal council. A year later, in 1923, the council rejected Waters and elected Allen J. Cuffee as chief of the Montauketts.

Early in 1923 Florence Pharaoh and her sister-in-law Pocahontas sent letters to E. B. Meritt, asking about the progress of the bill. Both of the letters are in Florence's handwriting (ibid., items 20, 21). He replied only that the bill was still before the Senate Committee on Indian Affairs. Florence wrote again in November, and this time the new Indian commissioner, Charles Burke, answered her, saying that the bill was still before the committee and "what further action, if any, Congress may take in the matter we are of course unable to say." The message was clear, but the Montauketts refused to acknowledge that Congress had turned a deaf ear to them. Florence wrote again on June 27, 1924, pleading for a settlement that would give her something to live on now that she had lost her husband. The reply was much more curt than before. The commissioner told Florence that any alleged rights or Indian benefits due to her from her husband were not "descendable" to her.

In the summer of 1924 James Waters, who had not taken his removal from office gracefully, sued Allen Cuffee, who had resigned as sachem in 1924, demanding that he turn over the tribal records to him. The judge agreed with Waters and ordered Cuffee to comply (QPL, clipping file). It seems clear that by this time Waters had alienated most of the Montauketts in the eastern enclaves. Unfortunately, there are no surviving records that might explain the context for the suit. According to Waters's grandnephew, his house burned down several years after his death, and all of his papers were lost (James Waters, letter, Dec. 30, 1996).

Waters suffered from heart disease and died in 1927 at the age of fifty-one. The last three years of his life were devoted to a struggle to save an Indian cemetery near his home in Little Neck. The burial ground, located on the edge of what is now Northern Boulevard, was scheduled to be moved to accommodate the widening of the street. Waters said he wanted to be buried there with his ancestors. He again went to the courts, and again he suffered a defeat. James Waters was buried in the AME Zion church cemetery in Douglaston. Ironically, Waters's wish to be buried with his ancestors was finally realized two years after his death when the remains of the Indians in the burial ground were relocated alongside Waters in the Douglaston cemetery (J. Strong 1997, 30).

The long struggle to reclaim their lands took a heavy toll on the Montauketts. Tribal affairs were neglected as the people turned to deal with the many other problems that faced the poor during the depression years. A number of significant changes took place on Montauk during this period. In 1926 Carl Fisher, the real estate developer who had created Miami Beach, purchased ten thousand acres of land on Montauk from the Benson estate for $3 million. This purchase must certainly have embittered the Montauketts, who barely survived on the margins of an economic system that so richly rewarded the Bensons. The Benson family had reaped great wealth from their initial purchase, yet they had invested very little of their time or resources in improving the Montauk lands.

Fisher launched a development scheme that rivaled the visions of Austin Corbin. He began to promote Montauk as the "Miami Beach of the North." Fisher also shared Corbin's aristocratic arrogance and his admiration for the English upper class. Montauk, said Fisher, was to be "as warm and gentle as the downs of England, where the real aristocrats of modern America may find new health, new relaxation, and new ways to play amid luxurious surroundings" (CPMCP, 18–19). Fisher built miles of roads, established a small resort community of Montauk, and constructed hotels, an elaborate equestrian complex with bridle trails, and other resort facilities. Fisher also constructed a polo field near Third House.

There were some things, however, that even the Corbins, the Bensons, and the Fishers could not control. The reckless extravagance and abuse of power by their own class brought down the economic system that had so generously rewarded them. Fisher, who had borrowed heavily to finance his playground for the rich, went bankrupt in 1929.

The small resort community of Montauk survived, but some of the other facilities were left to deteriorate. Ten years later developers turned the area around Third House into a dude ranch and renovated the building to give it a "Wild West" decor. They added several small "western-style" guest cabins to the Third House complex.

154

*The
Montaukett
Indians of
Eastern
Long Island*

In 1936 Maria Pharaoh-Banks died at the age of eighty-eight, leaving behind her third husband, Edward Banks; their son, Junius; and a daughter by her first marriage, Pocahontas Pharaoh. She had outlived two husbands and five of her ten children.

Maria's death marked the end of an important chapter in Montaukett history. It had been a frustrating time but one filled with high points of hope and excitement about their prospects. When their hopes were dashed once again, this time by the federal government, the Montaukett enclaves turned inward and focused on their families and their kinship obligations.

NINE

NADIR AND RESURGENCE
1940–1999

A LTHOUGH THE Montauketts withdrew from the public eye after they lost the struggle in the courts, they did not abandon their Indian cultural heritage. The Montaukett families continued to meet together for seasonal celebrations that were rooted in traditional Indian culture. Montauketts continued to attend the "June Meetings" and fall powwows that were held at Shinnecock and Poospatuck Reservations.

On occasion the Montaukett families in Freetown and Eastville met by the water at a place called "Springy Banks" on Three Mile Harbor in East Hampton, near Stephen Pharaoh's birthplace. The Montauketts did not dress in Indian regalia on these occasions, but the meetings themselves were expressions of an existing extended-family kinship system. These small gatherings are not well documented, but Olive Pharaoh said that she remembered going there for many family reunions (personal communication, May 1996). A photograph showing members of the Butler and Pharaoh families at a picnic at Springy Banks documents one such gathering in 1935 (Stone 1993a, 397).

Some of the meetings at Springy Banks were larger and included guests from other tribes. On these occasions most of the people who dressed in Indian regalia performed dances as a part of the program. In 1940 the Montauketts hosted two powwows that were attended by representatives of the Narragansett, Shinnecock, Matinecock, and several other southern New England tribes (Westez 1993, 291–94).

In August 1944 the Montauketts hosted a powwow organized by Red Thunder Cloud (Carlos Westez), who lived on eastern Long Island for many years. Although many have questioned his Indian

156

The
Montaukett
Indians of
Eastern
Long Island

ancestry, most agree that he was a tireless advocate for Indian causes. Even his critics among the Montauketts and the Shinnecocks acknowledge that he made a significant contribution to the survival of Indian culture of eastern Long Island. Red Thunder Cloud worked as a research assistant for Frank Speck, the pioneer ethnologist from the University of Pennsylvania, gathering ethnographic data on the Montauketts and Shinnecocks (ibid.; Carr and Westez 1980).

"Tez," as he was known to his friends, served as an important catalyst for the revival of interest in traditional culture on Long Island. At the 1944 powwow he invited a delegation of twelve Narragansetts to come to Springy Banks and sign a symbolic treaty of peace with their ancient Montaukett enemies in an effort to draw public attention to the continuing existence of Montauketts, and to encourage the Montauketts themselves to become more active in tribal affairs. East Hampton mayor Judson Bannister attended to witness the ceremony as a guest of honor (Stone 1993a, 396). Charles Butler, Olive Pharaoh, and Eliza Beaman represented the Montauketts.

Some traditional craft skills such as beadwork, basket making, and wood carving survived among the Montauketts (ibid., 577–82). Marguerite Fowler-LaPorte, Pocahontas Pharaoh, and Robert Butler were all accomplished beadworkers (Westez 1993, 293). Several baskets made in the early twentieth century by unidentified Montaukett artisans are now located in the East Hampton Historical Society collections (Stone 1993a, 570).

The Montauketts and Shinnecocks were skilled at carving "scrub brushes," a simple but very effective tool for scrubbing large pots. Samuel and Pocahontas Pharaoh, George and Charles Butler, George Fowler, and Walter Halsey were skilled wood carvers (Rabito-Wyppensenwah and Bacha 1993, 575). They made the scrub brushes out of oak staves by splitting one end of the stave into small splints and carving the other end to form a handle. The brushes, of course, are not aboriginal in origin, but they were part of a craft tradition that emerged soon after contact with the Europeans (Conkey, Boissevain, and Goddard 1978, 184). The scrub brushes were widely used on eastern Long Island until the middle of the twentieth century. Olive Pharaoh, Maria's great-granddaughter, said that her father, Samuel, had learned how to carve brushes from his father, Ebenezer, who was Wyandank's brother. She remembered helping her Aunt Pocahontas, who died in 1963, gather oak branches, and she watched her carve the brushes. Olive provided the following description of the process:

Pocahontas Pharaoh with scrub brush.
Courtesy of East Hampton Library.

158

The
Montaukett
Indians of
Eastern
Long Island

It was one of the only times I had to keep quiet. After the bark had been stripped off a piece of wood, she would take a small knife in one hand and begin to make small cuts, very thin cuts down the piece of wood for about three or four inches. The brush part took a very long time. If you were not careful, that knife could cut you, or if you made the wrong cut you would have to start over again. My aunt would not allow me to use the knife until I was eleven years old. It was slow going. A good scrub brush took three to four hours to make. After she smoothed the handle down, Pocahontas put two strings around the brush end, and she connected the two. The top string went around the brush, while the other string would go in and around the different brush sticks. (Rabito-Wyppensenwah and Bacha 1993, 575)

The Montauketts and Shinnecocks developed a small cottage industry of craft items, which they peddled in the villages on eastern Long Island. Olive Pharoah remembered going with her Aunt Pocahontas to sell her scrub brushes. "My aunt would take me along with her when she went to her friends' houses, where she would drop off scrubs that were requested. Other times she would go to the grocery store and leave some for sale. She always kept herself occupied by making scrubs, sewing, making quilts and cooking for the family" (ibid.). In addition to the scrub brushes, they sold baskets, wooden duck decoys, quilts, eel traps, table linens, beadwork, corn and herb mortars, and wooden ladles (Stone and Smith 1983, 291–93; Stone and Cuffee 1983, 303).

Pocahontas Pharoah also kept alive the Montaukett herbal traditions.[1] Her niece Olive recalled helping her collect the herbs near their home in Sag Harbor. "She used to tell the names of each one," said Olive. Pocahontas kept such herbs as bonset (*Eupatorium perfoliatum*), sassafras (*Sassafras albidium*), sweet fern (*Comptonia peregina*), white oak bark (*Quercus alba*), white pine bark (*Pinus strobus*), wild cherry bark (*Prubus serotina*), and plantain (*Plantago major*) in a walk-in pantry (Rabito-Wyppensenwah and Abiuso 1993, 586). Olive Pharoah remembered that Pocahontas would visit sick people who asked for her. Most of them were the older members

---

1. Eliza Beaman, who represented the Montauketts at the 1944 powwow, was also a highly respected herbalist during this period. Her father, George Fowler, was a Montaukett and her mother was a Shinnecock. Many of her herbal remedies were published in an article by ethnographers J. D. Carr and Carlos Westez (1980).

of the Montaukett community. After her death in 1963 the use of herbal medicines among the Montauketts gradually declined.

One of the most ironic developments during this period in Montaukett history was Suffolk County's purchase of a 1,157-acre parcel of land at Montauk that included most of Indian Fields and the Third House complex. The county made the purchase in a series of transactions beginning in 1971 and then established a county park on the parcel. The developers who successfully prevented the return of the Montauketts to Montauk never used the site.

In the years following World War II, the Bunns, Greens, Fowlers, Brewsters, and many of the other nonreservation Algonquian families in Suffolk County began meeting on the second Sunday in August at the picnic grounds in Sunken Meadow State Park on the north shore of Long Island (Leftenant, Bunn, and Pharaoh, personal communication, April 1997). These reunions, which sometimes drew as many as three or four hundred people, were primarily social gatherings, but the common bond that drew them together was a shared folk tradition asserting their Algonquian ancestry.

In the 1960s many of these people began to research their family genealogies to document their connection to historically known Algonquian communities. Some hoped to claim residence rights on the Poospatuck or Shinnecock Reservations or to qualify for state benefits. In response to this interest in validating their Indian ancestry, Ralph Bunn established the Native American Validation Alliance. Working with a small number of volunteers, Bunn has traveled all over Long Island gathering public records of births, deaths, weddings, military service, and Indian deeds. He has also examined family Bibles and photograph albums, and collected oral testimony. This task was not easy. The Montaukett families moved frequently, and documents were lost. Prior to World War I many children were born at home, and some had no birth certificates. There were also many common-law marriages where the children kept the mother's last name. Often people were reluctant to make their family histories public because they were embarrassed about these unions.

Sandi Brewster-Walker, whose family had lived in North Amityville for several generations, also began working on the genealogies of the Algonquian families in North Amityville and the nearby communities (personal communication, July 3, 1998). She was particularly interested in establishing a well-documented connection between these families and the Montaukett community in East Hampton and Sag Harbor. Unfortunately, neither she nor Ralph Bunn have been

160

The
Montaukett
Indians of
Eastern
Long Island

able to find a significant number of documents linking the two communities. There is, however, a great deal of oral testimony asserting close kinship ties with the core Montaukett families in Sag Harbor and East Hampton.

The Pharaoh and Fowler families in Eastville and Freetown made little overt show of their Indian heritage until the 1980s when developers threatened the ancient burial grounds at Montauk. In 1983 two development corporations, Fort Hill Associates and Signal Hill Associates, applied to the town of East Hampton for permission to build homesites on the top of the hill on North Neck, which overlooks Fort Pond and the present village of Montauk (*New York Times,* May 15, 1983).

The site, well known to the Montauketts, was an ancient burial ground that had first been documented by Long Island ethnographer William Wallace Tooker (1962, 143). At the end of the nineteenth century, Tooker reported seeing evidence of more than one hundred burials on the hill. More recent excavations by professional archaeologists confirmed Tooker's observations. Edward Johannemann, archaeologist for the Long Island Archaeological Project, reported that he had found evidence of hearths and habitation sites as well as grave sites (*Newsday,* Nov. 23, 1984). This information did not move the builders or some of the town officials. The attitude expressed by Ronald Greenbaum, the East Hampton town supervisor, shocked the Montauketts and many others. He summed up his position on the matter in a public meeting, asking, rhetorically, "Who cares about a bunch of dead Indians?" (*New York Times,* May 15, 1983).

As it turned out, many people cared. One of them was Robert Cooper. At the time Cooper was a member of the East Hampton Police Department. With assistance from Eugene Cuffee, a Shinnecock, and several members of the Montaukett community, he organized a protest at the site in May 1983 (ibid.). The Montauketts took the matter to court in July and won a temporary injunction blocking the developers from doing any construction until the following September (*Newsday,* July 14, 1983, p. 21).

In November 1983 the issue was finally resolved when the town board, under pressure from the Montauketts, environmentalists, and other interested citizens, voted to purchase the 30-acre site for $1.4 million and preserve the Indian burial ground (*Newsday,* Nov. 23, 1983). Robert Cooper was appointed chairman of the Fort Hill Cemetery

Robert Cooper. Photograph by John A. Strong.

Advisory Board of Trustees. The victory for the Montauketts encouraged many to consider becoming more active in tribal affairs.

The following March Cooper raised another issue of concern to the Montauketts. The federal government proposed to sell a 278-acre air force installation located south of Indian Fields to real estate developers. When New York State and the town of East Hampton sued to stop the sale, Robert Cooper asked them to assist him in a move to have the land turned back to the Montauketts (ibid., Mar. 2, 1984).

Cooper charged that the land had been taken from them illegally by Arthur Benson and repeated the arguments raised by the Montaukett lawyers in 1909. He pointed out that the federal court ruling in the 1975 Passamaquoddy case held that all transactions involving Indian lands that took place after the 1790 Non-intercourse Act had to be approved by the United States Congress. Cooper did not have the resources to press his claim, but he and the local officials were able to block the developers from getting the land. The New York State Park Service finally took over the property. It is possible, however, that the legal issues raised by the Montauketts will be pressed more vigorously in the future.

Two years later another piece of the ancient Montaukett lands came under the control of government agencies. New York State purchased about 1,000 acres of Hither Woods and created Hither Hills State Park. In 1988 the state purchased another 777 acres and added them to the park (*New York Times*, Dec. 22, 1988). The park now encompasses all but a few hundred acres of the land included in the gift deed of 1662 (see chapter 3). Ironically, nearly one-half of the land wrested away from the East Hampton town authorities by the proprietors in 1852 has now come back into the public domain.

In 1989 developers threatened another Montaukett burial ground on North Neck. One of the graves was the last resting place of Cyrus Charles, who had written the Montaukett petition to the governor of New York in 1764. Representatives from the Shinnecocks and many white supporters joined with three generations of Montauketts to hold a protest rally to save the site. Robert Cooper, Olive Pharaoh, and her sister Carolyn, the great-grandchildren of Maria Pharaoh; Olive's son, Robert; and his young daughter, Tami, all joined in the fight to preserve the site. Olive Pharaoh spoke out against the development project. "I think the cemetery should be preserved. At one time we were the owners of Montauk, and it was taken from us, and we have nothing. The least they can do is leave us alone" (*New York Times,* Oct. 22, 1989). The protest proved more successful than any of the demonstrations led by Cyrus Charles in the eighteenth century. The town government agreed to preserve the grave site, and in the process the town recognized "the continued existence" of the Montauketts (*Newsday,* Dec. 10, 1991).

The successful efforts to protect their burial grounds were undoubtedly a factor encouraging the renewal of interest in reviving Montaukett tribal structures. On February 24, 1990, the Reverend Sharon Jackson, a Montaukett descendant from the Amityville area, called a meeting of the families to discuss the problems faced by non-reservation Indians on Long Island. A small number of Brewster and Fowler family members attended and expressed particular concern about maintaining their cultural identity and preserving some of the family cemeteries in North Amityville (Field Notes, Feb. 24, 1990).[2]

Members of the Bunn, Green, Steele, Miller, Brewster, and other black and Algonquian families buried their dead in small plots near their residences during the nineteenth century. Many of the cemeteries were abandoned as neighborhoods went through changes in the early decades of the twentieth century.[3] The group established an informal committee chaired by Jackson, but there was no clear focus on what to do next.

The following summer the group met on the Southampton College campus and began to focus more on the problems related to petitioning the federal government for tribal recognition. Several people noted that they had documented kinship connections with two or three tribal groups on Long Island, and some had made a claim to residence rights on the Shinnecock Reservation. They knew, however, that the Bureau of Indian Affairs would not permit individuals to claim the rights of membership in more than one recognized Indian

2. Field Notes include notes taken at the following meetings of the Montaukett Tribe: Feb. 24, 1990; Aug. 1991; Feb. 28, 1993; Nov. 8, 1997; and Jan. 10, 1998; and informal interviews with the following Montauketts: Robert Cooper, Robert Pharaoh, Ralph Bunn, the Reverend Sharon Jackson, Phyllis Brewster-Toone, Sandi Brewster-Walker, Jo Ann Leftenant, James Devine, Olive Pharaoh, John Kenney, and Terrie Caldwell. These notes include videotapes taken by Ralph Bunn at the Montaukett meetings in February and May 1993. All these materials are in the East Hampton Library Collections or in the Suffolk County Historical Society Library in Riverhead, N.Y.

3. Two of these cemeteries have since been restored and marked with large granite slabs engraved with the words "In memory of the Native American Families of Long Island and those known only to the Great Spirit." The inscription forms the border around the figure of a turtle.

164

*The
Montaukett
Indians of
Eastern
Long Island*

community. Most indicated that they were willing to abandon all other tribal affiliations and claim only their Montaukett identity (ibid., Aug. 1991).

In November 1992 Robert Cooper, who had retired from the East Hampton police force, won election to the town board by a large margin. He was the first nonwhite to be elected for a full term on the board. Cooper's success in local politics increased his status in the Montaukett community. At a meeting held in Riverhead on May 3, 1993, when the group discussed the problem of tribal leadership, Cooper and Robert Pharaoh were the primary candidates. Cooper had been more active in tribal affairs up to that time, but the members believed that they would have to consult with Olive Pharaoh, the tribal matriarch. It was assumed that her preference

Robert Pharaoh and Olive Pharaoh. Courtesy of Toba Tucker and Pharaoh family.

would be for her son, Robert, but they knew that he had been distracted by personal problems and had not yet indicated his intentions. Cooper said that he would contact Olive Pharaoh and ask for her support. The Reverend Sharon Jackson told Cooper that he should get a letter from her endorsing him. Cooper agreed that Olive Pharaoh's endorsement was a necessary requirement for anyone who claimed tribal leadership. They took no further action on this issue at the meeting (ibid., Feb. 28, 1993; videotape, May 3, 1993).

Soon after the meeting Robert Pharaoh came forward, with his mother's endorsement, to claim the title of chief by right of inheritance from the Pharaoh line. Later that May Pharaoh invited tribal members and the public to Montauk County Park for a gathering that featured craft booths, informational exhibits, and traditional foods. The following year the activities included an ethnobotanical walk and dances performed by members of the Shinnecock Tribe. In 1994 Pharaoh circulated a copy of James Waters's 1919 Montaukett constitution for tribal consideration and urged the members to establish a formal tribal organization under his leadership.

Cooper, who was not willing to accept Pharaoh's claim, began to seek support among the Montauketts. Ironically, Cooper and Pharaoh are descended from the two families who had frequently been at odds over tribal leadership in the past. Cooper traces his Montaukett ancestry through his maternal line back to his great-grandmother, Maria, who was a Fowler. Cooper's great-grandfather, Edward Banks, Maria's third husband, was not a Montaukett. Robert Pharaoh's mother, Olive, was the great-granddaughter of Maria and her first husband, David Pharaoh. Olive's husband left the family soon after the marriage, and their son, Robert, kept the Pharaoh family name.

The tensions between the two men erupted in 1995 when the Smithsonian Museum of the American Indian in New York approached the Montauketts and asked them to accept the skeletal remains of three unidentified Indians for burial in the Fort Hill cemetery. Smithsonian director Richard West wanted to repatriate as many of the skeletal remains as possible to the appropriate tribal burial grounds. Many of the remains, however, were too fragmentary to identify or were refused by their own tribes for various reasons. Robert Pharaoh and East Hampton town supervisor Tony Bullock thought it would be a good gesture to bury them at Fort Hill. Pharaoh said that it would help the tribe in their petition for federal recognition (*Newsday*, June 24, 1995).

Robert Pharaoh and his daughter, Tami. Opening
Ceremony, Craft Fair, May 26, 1996, at Montauk
County Park. Photograph by John A. Strong.

Cooper, however, was adamantly opposed. He said that it
would not be appropriate to bury non-Montauketts in the section
of the cemetery reserved for Montauketts. Native American staff
members at Smithsonian were upset by the open debate. They had
hoped for a quiet transfer and reburial. In the face of the public con-
troversy, the museum officials quickly withdrew their request.

In 1996 Robert Pharaoh established the Friends of the Pharaoh
Museum and, with the help of Terrie Caldwell, who represented Montaukett families from the Amityville area, expanded the summer craft
fair to include a drum and dance group. The museum launched
another interesting project in the summer of 1996. Elizabeth Bowser,
who was president of the organization at that time, wrote a successful grant to establish an experimental garden using the traditional
techniques employed by the Montauketts before the arrival of the English in the seventeenth century. The garden plot was located on Hog

Creek Lane in East Hampton, a short distance from the birthplace of
Stephen Talkhouse Pharaoh. The group recruited Lamont Smith, a
Shinnecock who has planted traditional gardens on his land at Shinnecock for the past several years, to direct the project. With volunteer
help from interested local people, the staff from Quail Hill farm (a
community-supported organic-farming operation), and students from
the author's summer class on local Indian history, the project was a
modest success.

All of these developments were important to the resurgence of
the Montauketts, but Pharaoh has emphasized that his primary concern is to reclaim tribal land. "Our main goal is focused on Indian
Fields," said Pharaoh to a *Newsday* reporter (May 5, 1996). He sees
federal recognition as an important first step in the pursuit of that goal.

In the spring of 1996 Pharaoh, working with the Chicago-based
law firm of Bell, Boyd, and Lloyd, took the first step toward federal
recognition by filing a letter of intent with the Branch of Acknowledgment and Research (BAR), an agency established in the Bureau
of Indian Affairs (BIA) to review petitions for federal recognition. They
began work on a petition demonstrating that the Montauketts met the
seven mandatory criteria for federal acknowledgment (*Federal Register,* 1-25-98, CFR, pt. 83.7).

The first requirement calls for the Montauketts to provide
proof that they have had "substantially continuous" public recognition as an Indian community since 1900. The bureau considers references in the press and in scholarly publications and relations with
local governments as evidence. The obituaries and accounts of tribal
activities in the press cited in scholarly accounts by Stone (1993a)
and J. Strong (1996b; 1997) will help the Montauketts to meet this
criterion. The BAR does not consider occasional denials of tribal status, such as the 1909 pronouncements of Judge Blackmar or the
attacks on Montauk identity by the press, to be conclusive evidence
that the tribe no longer exists.

The second requirement calls for evidence that the petitioning
group comprises a distinct community with a continuous existence
from the time of first contact with European settlers to the present. The
BAR accepts such data as significant rates of marriage within the group
and evidence of other social relationships and kinship organizations.

The BAR also wants evidence that the group has some form of
political leadership that has been in place from colonial times to the
present. They do not demand minutes of meetings or uninterrupted
lists of tribal sachems, but they do ask for evidence that the group can

168

The
Montaukett
Indians of
Eastern
Long Island

organize itself to carry out specific goals, such as the campaign to reclaim the land or the struggle to gain federal recognition. Ironically, one of the factors that demonstrates the existence of a viable political system is evidence that there are internal conflicts over group goals or policies. The tension between Cooper and Pharaoh will have at least one positive effect. At the same time, however, the group must demonstrate that they have the capacity to settle disputes by mediation.

Fourth, the group must produce a written or an oral description of their membership criteria and system of governance. The fifth requirement asks for a membership list consisting of members who are descended from a tribe that existed at the time of European arrival. The BAR does not require professional genealogies for each member. A group may submit such data as tribal rolls, affidavits of recognition from tribal elders, or leaders identifying individual members. The group must submit an official membership list, certified by the group's leaders, which includes the full name and maiden name, date of birth, and current address. The petitioners must also explain how they prepared the list and define their criteria for membership.

The sixth requirement stipulates that the group must be composed of persons who are not members of any other federally recognized tribe. The last criterion prohibits any tribe previously terminated by congressional legislation from consideration for federal recognition. These last two criteria do not apply to the Montauketts.

History has come full circle for the Montauketts. They now find themselves poised, as they were at the end of the nineteenth century, hoping to recover their tribal land on Montauk. Once again they have been asked to demonstrate that they exist as a tribe. This time, however, an abundance of historical data is available. The seven-hundred-page *History and Archaeology of the Montauk,* edited by Gaynell Stone and published by the Suffolk County Archaeological Society in 1993, has provided considerable evidence to support their petition.

Early in June 1996 Olive Pharaoh, the tribal matriarch, died. A month earlier, when a reporter asked her about Indian Fields, Olive said, "I want to see it . . . see it back in the hands of its rightful owners—before I die" (*Newsday,* May 5, 1996). Unfortunately, she passed away with her dying wish unfulfilled.

The tension between Cooper and Pharaoh continued. Cooper charged that Robert Pharaoh had gone ahead on his own without consulting regularly enough with the other Montauketts. He also charged that the tribe had not yet selected a chief. Cooper argued that the tribe should ratify a constitution and hold elections for a chief and a tribal council. He said that he was concerned about the contract that Pharaoh had made with Bell, Boyd, and Lloyd. Cooper expressed a fear that a commitment might have been made for tribal involvement in gambling operations. If our petition is denied, asked Cooper, will the tribal members be liable for all of the law firm's expenses?

Pharaoh responded to the charges, stating that he took the initiative because of the frustratingly slow pace of progress over the previous five years. Neal Bermis, a representative with Bell, Boyd, and Lloyd, assured the Montauketts that the firm was working on a contingency basis. If the Montauketts won federal recognition and, with the help of government lawyers, won a land claim, the firm would expect to be paid from those revenues. If they did not win, the firm would simply write it off as they would in any contingency case. Bermis also said that his firm had no plans for casinos. That idea, he said, would be a matter for the tribe to discuss after they won recognition and resolved their land claims. Robert Stearns, an anthropologist for the BIA, said the evaluation and review process could easily take five more years (*East Hampton Star,* Nov. 7, 1996).

The conflict between the factions had become public, making it more difficult for the tribe to resolve the differences quietly. Cooper argued that he had worked for many years on the Montaukett cause before Robert Pharaoh appeared on the scene. Pharaoh countered, saying he had been working on tribal affairs for the past fifteen years and added that Cooper had accomplished very little over the previous five years. Both men, however, assured the *East Hampton Star* reporter that they would put aside their personal differences for the good of the tribe (ibid.). These differences, however, increased over the next few months as casino interests intruded themselves into Montaukett affairs.

In the fall of 1997 Cooper had discussions with a group of investors who called themselves the Dreamcatchers. They talked about huge profits that could be made from gambling operations at a site in the town of Riverhead. The organization wanted a partnership with an Indian community who could make a credible claim to land in Riverhead on the former Grumman site that was being closed by the navy. Cooper had previously voiced opposition to casinos at Montauk, but he did not oppose casinos in principle. The success of the Pequots and a few other tribal gambling operations feeds the hopes of Indian peoples throughout the United States.

The Dreamcatchers had earlier approached the Unkechaugs and the Shinnecocks with promises of huge profits if they would pursue a claim to a three-thousand-acre parcel of land in the town of

170

The
Montaukett
Indians of
Eastern
Long Island

Riverhead owned by the United States Navy. The Grumman Corporation, a major manufacturer of military aircraft, occupied the land until the company closed its operations shortly after the end of the cold war. The federal government is in the process of turning the property over to the town of Riverhead. A substantial claim by an Indian tribe, however, could halt the process and open the way for a return of some land to them. In the seventeenth century several sachems, including Wyandanch of the Montauketts; Unkechaug sachems Gie, Tobaccus, and Wiangonhut; and Weany, the Shinnecock sunksquaw, claimed to exercise authority at various times over land in this general area (J. Strong 1983, 73–94). The Unkechaugs, whose reservation at Poospatuck is located less than ten miles to the southwest of the Grumman site, clearly have the strongest claim.

Charles Rogers, a real estate developer from Queens, and William D. Talmage, a real estate broker from Riverhead, who had worked together to build Tanger Mall, a large shopping mall near the Grumman property, founded Dreamcatchers to finance any Indian group who could initiate a successful claim to the Grumman property. They envisioned a casino complex near the Tanger Mall that would draw people from New York City, Long Island, and southern New England. They chose the name "Dreamcatchers" as a calculated public relations gimmick to associate themselves with the sacred Native American amulet believed to protect sleepers from evil spirits. They were apparently unaware that some Native Americans deeply resent the commercialization of all sacred amulets, while others argue that the dreamcatchers are nothing more than a "new age" fad.

When representatives from the Dreamcatchers approached Chief Harry Wallace, the Unkechaug chief, he and his council went over their proposal with great care and decided that it was far too speculative for serious consideration. Wallace, who is a lawyer by training and has several council members with business experience to advise him, believed that the Dreamcatcher organization was not well-enough informed about land claims procedures and that their projections of profits and timetables for returns on investments were overly optimistic (personal communication, Feb. 21, 1998). He also remarked that he was put off by the developers' use of the name "Dreamcatchers," which he believed was offensive and patronizing.

In the fall of 1997 Robert Cooper and representatives from Dreamcatchers began discussing the possibility of making a claim for the Grumman site. On November 7, 1997, Pharaoh held a meeting to inform the membership about the progress of work on the petition.

Cooper and his supporters did not attend. Neal Bermis reviewed the progress on the document and answered questions about the procedures for recognition. He repeated that his law firm was working on a contingency basis and that there were no binding agreements with the tribe about any form of gaming. Any discussion of gambling casinos, he said, would jeopardize their petition for recognition. Bermis believed that the BAR might hesitate to grant recognition to a tribe that appeared to have gambling as its major goal.

William Talmage assured Robert Cooper that the welfare of the Montauketts was the Dreamcatchers' "paramount concern." Cooper disagreed with Bermis's contention that any hint of an interest in gambling would undermine the petitioning process. Cooper made it clear that he did not want a casino on Indian Fields at Montauk, but he believed that the tribe should explore the possibility of a gambling operation on the Grumman site. A week later Cooper met with representatives of the Dreamcatchers and discussed the

Robert Cooper and John Fowler at Nunnowa Ceremony, November 1997. Photograph by John A. Strong.

172

The
Montaukett
Indians of
Eastern
Long Island

plans for the Grumman site. Cooper agreed to present their claim to the Naval Facilities Engineering Command, which was supervising the transfer process. Cooper did send a statement of concern to the naval authorities but made no formal claim to the land.

Two weeks later, on November 22, Cooper called a tribal meeting. Robert Pharaoh and a small number of his supporters attended, but the majority of members who came were Cooper's people. Thirty-seven of the forty-five people in attendance ratified a tribal constitution, based on the Montaukett constitution written by James Waters in 1919, and voted for Cooper to serve as tribal chairperson and secretary. They also elected a tribal council, which included Gail Boyd, assistant chairperson; Kenneth Nelson, assistant secretary; Phyllis Brewster-Toone, treasurer; Deloris Vaughan, shaman; and two members at large, John Fowler and Cheryl Cuffy-Carion. These officers, said Cooper, would serve until the formal elections at the June 1998 meeting (*Sag Harbor Independent*, Dec. 3, 1998). Pharaoh rejected the vote, arguing that he and his supporters had not been notified of the election in a timely fashion.

In an effort to bring the two factions together, John Kenney, a tribal member, wrote an open letter appealing for unity (Dec. 30, 1997). This period is not a time for "confrontation and mutually destructive behavior," wrote Kenney; it is a time for "cooperation, good will, and reason." He called for better attendance at the tribal meetings and open discussions about the issues dividing the tribe. The tensions, he said, are superficial. Much of the misunderstanding, he continued, could be resolved with better communications. Although Kenney's appeal called for the leaders to work together, he was quite critical of Cooper in the process. Cooper rejected Kenney's appeal because he believed that it placed the blame on him for the tribal divisions.

In spite of these difficulties, Pharaoh's consultants completed the preliminary work on the petition and presented it to the tribe at a meeting in the Amityville Public Library on January 10, 1998, at 1 P.M. About sixty people attended the meeting (Field Notes). Cooper again pressed the issue of leadership by scheduling his own meeting on the same day a short distance away in the North Amityville American Legion Hall at 2 P.M. Several Montauketts, in an effort to promote unity, came to Pharaoh's meeting and indicated that they would go to the Legion Hall for Cooper's session afterward. Phyllis Brewster-Toone, who had been elected treasurer in Cooper's council, was among the peacemakers.

Pharaoh surprised many who had been skeptical of the reports that he was not making progress toward recognition. Pharaoh invited everyone to examine the document, and Neal Bermis briefly outlined its contents. The petition included a lengthy history of the Montaukett Tribe and about ninety genealogies. Pharaoh offered the document as evidence that he and his consultants were making significant progress toward the goal of federal recognition.

Although there was general approval and appreciation for Pharaoh's accomplishment, several people raised the question of the split between Pharaoh and Cooper. Phyllis Brewster-Toone, Albert Miller, and Jerry Witaker called for a joint meeting of the two factions to make another attempt at tribal unity. Many in the room agreed that a call for unity was in order, and Pharaoh agreed but made it clear that he would not recognize the November election (ibid.).

Miller and Brewster-Toone did attend Cooper's meeting, which also drew about sixty people. Cooper agreed that unity was necessary, but remained convinced that he and his council should stay in office until the June 1998 tribal elections. Cooper argued that Pharaoh's petition was poorly prepared and did not present a strong-enough database to win tribal recognition. He said that he was beginning work on a separate petition to the BAR that would provide a much more comprehensive response to all of the criteria required by Washington.

At this same meeting Cooper invited William Talmage to discuss his company's proposal for the Grumman site. After several months of negotiations, Cooper and his council had some of the same questions raised by the Unkechaugs about the Dreamcatchers' proposal. Cooper said later that though Talmage's presentation was forthright and thorough, several questions remained. According to Cooper he and his council decided to end their negotiations with Dreamcatchers (personal communication, Feb. 20, 1998).

Sometime afterward a Dreamcatchers' representative contacted Robert Pharaoh, who told him that Cooper had no authority to speak for the Montaukett Tribe. Pharaoh said that he did not want to discuss gambling prospects or land claims until the recognition process was completed. The whole matter became public on February 19, 1998, when the *East Hampton Star* ran a front-page article with the headline, "Montauk Factions at Odds over Gambling." In an interview with a reporter, Pharaoh denounced Cooper's contacts with gambling interests and again expressed concern that his discussions with the Dreamcatchers might undermine the Montauketts' petition

174

The
Montaukett
Indians of
Eastern
Long Island

for recognition. Cooper told the same reporter that he had made no deal with Dreamcatchers and that he deplored the publicity about internal tribal affairs. "As Native Americans," said Cooper, "we have a right to do what we want to do as a family. If we think it is a public concern, we will give it to the public."

Holly Reckord, a BAR staff member, noted that such divisions often occur early in the petitioning process but warned that the Montauketts should make every effort to reconcile their differences. "We prefer that they come together," she said, "but if they are fighting we will have to accept two different applications." She warned that this split would waste a great deal of time and energy that could be better used to move the petition forward (*East Hampton Star,* Feb. 19, 1998).

Robert Cooper was reelected as chief in a second election at a meeting of his group on June 13, 1998. According to Cooper seventy members were present, and all of them had genealogical documents verifying their Montaukett ancestry (personal communication, July 22, 1998). Robert Pharaoh took the position that he had inherited the title of chief from his mother's lineage. There was no need, therefore, for an election. Olive's grandfather David was a Pharaoh, and her grandmother Maria was a Fowler. The marriage linked together the two more prominent Montaukett families of that period. Pharaoh argued that Cooper's lineage was weaker because his lineage came through Maria's third husband, Edward Banks. Cooper, therefore, can claim descent only through the Fowler line. Similar conflicts between elected and traditional chiefs are not uncommon in Indian tribes. The question can be resolved only by the members, who have to make a choice about which man they will follow. It is the Montaukett people who will make the final determination and vote with their feet. Some Montauketts have taken the position that they will wait and see who "brings home the bacon."

Pharaoh made an important move in that direction by submitting his petition for federal recognition to the BAR on June 23, 1998. Robert Cooper's group is still in the process of preparing their own petition, which Cooper argues will be more complete than Pharaoh's. The second petition may cause some problems for the recognition process. At this time, however, there is no established BAR policy on such situations.

The BAR procedures for processing petitions from tribes begin with a lengthy preliminary review after which a letter of technical assistance is sent to the petitioners. The letter provides the petitioner with a list of areas that require more documentation. In January

1999 Robert Pharaoh received a ten-page letter from the BAR requesting additional documentation about tribal activities, decision-making processes, patterns of leadership, and membership lists for the period between 1945 and 1980.

This task will not be easy for the Montauketts because during this time they met informally at family gatherings, and no official minutes were kept. The bureau suggested that the Montauketts search for photos of family gatherings, and evidence that tribal members often married within the tribe and lived in close proximity with each other. The BAR also asked for a copy of the tribes' membership application. They wanted to see how the group defined their criteria for membership. Tribal members, with the help of volunteer graduate students from the University of Connecticut, are in the process of gathering these materials, but it will not be an easy task

Robert Pharaoh and the first draft of the BAR petition.
Photograph by John A. Strong.

because the Montauketts, as is the case with many Indian communities, have never kept extensive written records.

Even under the best of circumstances, the review process is long and arduous. The research required in response to the letter of technical assistance will take a year or more to complete. When the amended petition is submitted, the tribe will have to submit a written request for a second review. If the petition is approved after the review, the petition will be placed on the list of petitioners waiting for active consideration. There are now about fifteen tribes on the list awaiting consideration. According to the BAR staff they may not get to the Montaukett petition for another two or three years after that. In other words, if all goes well, and it seldom does in these matters, the Montauketts cannot expect to hear a final decision until 2004 or 2005.

As this book goes to press, the two factions remain unreconciled. Robert Cooper has not submitted his petition to the BAR. The Montauketts have traveled a long and difficult road, and they now face two of their greatest challenges. They must resolve their internal differences and then endure a long waiting period while their petition is under review. If they can meet these challenges, then they may one day reclaim their homeland and fulfill Maria Pharaoh's vision and Olive Pharaoh's dying wish.

WORKS CITED
INDEX

WORKS CITED

Ales, Marion Fisher. 1993. "A History of the Indians on Montauk, Long Island." In *The History and Archaeology of the Montauk Indians,* edited by Gaynell Stone, 5–67. Stony Brook: Suffolk County Archaeological Association.

Axtell, James. 1985. *The Invasion Within: The Contest of Cultures in Colonial North America.* New York: Oxford Univ. Press.

Bailey, Paul, ed. 1949. *Long Island: A History of Two Great Counties, Nassau and Suffolk.* New York: Lewis Historical Publishing.

———. 1956. "Decline and Fall of Tribal Life." *Long Island Forum* 19, no. 9: 165–66, 175–77.

———. 1982. *The Thirteen Tribes of Long Island.* 1959. Reprint. Syosset, N.Y.: Friends for Long Island's Heritage.

Bartlett, John R, ed. 1968. *Records of the Colony of Rhode Island and Providence Plantations in New England.* 10 vols. 1850–1865. Reprint. New York: AMS Press.

Beecher, Lyman. 1993. "Montauk." In *The History and Archaeology of the Montauk,* edited by Gaynell Stone, 289. Stony Brook, N.Y.: Suffolk County Archaeological Association.

Bernstein, David. 1990. "Trends in Prehistoric Subsistence on the Southern New England Coast: The View from Narragansett Bay." *North American Archaeologist* 11, no. 4: 321–52.

Blackwood, Robert T. 1993. "Samson Occom and Brothertown, New York." In *The History and Archaeology of the Montauk,* edited by Gaynell Stone, 535–39. Stony Brook, N.Y.: Suffolk County Archaeological Association.

Blodgett, Harold. 1935. *Samson Occom.* Dartmouth College Manuscript Series No. 3, Hanover, N.H.

Bolton, Reginald Pelham. 1975. "New York in Indian Possession." In *Indian Notes and Monographs.* Vol. 2, no. 7. 1920. Reprint. New York: Museum of the American Indian, Heye Foundation.

Bragdon, Kathleen J. 1996. *Native People of Southern New England, 1500–1650.* Norman: Univ. of Oklahoma Press.

Brasser, T. J. 1971. "The Coastal Algonquians: People of the First Frontiers." In *North American Indians in Historical Perspective,* edited by Eleanor Leacock and Nancy Laurie, 64–91. New York: Random House.

————. 1978. "Early Indian-European Contacts." In *Handbook of North American Indians.* Vol. 15, *The Northeast,* edited by Bruce Trigger, 78–88. Washington, D.C.: Smithsonian Institution Press.

Brodhead, John Romeyn. 1853–71. *History of the State of New York.* 2 vols. New York: Harper Brothers.

Campisi, Jack. 1982. "The Iroquois and the Concept of Tribe." *New York History* 43, no. 2: 165–82.

Carr, J. D., and Carlos Westez. 1980. "Surviving Folktales and Herbal Lore among the Shinnecock Indians of Long Island." In *Languages and Lore of the Long Island Indians,* edited by Gaynell Stone and Nancy Bonvillain, 278–83. Stony Brook, N.Y.: Suffolk County Archaeological Association.

Cave, Alfred. 1996. *The Pequot War.* Amherst: Univ. of Massachusetts Press.

Ceci, Lynn. 1977. "The Effect of European Contact and Trade on Settlement Patterns of Indians in Coastal New York, 1524–1664." Ph.D. diss., City Univ. of New York. (Published by Garland Publishing in 1990).

Christoph, Peter. 1999. "Thomas Dongan and Charter of East Hampton." In *Awakening the Past: East Hampton's 350th Anniversary Lecture Series,* edited by Tom Twomey, 173–90. New York: Newmarket Press.

————, ed. 1980. *Administrative Papers of Governors Richard Nicolls and Francis Lovelace, 1664–1673.* Baltimore: Genealogical Publishing.

Christoph, Peter, and Florence Christoph, eds. 1982. *Books of General Entries of the Colony of New York, 1664–1673.* Baltimore: Genealogical Publishing.

Clark, Julia, ed. 1993. "Samson Occum's Diary." In *The History and Archaeology of the Montauk,* edited by Gaynell Stone, 223–83. Stony Brook, N.Y.: Suffolk County Archaeological Association.

Coles, Robert. 1954. *The Long Island Indians.* Glen Cove, N.Y.: Little Museum.

Conkey, Laura, Ethel Boissevain, and Ives Goddard. 1984. "Indians of Southern New England and Long Island." In *Handbook of North American Indians.* Vol. 15, *The Northeast,* edited by Bruce C. Trigger, 177–89. Washington, D.C.: Smithsonian Institution Press.

Cook, Sherburne F. 1973. "The Significance of Disease in the Extinction of the New England Indians." *Human Biology* 45, no. 3: 485–508.

Cooper, Thomas, ed. 1993. *The Records of the Court of Session of Suffolk County in the Province of New York, 1670–1688.* Bowie, Md.: Heritage Books.

Cornelius, Carol. 1993. "An Interview with June Ezold, the Tribal Chairperson of the Brotherton Indians of Wisconsin." In *The History and Archaeology of the Montauk,* edited by Gaynell Stone, 565–68, Stony Brook, N.Y.: Suffolk County Archaeological Association.

Cronon, William. 1983. Changes in the Land. N.Y.: Hill and Wang.

De Laet, Johannes. 1909. "New World, or Description of West-India." In *Narratives of New Netherland,* edited by J. Franklin Jameson, 31–60. 1625. Reprint. New York: Charles Scribner.

Denton, Daniel. 1968. "A Brief Description of New York, 1670." In *Historical Chronicles of New Amsterdam, Colonial New York, and Early*

Long Island, edited by Sidney Pomerantz, 1–22. New York: Empire State Historical Publications.

Dexter, Franklin B., ed. 1899. *Diary of David McClure.* New York: Knickerbocker Press.

Dominy, Nathaniel, Sr. 1887–1909. "Wind, Feathers and Doings." East Hampton, N.Y.: East Hampton Library, Long Island Collections.

Edwards, Everett, and Jeanette Rattray. 1956. *Whale-off: The Story of American Shore Whaling.* New York: Coward and McCann.

Flint, Martha. 1967. *Long Island Before the Revolution.* 1896. Reprint. Port Washington, N.Y.: Ira J. Friedman.

Forbes, Allyn B., ed. 1929–47. *The Winthrop Papers.* 5 vols. Boston: Massachusetts Historical Society.

Ford, Richard. 1981. "Gardening and Farming Before A.D. 1000: Patterns of Prehistoric Cultivation in North America." *Journal of Ethnobiology* 1: 6–27.

Fried, Morton. 1975. *The Notion of Tribe.* Menlo Park, Calif.: Cummings Publishing.

———. 1976. *The Evolution of Political Society.* New York: Random House.

Furman, Gabriel. 1874. *Antiquities of Long Island.* New York: J. W. Bolton.

Gardiner, David. 1973. *Chronicles of the Town of East Hampton.* 1840. Reprint. Sag Harbor, N.Y.: Isabel Gardiner Mairs.

Gardiner, John Lyon. 1798. *The Journal and Farm Book of John Lyon Gardiner.* East Hampton, N.Y.: East Hampton Public Library Collections.

———. 1980. "Montauk Vocabulary, Recorded from George Pharaoh, March 25, 1798." In *Languages and Lore of the Long Island Indians,* edited by Gaynell Stone Levine and Nancy Bonvillain, 15–16. Stony Brook, N.Y.: Suffolk County Archaeological Association.

Gardiner, Lion. 1980. "Relation of the Pequot Wars." In *The History of the Pequot War,* edited by Charles Orr, 112–49. 1897. Reprint. New York: AMS Press.

Goddard, Ives. 1978a. "Delaware." In *Handbook of the North American Indians.* Vol. 15, *The Northeast,* edited by Bruce Trigger, 213–39. Washington, D.C.: Smithsonian Institution Press.

———. 1978b. "Eastern Algonquian Languages." In *Handbook of the North American Indians.* Vol. 15, *The Northeast,* edited by Bruce Trigger, 70–77. Washington, D.C.: Smithsonian Institution Press.

Gombieski, Jane. 1993. "Klokards, Kleagles, Kludds, and Kluxers: The Ku Klux Klan in Suffolk County, 1915–1928, Part One." *Long Island Historical Journal* 6, no. 1: 41–62.

Gonzales, Ellice. 1984. "From Unkechaug to Poospatuck." National Park Service, Fire Island National Seashore, Patchogue, N.Y.

———. 1993. "Montauk Ethnological Sources." In *The History and Archaeology of the Montauk,* edited by Gaynell Stone, 67–77. Stony Brook, N.Y.: Suffolk County Archaeological Association.

Grim, John A. 1987. *The Shaman.* Norman: Oklahoma Univ. Press.

Grumet, Robert Steven. 1979. "We Are Not Such Great Fools: Changes in Upper Delawaran Socio-Political Life, 1630–1758." Ph.D. diss., Rutgers Univ.

———. 1980. "Sunksquaws, Shamans, and Tradeswomen: Middle Atlantic Coastal Algonkian Women During the Seventeenth and Eighteenth Centuries." In *Women and Colonization: Anthropological Perspectives,* edited by Mona Etienne Lurie and Eleanor Burke Leacock, 43–62, New York: Praeger Scientific.

———. 1991. "William Wallace Tooker: Pioneer Algonkinist." In *The Wabnaki Collection and the William Wallace Tooker Papers in the Huntington Free Library: A Guide to the Microfilm Edition,* edited by Mary B. Davis, 23–31. New York: Huntington Free Library.

Gwynne, Gretchen. 1982. "The Late Archaic Archaeology of Mount Sinai Harbor, New York: Human Ecology, Economy and Residence Patterns on the Southern New England Coast." Ph.D. diss., SUNY, Stony Brook. Ann Arbor: University Microfilms, no. 8218079.

Hagan, William T. 1992. "Full Blood, Mixed Blood, Generic, and Ersatz: The Problem of Indian Identity." In *The American Indian Past and Present,* edited by Roger Nichols, 278–88. New York: McGraw-Hill.

Hauptman, Laurence. 1980. "Refugee Havens: The Iroquois Villages of the Eighteenth Century." In *American Indian Environments,* edited by Christopher Vescey and Robert Venables, 128–39. Syracuse: Syracuse Univ. Press.

Hawke, David Freeman. 1988. *Everyday Life in Colonial America.* New York: Harper and Row.

Hedges, Henry. 1897. *A History of the Town of East Hampton.* Sag Harbor, N.Y.: J. H. Hunt.

Hendricks, Gordon. 1979. *The Life and Works of Winslow Homer.* New York: Harry Abrams.

Hicks, Benjamin, ed. 1896–1904. *Records of the Town of North and South Hempstead.* 8 vols. Jamaica, N.Y.: Long Island Farmer Print.

Hoadly, Charles J., ed. 1857. *Records of the Colony and Plantation of New Haven from 1638–1649.* 2 vols. Hartford, Conn.: Case Tiffany.

Horton, Azariah. 1993. "Journals, 1741–44." In *The History and Archaeology of the Montauk,* edited by Gaynell Stone, 195–220. Stony Brook, N.Y.: Suffolk County Archaeological Association.

Hoxie, Fred. 1984. *A Final Promise: The Campaign to Assimilate the Indians, 1880–1920.* Lincoln: Univ. of Nebraska Press.

Huden, John C. 1946. "David Fowler, Montauk Indian." *Long Island Forum* 9, no. 4:153–56.

Jameson, J. Franklin. 1883. "Montauk and the Commonlands of Easthampton." *Magazine of American History* 9, no. 4: 225–39.

Jennings, Francis. 1976. *The Invasion of America: Indians, Colonialism and the Cant of Conquest.* New York: W. W. Norton.

Jennings, Jessie. 1989. *Prehistory of North America.* Mountain View, Calif.: Mayfield Publishing.

Johannemann, Edward. 1993. "Indian Fields Site, Montauk, Suffolk County, New York, Part One." In *The History and Archaeology of the Montauk,* edited by Gaynell Stone, 643–54. Stony Brook, N.Y.: Suffolk County Archaeological Association.

Johnson, Eric. 1996. "Uncas and the Politics of Contact." In *Northeast*

Indian Lives, 1632–1816, edited by Robert S. Grumet, 29–47. Amherst: Univ. of Massachusetts Press.

Jones, William. 1905. "The Algonkin Manitou." *Journal of American Folklore* 18: 183–90.

Journal of the Assembly of the State of New York. 1818. Albany: John Barber, Printer.

Journal of the Assembly of the State of New York. 1822. Albany: John Barber, Printer.

Journal of the Senate of the State of New York. 1808. Albany: John Barber, Printer.

Kavenagh, W. Keith, ed. 1973. *Foundations of Colonial America.* 3 vols. New York: Chelsea House.

Kawashima, Yasuhide. 1986. *Puritan Justice and the Indian: White Man's Law in Massachusetts, 1670–1763.* Middleton, Conn.: Wesleyan Press.

Kraus, Scott D., et al. 1986. "Migration and Calving of Right Whales *(Eubalaena glacialis)* in the North Atlantic." In *Right Whales: Past and Present Status,* edited by Robert I. Brownell, Peter B. Best, and John H. Prescott, 201–20. Special issue no. 10. Cambridge, Mass.: International Whaling Commission.

Latham, Roy. 1935. "Orient Number 2 Site." Field notes in Southold Indian Museum Archives, Southold, N.Y.

Laufer, Berthold. 1917. "Origin of the Word Shaman." *American Anthropologist* 19: 361–71.

Laws of the State of New York. 1852. Seventy-fifth Session of the Legislature. Buffalo: Jewett, Thomas.

Leone, Mark, and Parker B. Potter, eds. 1988. *The Recovery of Meaning, Historical Archaeology in the Eastern United States.* Washington, D.C.: Smithsonian Institution Press.

Levine, Gaynell, and Nancy Bonvillian, eds. 1980. *Languages and Lore of the Long Island Indians.* Stony Brook: Suffolk County Archaeological Association.

Levine, Gaynell Stone, ed. 1977. *Early Papers in Long Island Archaeology.* Stony Brook, N.Y.: Suffolk County Archaeological Association.

———. 1978. *The Coastal Archaeology Reader.* Stony Brook, N.Y.: Suffolk County Archaeological Association.

Lincoln, Charles Z. 1894. *The Colonial Laws of New York from 1664 to the Revolution.* Albany, N.Y.: James B. Lyton.

———. 1906. *The Constitutional History of New York.* 5 vols. Rochester, N.Y.: Lawyer's Cooperative.

Love, W. De Loss. 1899. *Samson Occom and the Christian Indians of New England.* Boston: Pilgrim Press.

Mannello, George. 1964. *Our Long Island.* New York: Noble and Noble. Reprint, 1984.

Matthiessen, Peter. 1986. *Men's Lives.* New York: Random House.

McBride, Kevin. 1994. "The Source and Mother of the Fur Trade: Native-Dutch Relations in Eastern New Netherland." In *Enduring Traditions,* edited by Laurie Weinstein, 31–51. Westport, Conn.: Bergin and Garvey.

Miller, Karla, and Eugene Cuffee. 1993. "The Montauk Tribal Role." In *The*

History and Archaeology of the Montauk, edited by Gaynell Stone, 489–500. Stony Brook, N.Y.: Suffolk County Archaeological Association.

Morice, John. 1949. "The Indians of Long Island." In *Long Island: A History of Two Great Counties,* edited by Paul Bailey, 1: 107–46. New York: Lewis Historical Publishing.

Nash, Gary. 1982. *Red, White, and Black: The Peoples of Early America.* Englewood Cliffs, N.J.: Prentice-Hall.

New York Historical Society. 1912. "Proceedings of the General Court of Assizes, 1680–82." In *Collections, 1912.* New York: New York Historical Society.

O'Callaghan, Edmund Bailey, ed. 1849. *Documentary History of the State of New York.* 4 vols. Albany: Weed, Parsons.

O'Callaghan, Edmund Bailey, and Berthold Fernow. 1856–1887. *Documents Relative to the Colonial History of the State of New York.* 15 vols. Albany: Weed, Parsons.

Occom, Samson. 1993. "An Account of Montauk Indians on Long Island." In *The History and Archaeology of the Montauk,* edited by Gaynell Stone, 151–53. Stony Brook, N.Y.: Suffolk County Archaeological Association.

Osborne, Joseph, ed. 1887. *Records of the Town of East Hampton.* 5 vols. Sag Harbor, N.Y.: Hunt.

Ottery, Rudi, and Will Ottery. 1993. "Where Did All the Montauk Go?" In *The History and Archaeology of the Montauk,* edited by Gaynell Stone, 315–49. Stony Brook, N.Y.: Suffolk County Archaeological Association.

Overton, Jacqueline. 1963. *Indian Life on Long Island.* Port Washington, N.Y.: Ira J. Friedman. Reprint, 1969.

Pelletreau, William. 1882. "The Town of Southampton." In *The History of Suffolk County,* edited by W. W. Munsell, 1–54. New York: W. W. Munsell.

———. 1903. *The History of Long Island.* 2 vols. New York: Lewis Publishing.

———, ed. 1874–77. *Records of the Town of Southampton.* 8 vols. Sag Harbor, N.Y.: Hunt.

———, ed. 1898–1931. *Town Records of Smithtown.* 3 vols. Sag Harbor, N.Y.: Hunt.

Pilkington, Walter, ed. 1980. *The Journals of Samuel Kirkland: Eighteenth-Century Missionary to the Iroquois, Government Agent, Father of Hamilton College.* Clinton, N.Y.: Hamilton College.

Prime, Nathaniel. 1845. *A History of Long Island, from Its First Settlement by Europeans to the Year 1845, with Special References to Ecclesiastical Concerns.* New York: Robert Carter.

Pulsifer, David, ed. 1968. *Records of the Colony of New Plymouth.* 10 vols. 1859. Reprint. New York: AMS Press.

Rabito-Wyppensenwah, Philip. 1993a. "Discovering the Montauketts in Rediscovered Documents." In *The History and Archaeology of the Montauk,* edited by Gaynell Stone, 423–27. Stony Brook, N.Y.: Suffolk County Archaeological Association.

————. 1993b. "Disease among the Montauketts." In *The History and Archaeology of the Montauk,* edited by Gaynell Stone, 415–18. Stony Brook, N.Y.: Suffolk County Archaeological Association.

————. 1993c. "Eighteenth- and Nineteenth-Century Native American Whaling of Eastern Long Island." In *The History and Archaeology of the Montauk,* edited by Gaynell Stone, 437–44. Stony Brook, N.Y.: Suffolk County Archaeological Association.

————. 1993d. "The Hannibals: A Montaukett Family." In *The History and Archaeology of the Montauk,* edited by Gaynell Stone, 349–55. Stony Brook, N.Y.: Suffolk County Archaeological Association.

————. 1993e. "Montauk Censuses." In *The History and Archaeology of the Montauk,* edited by Gaynell Stone, 409–11. Stony Brook, N.Y.: Suffolk County Archaeological Association.

————. 1993f. "Montaukett/Brotherton Participation in the Civil War." In *The History and Archaeology of the Montauk,* edited by Gaynell Stone, 553–55. Stony Brook, N.Y.: Suffolk County Archaeological Association.

————. 1993g. "The Montaukett in the Colonial Wars." In *The History and Archaeology of the Montauk,* edited by Gaynell Stone, 433–34. Stony Brook, N.Y.: Suffolk County Archaeological Association.

————. 1993h. "The Recorded Evidence of Montaukett Marriages." In *The History and Archaeology of the Montauk,* edited by Gaynell Stone, 419–21. Stony Brook, N.Y.: Suffolk County Archaeological Association.

————. 1993i. "Those Days Will Never Return: The Autobiography of Maria Pharaoh." In *The History and Archaeology of the Montauk,* edited by Gaynell Stone, 365–67. Stony Brook, N.Y.: Suffolk County Archaeological Association.

————. 1993j. "Town Montaukett Economic Survival." In *The History and Archaeology of the Montauk,* edited by Gaynell Stone, 445–56. Stony Brook, N.Y.: Suffolk County Archaeological Association.

Rabito-Wyppensenwah, Philip, and Edwin Bacha. 1993. "Scrubs: A Traditional Montaukett Craft." In *The History and Archaeology of the Montauk,* edited by Gaynell Stone, 575–76. Stony Brook, N.Y.: Suffolk County Archaeological Association.

Rabito-Wyppensenwah, Philip, and Robert Abiuso. 1993. "The Montauk Use of Herbs: A Review of the Recorded Material." In *The History and Archaeology of the Montauk,* edited by Gaynell Stone, 585–87. Stony Brook, N.Y.: Suffolk County Archaeological Association.

Rattray, Jeannette Edwards. 1938. *Montauk: Three Centuries of Romance, Sport, and Adventure.* East Hampton, N.Y.: Rattray.

————. 1953. *East Hampton History.* Garden City, N.Y.: Country Life Press.

————. 1985. "Montauk's First Three Houses." *East Hampton Star,* May 9.

Richardson, Leon Burr, ed. 1933. *An Indian Preacher in England.* Dartmouth College Manuscript Series no. 2. Hanover, N.H.: Dartmouth College Publications.

Ritchie, Robert C. 1977. *The Duke's Province: A Study of New York Politics and Society, 1664–1691.* Chapel Hill: Univ. of North Carolina Press.

Ritchie, William. 1969. *The Archaeology of New York State.* Garden City, N.Y.: Natural History Press.

Rosier, James. 1930. "Report on Weymouth's Voyage to New England, 1605." In *Early English and French Voyages, 1534–1608,* edited by Harry Burrage, 355–94. 1907. Reprint. New York: Scribner.

Ross, Peter. 1902. *A History of Long Island.* New York: Lewis Publishing.

Sainsbury, John. 1971. "Miantonomo's Death and New England Politics 1630–1645." *Rhode Island History* 30, no. 4:111–23.

Salisbury, Neal. 1984. *Manitou and Providence, Indians, Europeans, and the Making of New England, 1500–1643.* New York: Oxford Univ. Press.

Salwen, Burt. 1978. "Indians of Southern New England and Long Island." In *Handbook of the North American Indians.* Vol. 15, *The Northeast,* edited by Bruce Trigger, 160–89. Washington, D.C.: Smithsonian Institution Press.

Sayville, Foster. 1993. "A Montauk Cemetery at East Hampton, Long Island." In *The History and Archaeology of the Montauk,* edited by Gaynell Stone, 615–29. Stony Brook, N.Y.: Suffolk County Archaeological Association.

Schur, Robert. 1942. "The Long Island Indians." *Long Island Forum* 5: 105–8.

Second Annual Report of the State Historian of the State of New York. 1897. Albany: Wynkoop Hallenbeck Crawford.

Service, Elman. 1962. *Primitive Social Organization.* New York: Random House.

Sesso, Gloria, and Regina White. 1990. *The Long Island Story.* Austin, Tex.: Steck-Vaughn Publishers.

Seyfried, Vincent. 1974. *The Long Island Railroad: A Comprehensive History.* 7 vols. Garden City, N.Y.: Vincent Seyfried.

Shepherd, Edith H. 1981. "The Funeral of a Pharaoh." *Long Island Forum* 44, no. 2: 38–41.

Simmons, William. 1978. "Narragansett." In *Handbook of the North American Indians.* Vol. 15, *The Northeast,* edited by Bruce Trigger, 190–97. Washington, D.C.: Smithsonian Institution Press.

Sleight, Harry. 1931. *Whale Fishing on Long Island.* Bridgehampton, N.Y.: Hampton Press.

———, ed. 1926–27. *Journal of the East Hampton Trustees.* 7 vols. East Hampton, N.Y.: Town of East Hampton.

Smith, Carlyle. 1950. "The Archaeology of Coastal New York." *Anthropological Papers of the American Museum of Natural History* 43, pt. 2.

Smith, Raymond, ed. 1926. *In Re Montauk.* East Hampton, N.Y.: East Hampton Town Trustees.

Snyder, Robert. 1979. "Women, Wobblies, and Worker's Rights." *New York State History* 61: 29–57.

Snyderman, George S. 1951. "Concepts of Land Ownership among the Iroquois and Their Neighbors." *Bulletin of the Bureau of American Ethnology* 149, no. 2: 15–38.

Stone, Gaynell. 1993a. *The History and Archaeology of the Montauk.* Stony Brook, N.Y.: Suffolk County Archaeological Association.

———. 1993b. "Later Ethnographic Statements about the Montauk." In *The History and Archaeology of the Montauk,* edited by Gaynell Stone, 285–302. Stony Brook: Suffolk County Archaeological Association.

———. 1993c. "Montauk Material Culture-Visual Record." In *The History and Archaeology of the Montauk,* edited by Gaynell Stone, 577–83. Stony Brook, N.Y.: Suffolk County Archaeological Association.

———, ed. 1983. *The Shinnecock Indians: A Culture History.* Stony Brook, N.Y.: Suffolk County Archaeological Association.

Stone, Gaynell, and Eugene Cuffee. 1983. "Economic Activities." In *The Shinnecock Indians: A Culture History,* edited by Gaynell Stone, 303–7. Stony Brook, N.Y.: Suffolk County Archaeological Association.

Stone, Gaynell, and Josephine Smith, with Alice Martinez, Harriett Gumbs, and Alice Phillips. 1983. "Material Culture." In *The Shinnecock Indians: A Culture History,* edited by Gaynell Stone, 291–96. Stony Brook, N.Y.: Suffolk County Archaeological Association.

Street, Charles R., ed. 1887–1889. *Huntington Town Records.* 3 vols. Huntington, N.Y.: Town of Huntington.

Strong, Lara M., and Selcuk Karabag. 1991. "Quashawam: Sunksquaw of the Montauk." *Long Island Historical Journal* 3, no. 2: 189–204.

Strong, John A. 1983. "The Evolution of Shinnecock Culture." In *The Shinnecock Indians: A Culture History,* edited by Gaynell Stone, 7–94. Stony Brook, N.Y.: Suffolk County Archaeological Association.

———. 1990. "The Pigskin Book: Records of Native American Whalemen." *Long Island Historical Journal* 3, no. 1: 29–40.

———. 1992. "The Thirteen Tribes of Long Island: The History of a Myth." *Hudson Valley Regional Review* 9, no. 2: 39–73.

———. 1993. "How the Montauk Lost Their Land." In *The History and Archaeology of the Montauk Indians,* edited by Gaynell Stone, 77–116. Stony Brook, N.Y.: Suffolk County Archaeological Association.

———. 1994a. "Detribalization by the Courts: The Montaukett (1909) and Mashpee (1978) Cases Compared." Paper presented at the Forty-eighth International Congress of Americanists, Stockholm, Sweden. July 5.

———. 1994b. "The Imposition of Colonial Jurisdiction over the Montauk Indians of Long Island." *Ethnohistory* 41, no. 1: 561–90.

———. 1994c. "The Reaffirmation of Tradition among the Native Americans of Eastern Long Island." *Long Island Historical Journal* 7, no. 1: 42–67.

———. 1995. "Indian Labor During the Post-Contact Period on Long Island." In *To Know the Place,* edited by Joann Krieg, 13–39. Hempstead, N.Y.: Long Island Studies Institute.

———. 1996a. "The Role of Algonquian Women in Land Transactions on Long Island, 1639–1859." Conference on Long Island Women, Long Island Studies Institute, Hofstra Univ. March.

———. 1996b. *"We Are Still Here!" The Algonquian Peoples of Long Island Today.* Interlaken, N.Y.: Heart of the Lakes Press.

———. 1996c. "Wyandanch, Sachem of the Montaukett." In *Northeastern Indian Lives,* edited by Robert Grumet, 48–73. Amherst: Univ. of Massachusetts Press.

———. 1997. *The Algonquian Peoples of Long Island from Earliest Times to 1700.* Interlakin, N.Y.: Heart of the Lakes Press.

Strong, John A., and Zsuzsanna Török. 2000. "Taking the Middle Way: Algonquian Responses to the Reverend Azariah Horton's Mission on Long Island." *Long Island Historical Journal* 12, no. 2:145–58.

Sturtevant, William. 1983. "Tribe and State in the Sixteenth and Twentieth Centuries." In *The Development of Political Organization in Native North America*, edited by Elisabeth Tooker, 3–16. Washington, D.C.: American Ethnological Society.

Sullivan, James, ed. 1921–1965. *The Papers of Sir William Johnson.* 14 vols. Albany: State Univ. of New York.

Taylor, Samuel. 1980. "A Pow-Wow on Long Island, 1659." In *The Language and Lore of the Long Island Indians*, edited by Gaynell Stone and Nancy Bonvillian, 285–86. Stony Brook, N.Y.: Suffolk County Archaeological Association.

Thomas, Peter. 1976. "Contrastive Subsistence Strategies and Land Use as a Factor for Understanding Indian-White Relations in New England." *Ethnohistory* 26, no. 1: 1–18.

Thompson, Benjamin. 1838. *History of Long Island from Its Discovery and Settlement to the Present Time.* 3rd ed. Revised and enlarged by Charles Warner, 1918. New York: Robert H. Dodd.

Tooker, Elizabeth, ed. 1979. *Native North American Spirituality of the Eastern Woodlands.* Mahwah, N.J.: Paulist Press.

Tooker, William Wallace. 1962. *Indian Place Names on Long Island.* Port Washington, N.Y.: Ira Friedman.

———. 1980. "John Eliot's First Indian Teacher and Interpreter, Cockenoe de Long Island." In *Languages and Lore of the Long Island Indians*, edited by Gaynell Stone Levine and Nancy Bonvillain, 176–89. Stony Brook, N.Y.: Suffolk County Archaeological Association.

———. 1993. "The Last of the Montauks: In Defense of Their Claims of Montauk Lands." In *The History and Archaeology of the Montauk*, edited by Gaynell Stone, 287–88. Stony Brook, N.Y.: Suffolk County Archaeological Association.

Trelease, Allen W. 1971. *Indian Affairs in Colonial New York: The Seventeenth Century.* New York: Kinnikat Press.

Truex, James, ed. 1982. *The Second Coastal Archaeology Reader: 1900 to the Present.* Stony Brook, N.Y.: Suffolk County Archaeological Association.

Trumbull, J. Hammond, ed. 1968. *The Public Records of the Colony of Connecticut.* 15 vols. 1850–1890. Reprint. New York: AMS Press.

United States Reports. 1901. Vol. 180. New York: Banks Law Publishing.

Venables, Robert W. 1993. "A Chronology of Brotherton History to 1850." In *The History and Archaeology of the Montauk*, edited by Gaynell Stone, 515–32. Stony Brook, N.Y.: Suffolk County Archaeological Association.

Weatherhead, L. R. 1980. "What Is an Indian Tribe? The Question of Tribal Existence." *American Indian Law Review* 8: 1–47.

Weeks, Philip. 1990. *Farewell, My Nation: The American Indian and the United States, 1820–1890.* Arlington Heights, Ill.: Harlan Davidson.

Westez, Carlos. 1993. "An Ethnographical Introduction to the Long Island Indians." In *The History and Archaeology of the Montauk*, edited by Gaynell Stone, 291–94. Stony Brook, N.Y.: Suffolk County Archaeological Association.

White, Richard. 1991. *The Middle Ground, Indians, Empires, and Republics in the Great Lakes Region, 1650–1815*. New York: Cambridge Univ. Press.

Williams, James Homer. 1995. "Great Doggs and Mischievous Cattle: Domesticated Animals and Indian-European Relations in New Netherland and New York." *New York History* 76, no. 3: 245–64.

Williams, Roger. 1963. *Complete Writings of Roger Williams*. 7 vols. New York: Russell and Russell.

———. 1973. *A Key to the Language of America, 1643*. With notes by John J. Teunissen and Evelyn J. Hinz. Detroit: Wayne State Univ. Press.

Wonderly, Anthony. 1997. "Montauketts among the Brothertons, in the Lands of the Oneidas." Paper presented at the New York State History Conference, Saratoga, N.Y.

Wood, Silas. 1826. *A Sketch of the First Settlement of the Several Towns on Long Island*. Rev. ed. Brooklyn: Alden Spooner.

Wooley, Charles. 1968. "A Two Years Journal in New York, 1678–80." In *Historic Chronicles of New Amsterdam, Colonial New York and Early Long Island*, edited by Cornell Jaray, 1–97. Port Washington, N.Y.: Ira J. Friedman.

Wyatt, Ronald. 1982. "The Archaic on Long Island." In *The Second Archaeological Reader: 1900 to the Present*, edited by James Truex, 70–78. Stony Brook, N.Y.: Suffolk County Archaeological Association.

INDEX

African Americans, 71; excluded from Brothertown, 77; intermarriage with Montauketts, 88, 144; and Mashpee case, 138n, prohibited from gathering with Indians, 78
African Methodist Episcopal Church, 90
Akomias, 37, 39
Alcohol abuse, 65–66, 85, 110
Ales, Marion Fisher, xiv
Algonquian culture, language, 6–8
Aquash (Montaukett sachem), 55, 56. *See also* Wyandanch
Archaic period, 5

Baker, Thomas, 35, 38, 40–41
Banks, Edward, 114
Banks, Junius, 114
Barnes, Benjamin, 132
Beecher, Reverend Lyman, 85
Belford, Joseph, 128–29, 132–36
Benson, Arthur, buys Montauk, 105, 108–10; death of, 114
Benson, Mary, 146
Bermis, Neal, 169
Blackmar, Judge Abel, 128, 137–40
Block Island raid, 21
Bowser, Elizabeth, 166
Branch of Acknowledgement and Research (BAR), 167
Brewster family, 163
Brewster-Toone, Phyllis, xiv, 173

Brewster-Walker, Sandi, 159
Brooklyn Daily Eagle, 123, 125, 127
Brothertown (Brotherton), 71, 80–81, 142, 143
Bunn, Ralph, xv, 159
Burke, Charles, 152
Burr, Judge Joseph, 144
Butler, John J., 127
Butler, William, 110n
Buttz v. Northern Pacific Railroad (1911), 144

Caldwell, Terrie, xiv, 166
Caruthers, Allen, 141
Cattle grazing, 66–67
Charles, Silas (Cyrus), burial site of, 162–63; and Sir William Johnson, 76–77; signs 1754 agreement, 71; petition to governor of, 73–74
Chatfield, Thomas, 67–68
Civil War, 95
Clans, 160
Cockenoe, 15, 15n; accommodationist policy, 21, 22, 25; gift deed, 28–29, 47, 56
Colden, Governor Cadwallader, 72–73
Commission on Indian Affairs, 35, 39
Cooper, John, 26